guru
in a bottle ®

KU-593-136

The Art of Influencing and Selling

Ardi Kolah

KoganPage

LONDON   PHILADELPHIA   NEW DELHI

First published in Great Britain and the United States in 2013 by Kogan Page Limited

120 Pentonville Road	1518 Walnut Street, Suite 1100	4737/23 Ansari Road
London N1 9JN	Philadelphia PA 19102	Daryaganj
United Kingdom	USA	New Delhi 110002
www.koganpage.com		India

© Ardi Kolah, 2013

ISBN   978 0 7494 6448 6
E-ISBN   978 0 7494 6449 3

British Library Cataloguing-in-Publication Data

A CIP record for this book is available from the British Library.

Library of Congress Cataloging-in-Publication Data

Kolah, Ardi.
    The art of influencing and selling / Ardi Kolah.
       p. cm.
       Includes index.
    ISBN 978-0-7494-6448-6 – ISBN 978-0-7494-6449-3 (ebook)   1. Selling.   2. Selling–Psychological aspects.   3. Sales presentations.   4. Business networks.   I. Title.
    HF5438.25.K647 2012
    658.85–dc23
                                                              2012039391

Typeset by Graphicraft Limited, Hong Kong
Print production managed by Jellyfish
Printed and bound in Great Britain by CPI Group (UK) Ltd, Croydon, CR0 4YY

For Fenella, Zara and Aviva,
who are my inspiration every day

Contents

8 The power of business networking 207

9 How to get senior-level appointments in your diary 239

10 Closing a sale and follow-up 255

About the author

Ardi Kolah, BA, LLM, FCIM, FCIPR, FRSA is director of communications for a financial services Fortune 500 company in Europe.

He began his career as a TV and radio reporter/producer at the BBC, working in network news and current affairs and BBC World Service before embarking on a career within public relations, marketing and sponsorship, working with some of the world's most successful brands including Accenture, Logica plc, Disney, Ford of Europe, Speedo, Standard Chartered Bank, Shell, Procter & Gamble, Yahoo, Reebok, Pepsi, Reliance, Emirates, Great Wheel Corporation, MOBO, YouGov, QBE, Brit Insurance, WHO, the Royal Navy and the Royal Air Force.

He's a former visiting lecturer on MBA programmes at Cranfield School of Management, Imperial College Business School, and Judge Business School, Cambridge University.

A prolific author, he's written some of the leading works on brand marketing, public relations, sponsorship and the legal aspects of marketing, with combined sales in excess of £2.5 million worldwide. He writes a regular blog for the UK's leading sales and marketing portal Brand Republic and has been a regular contributor to *Sponsorship News*, *Financial Times*, *Wall Street Journal*, *Bloomberg News*, CNN and BBC World Business Report and is on the editorial board of the *Journal of Brand Strategy*.

He holds several industry awards including the Hollis Award for 'Best Low Budget Sponsorship' for his work on the British Independent Film Awards and CIPR Excellence Award for Outstanding Individual in education and training.

He's a Fellow of the Chartered Institute of Marketing and the Chartered Institute of Public Relations, a Member of the Public Relations Consultants Association and a Liveryman of the Worshipful Company of Marketors, an elected member of BAFTA and a member of the Society of Authors. In 2003 Ardi was independently ranked by the CIM as one of the top 50 gurus in the world – and he's been trying to live this down ever since!

He's a frequent speaker at conferences around the world and has been a judge on numerous industry panels including CIPR Excellence Awards, New Media Age Awards, National Business Awards and Scottish Newspaper of the Year Awards. A former Board Director of the CIPR and the European Sponsorship Association, he's been a visiting lecturer at the Judge Business School, Cambridge University, Oxford College of Marketing, Oxford, and Imperial College Business School.

He studied law at Kingston University London and then was awarded a scholarship to study for an international Master's degree in law at King's College London and University College London.

He lives in Wimbledon, south-west London, with his wife Fenella and their two children, Zara and Aviva.

About Guru in a Bottle®

Guru in a Bottle® is about taking technical, high-level subjects and making them clear, human and accessible.

Unlike Dummies®, which tends to treat the reader as a blank canvas for much of the content presented, the approach taken by Guru in a Bottle® is to guide the reader through technical subjects as their friend and personal guru. Buying a Guru in a Bottle® book gets the guru out of the bottle, empowering the business manager and student to tackle technical subjects and enhance their working and learning experience.

Ardi Kolah created the iconic character Guru in a Bottle® with cartoonist Steve Marchant and the unique approach has helped make the Guru in a Bottle® Series extremely popular throughout Europe, the United States and India.

Voice over: "And now a word from our sponsors..."

Introduction

The art of influencing and selling is neatly summarized by this quote taken from the book *How to Win Friends and Influence People* by US sales guru Dale Carnegie: 'When dealing with people, let us remember we are not dealing with creatures of logic. We are dealing with creatures of emotion, creatures bristling with prejudices and motivated by pride and vanity.' What's fascinating is that this was written in 1953 and well before access to the powerful databases we have today, which contain millions of bits of data on just about every aspect of our lives that it is legally possible to hold.

What Dale Carnegie said then holds true today. If we only operate on a rational basis in order to try to influence our desired customer or client to purchase our product or service, then we'll fail miserably.

It's true that we mustn't ignore logic or the ability of critical argument and evaluation that dominates so much of the way in which we are taught to think and make decisions. Just look at the soap powder TV commercials of the 1950s and 1960s, where consumers were blinded with the power of the technology to make their clothes 'whiter than white'! There was almost a messianic obsession about selling features rather than benefits. And if you think times have changed and that approach is dead and buried along with the cheesy commercials with women restricted to the role of housewives, well I'm afraid it's still alive and kicking amongst some businesses! The problem is that the traditional thinking we apply to today's sales challenges just isn't up to the job any more.

What many of the most successful businesses on the planet have in common is the ability to challenge the conventional wisdom that has for too long dominated the way we think. In essence, these organizations have replaced one-dimensional with multidimensional thinking.

Much of our thinking is done in a disorganized, inefficient way. We often try to do too much at once. Emotions, information, logic, hope, risk and creativity are all mixed up together. It's like juggling too many balls all at once, and some end up getting dropped. As a result of this juggling act, we begin to limit our thinking and make poor decisions. Often, we tend to use only one type of thinking at any given moment. Yet one type of thinking is no longer adequate to cope with today's rapidly changing and challenging commercial environment. Judgement and argument can no longer solve all problems or move us forward. We need a multidimensional approach in order to succeed.

And this is what this book is about. We need to think about influencing and selling in 3D and not just online! We need to be collaborative, focused and directed. We need, in short, to rewire our thinking about how to influence and sell to our desired customer and client segments wherever we are and whatever business we happen to be in. We need to be able to navigate different avenues of thought to build insight, creative ideas and effective sales solutions if we want to be successful in this endeavour.

If you follow the approach we advocate here in this book, then you'll be on your way to creating more sales for your business. And the guru won't just be out of the bottle. The guru will be you!

About this book

Chapter 1: Psychology of selling a product or service or yourself
In this chapter, we'll look at the psychology of influence and the role that you play regardless of the product or service you're trying to sell.

Chapter 2: The sales pipeline and how to ensure it's realistic
In this chapter, we'll show you how to put together a realistic rather than pie-in-the-sky sales pipeline where the chances of success are greater and will keep a smile on the face of your boss!

Chapter 3: Up-selling, cross-selling, cold calling and warm calling
In this chapter, we'll analyse and rehearse the key skills you need to be effective in getting a chance of making a sale with a desired customer or client prospect.

Chapter 4: Effective approaches to prospective customers and clients
In this chapter, having discussed how the tools work and what you need to make a sale, we'll show you how to strut your stuff.

Chapter 5: How to interrogate a database of contacts to get more sales
In this chapter, we'll take a no-fuss look at database marketing without making you glaze over in the process!

Chapter 6: Making an effective sales presentation
In this chapter, we'll take you through some of the best ways in which to make a first impression in a sales presentation by looking at some of the tips and tricks used by seasoned sales presenters.

Chapter 7: How to write effective sales materials
In this chapter, we'll show you the way you should approach having to write sales brochures, newsletters and flyers that are aimed at customers and clients and reduce the chance of them being deleted or ending up in the waste bin!

Chapter 8: The power of business networking
In this chapter, we'll show you how to use the power of online and offline networking, as well as the importance of being recommended by other customers and clients, which could be your most powerful sales weapon.

Chapter 9: How to get senior-level appointments in your diary
In this chapter, we'll show you how to get past the 'gatekeeper' and get that all-important appointment with the key decision maker who can authorize to spend budget with you!

Chapter 10: Closing a sale and follow-up
In this chapter, we'll show you, once you've succeeded in opening a sale, how to close it successfully, as well as what to do after the sale has been made.

"And would Sir like to see something
more expensive that's not on the menu?"

Psychology of selling a product or service or yourself

The art of persuasion

Shortly after British prime minister Gordon Brown called the 2010 general election, the Conservative Party leader David Cameron took a trip to the Variety bakery in Bolton, England. With shirt sleeves rolled up, the 'prime-minister-in-waiting' stood on a plastic crate to speak to a group of bemused

Warburtons employees. It was a clear clash of cultures: David Cameron with his upper-class vowels addressing a group of about 100 no-nonsense bakers in blue boiler suits. A couple of TV crews were on standby to record David Cameron's blushes.

You could call it a high-risk strategy. Already well ahead in the public opinion polls, David Cameron had much to lose and little to gain from such stark exposure on national television. Yet the Conservative leader's campaign was full of similarly high-risk public appearances and photo opportunities.

After Warburtons, David Cameron visited a west London brewery, a branch of DIY shop B&Q and a Bestway Cash and Carry warehouse. It was a schedule designed to evoke the more prosaic qualities of life. Beer, white bread, DIY – the message was delivered straight into our subconscious: 'I'm more like you than you think.' Well, that was the idea. And of course, after he was elected, David Cameron unveiled his 'Big Society' vision, which became much derided.

But back to life on the campaign trail. All of these photo opportunities raised the one question that was nagging away at David Cameron: could the British public be persuaded to trust him?

This episode is relevant when considering the art of influencing and selling within a business context, and we'll get back to David Cameron in a moment.

The big issue

The biggest issue in business right now isn't lack of lending by the banks, decrease in disposable incomes and the depressed state of the developed economies of the West – although of course all of these issues combine to have an impact on business and the survival of companies in certain sectors.

The biggest issue is trust or, put another way, lack of trust.

Every day, we wake up to news stories about those whom we thought we could trust – bankers, MPs, lords, judges, the jury system, big corporations and business leaders – only to find that individuals and even whole organizations fall far short of how we expect them to behave and as a result can't be trusted any more. When bosses talk of pay restraint required from the workforce and then reward themselves eye-watering bonuses, who can trust them?

From a sales point of view, trust or the lack of trust is a major issue. If people don't trust us, they won't buy from us. It's as simple as that.

In order to build trust we need to be able to communicate, and increasingly that means being not just in 'transmit mode' but more importantly in 'receive mode'. A successful salesperson is someone who listens.

So there's no point shouting ever louder at the top of our voice if no one is bothering to listen to us. And it doesn't win friends or influence people, does it? Worse still, it makes us look ineffective and desperate. Try this simple test: walk down your local high street before Christmas and then return home and write down the names of the furniture stores that had 'SALE NOW ON' signs in their windows. It's likely you won't remember all of them, as we are conditioned now to screen out messages rather than screen them in. It all becomes a bit of a blur, doesn't it?

Trust builder

It follows that selling a product or service is inextricably linked to whether customers, clients, consumers and prospects can trust the person or organization making that offer. This move to the source of the offer rather than just focusing on the features and benefits of a product or service is now core to the thinking of several global brand owners, including Procter & Gamble, Unilever and Coca-Cola, which are now placing much more emphasis on the 'corporate brand' as a key to building trust with their customers in order to drive incremental sales.

The psychology of selling is shifting away from being transactional towards building a meaningful dialogue with customers, clients, consumers and prospects that's built on trust.

David Cameron's attempt to portray himself as a 'man of the people' in the hope that voters would see him as their future prime minister was fuelled in part by his belief that he wanted to be liked.

We tend to be influenced by people who are similar to us. David Cameron, with his Etonian upper-class pedigree and charming looks, is arguably quite different from the voters who live in Kilmarnock, East Ayrshire in Scotland. But his campaign strategy was to break down the perception of disparity.

According to British business psychologist Stuart Duff, David Cameron wanted voters to trust him even though he'd never held ministerial responsibility in his relatively short political career. 'If I can convince you that you're more like me, you'll start to tolerate me more for the things that I do wrong; you'll start to tolerate me more and start to notice the positive things I do rather than the negative things', observes Stuart Duff.

Clearly, David Cameron had thought about the barriers that separated him from the public, and his campaign strategy was to remove those negative stereotypes that surround a person of privilege and power, including their name – hence he wanted henceforth to be referred to in the media as 'Dave' rather than David. What next? Fluffy dice with the moniker 'Dave and Sam' (Samantha is his wife) hanging from the rear-view mirror of his Ford Escort? Such a folksy strategy has long been abandoned. And in any event such a strategy was doomed to fail before it had begun.

David Cameron had received a mixed reception in Bolton. His approach was solid enough, but he muddled his tactics. Starting with a cringe-making joke about bakers, his self-deprecation felt false. He was a politician desperate to be liked, which is a common mistake of leaders, who frequently believe the best way to gain influence is to make themselves likeable.

According to British business academic Steve Martin, likeability as a method of persuasion isn't that effective:

> We are conditioned to be more likely to say 'yes' to those people who like us and who tell us they like us, because we've been taught that they have our best interest at heart. Leaders seeking to build networks of followers should spend less time trying to be liked and put more effort into highlighting characteristics of followers that they genuinely admire. Most sales training programmes say that the first thing you need to do is to get your customer to like you. That's not true. The first thing you should do is learn to like your customer.

The transactional approach to selling is far from dead and buried. Evidence of this can be found in the poor sales performance of many businesses struggling to keep afloat in these turbulent economic times as well as on the web.

According to Wikipedia, 'selling' is defined as:

> Offer to exchange something of value for something else. The something of value being offered may be tangible or intangible. Buying and selling are understood to be two sides of the same coin or transaction. Both seller and buyer are in a process of negotiation to consummate the exchange of values. The exchange, or selling, process has implied rules and identifiable stages. It is implied that the selling process will proceed fairly and ethically so that the parties end up nearly equally rewarded. The stages of selling, and buying, involve getting acquainted, assessing each party's need for the other's item of value, and determining if the values to be exchanged are equivalent or nearly so, or, in buyer's terms, 'worth the price'.

What the definition doesn't get into is the relative bargaining positions of the buyer and seller – and this varies widely between industry sectors and markets. Not everyone is equal, of course.

Celebrated US psychologist Abraham Maslow believed that all of us strive to satisfy certain basic needs (Figure 1.1), and these needs he placed at the bottom of the hierarchy of needs all of us have.

According to Maslow, once all the basic needs have been satisfied, they no longer motivate individuals in terms of their behaviour. In contrast, more deep-rooted needs, such as self-expression, are self-propelling, and there is a continuous desire within us to 'be all that we can be'. This state is described as self-actualization, and focusing on satisfying the psychological desires of our customers, clients and prospects rather than just their basic needs is likely to result in more sales. The transactional view of selling, exchanging goods or services for money, is now outmoded. Customer, clients and prospects want and expect much, much more! It's time to rewire our thinking and redefine what we mean by 'selling'.

Figure 1.1   Maslow's hierarchy of needs

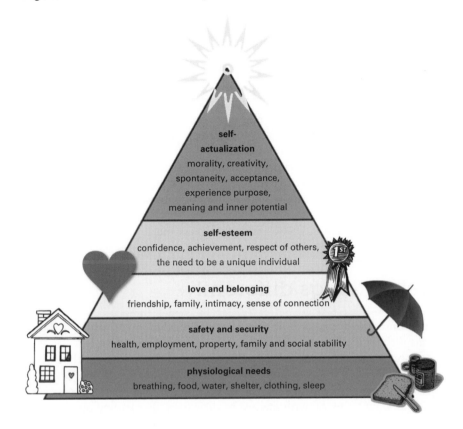

Redefinition of selling

In many sales contexts, both parties often struggle to understand complex offerings and so instead end up focusing on price. Part of the problem is that some sales professionals tend to treat everyone the same, with the result that they often fail to close the sale.

There's no such thing as an 'average' customer or client, and we need to shift our thinking from mass to niche if we want to achieve success in our sales and marketing efforts.

As a result, there's been a fundamental shift in our obsession with customers or clients. After all, it's much more profitable focusing on their attitudes, values, beliefs and behaviours than our own. If we are prepared to go to customers or clients rather than push product at them in the hope they will open their wallets, then this will create a new dialogue from which we can grow any business. The starting point is the customer or client's point of view (POV).

'Walmartizing' open-heart surgery

Take open-heart surgery. Yes, really! You may not have heard of Dr Devi Shetty, but he's fast becoming a household name in India. He's reinterpreted our understanding of 'medical care' not just in his native India, but the whole world. He runs a 1,000-bed hospital that provides affordable open-heart surgery and other medical treatment for a fraction of the price in other countries – making the family-owned hospital the biggest of its kind in the world.

Devi Shetty has personally carried out over 15,000 heart ops, and calls his approach 'Walmartization', which is a pun on Walmart, the world's largest discount department and warehouse chain.

His critics say that processing patients in such numbers is dangerous. A quick check of the statistics tells a very different story. His hospital reports a 1.4 per cent mortality rate within 30 days of coronary artery bypass graft surgery, one of the most common procedures. That's better than the 1.9 per cent average reported in US hospitals that carry out fewer operations.

Seeing things differently

The second thing we need to do as part of our redefinition of 'selling' is to see things differently. British sales and marketing guru Peter Fisk believes that successful organizations 'see things differently and think different things'.

Devi Shetty is a good example of this. He's sympathetic to the needs of patients who are tired of waiting for an appointment for open-heart surgery and who want to get on with the rest of their lives. By carrying out so many operations the hospital is able to reduce its costs because of economies of scale, pass on cost savings to patients, resulting in lower hospital bills, and treat patients on very low incomes free of charge. Arguably, these outcomes couldn't be achieved if Devi Shetty and his family managed the hospital along traditional lines.

Another innovative approach that has turned into a mega-successful sales operation is Zipcars. The company started off as an idea in a bar in Berlin over a decade ago. Today it provides cars for use by the hour and has over 560,000 members and 8,541 vehicles in several cities around the world. In 2010, it achieved a turnover of around US$186 million across all its operations, and a few years ago it acquired its rival Streetcar. The founders didn't understand why people had to buy cars – why not just rent one when you need it?

Customers get a membership card and can find the nearest Zipcar from their mobile phone. The swipe card opens the electronic door and operates the vehicle. Customers are charged by the minute and the miles travelled. The car is already cleared for congestion charge and has petrol in the tank as well as insurance. It's a business model that couldn't have been conceived without the internet and mobile devices, appealing to those who can't afford

Figure 1.2 Compound annual growth rate (percentage)

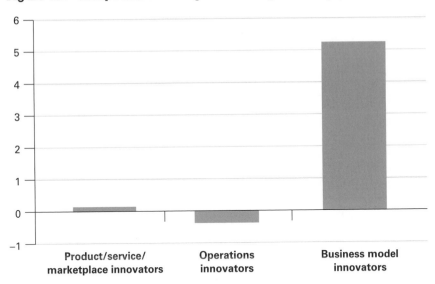

Source: Judge Business School, Cambridge University, 2010

a car – such as students – and the environmentally conscious, as well as those for whom the economics and the costs of running a private vehicle are now prohibitive.

Research by Judge Business School, Cambridge University has shown that such an approach in business is so much more successful than those that simply make incremental improvements to their products and services with extra 'bells and whistles'.

Businesses that are genuine innovators like Zipcar enjoy a significantly higher compound annual growth rate (CAGR) of five times that of their competitors (Figure 1.2). This study was based on a survey of over 4,000 businesses in 17 countries across Europe, the United States and Asia, so it's a compelling piece of evidence that we can't ignore.

Collaboration is the future of selling

The third thing we must do as part of redefining our approach to 'selling' is to collaborate with our customers, clients and prospects. It's not something that we are naturally good at, so for most companies this is still work in progress.

Threadless (2012)

One of the best examples of collaborative selling is US-based T-shirt company Threadless, which has grown to become an annual US$1 billion turnover business in less than five years since its launch. Threadless gets its customers to design a new range of T-shirts every week, which are sold through its website as well as retail stores. The best designs submitted win a US$2,000 cash prize, which the online community vote for.

T-shirts cost US$3 to produce and retail for US$15, which shows that customers are prepared to pay a premium for collaboration. What's really cool is that they keep coming back for more – as the community of customers want the latest designs. This is a great example of doing things differently – and more profitably.

This may strike you as being a new wave of thinking about how to sell more stuff – but in fact the founding members of iconic rock band the Grateful Dead set out to do just that in their quest to be the most commercially successful band in the world.

Grateful Dead (2012)

Before the internet, bands promoted their new albums by scheduling tours across the United States and around the world. Fans paid top dollar to attend sold-out shows where they were treated to pyrotechnics, light shows and of course music. Concerts were the same every night and included the band's 'best of' songs with cuts from the latest album mixed throughout the set.

The goal of these concert tours was to sell as many records as possible to ensure that an album went gold or platinum. Fans bought the albums at their local record store, where they would find the list of top albums that week taped to the wall next to the cash till. For an album to go gold in 1975, a band had to sell 500,000 records and hit US$1 million in sales. To be awarded the coveted platinum disc, bands had to shift in excess of 1 million units and US$2 million in sales.

Since those days the business model for the music industry has been turned on its head. Whereas in the past bands used tours to promote money-making albums, today albums are used to promote highly lucrative tours, where ticket sales run into hundreds of millions of dollars for bands like the Rolling Stones and U2.

The Grateful Dead weren't a conventional band in any sense way back in 1965, and rather than focusing on selling albums like other bands they generated revenues from ticket sales, merchandising and licensing by turning their shows into a totally unique fan experience and encouraging fans to create their own bootleg copies of their concerts and sell merchandise that they had made themselves using the band's distinctive logo! This radical marketing approach enthralled the Flower Power Generation and rapidly propelled 'official' merchandise and record sales through the stratosphere.

The fans' own enterprising activities didn't dent sales. Quite the reverse in fact, and it's fuelled a continuing interest in the band amongst existing and new audiences for the last 50 years. The result is that the band is the most commercially successful in the world today – a spectacular achievement considering that the band recorded its last album back in 1995.

The Grateful Dead broke almost every rule in the music industry book by encouraging their fans to record shows and trade tapes; they built a mailing list and sold tickets to their shows directly to fans so they wouldn't get ripped off by ticket touts. In short, the band built their business model on live concerts and merchandise, not album sales.

Hypnotizing the audience to fall under your spell!

Selling is incredibly personal and often depends on the ability of the seller, so selling yourself has become much more important – whether in a business-to-consumer (B2C) or business-to-business (B2B) context. Today, selling isn't just about the goods and services those prospective customers and clients are buying. Increasingly, they are buying you.

Communication within a sales context must therefore work at both a conscious and an unconscious level. Increasingly, sales professionals are turning to hypnosis as a strategy for helping to drive sales.

Hypnosis works on influencing the unconscious mind in order to facilitate changes in patterns of thinking and behaviour. When people are under hypnosis they have entered a dream-like state where their mind is relaxed. By unlocking the power of the unconscious mind, a professional salesperson can make suggestions that can have a profound impact on the prospective customer or client.

This is relevant in a selling context, as during the normal course of a day all of us have the capacity to drift in and out of consciousness. It's the brain's way of dealing with information overload! Going into a trance-like state allows people to relax and makes them open to new ideas – something that a professional salesperson would regard as a useful state.

The following checklist is a summary of the key points covered:

- The key to success in selling your product, your service or yourself is to listen to your customers, clients, prospects and fans.
- Try to see things differently and think different things.
- Like the Grateful Dead, cultivate a dedicated, active community, collaborating with them to co-create a lifestyle and give away 'freemium' content.
- Use social media and inbound marketing concepts to help drive incremental sales.
- Consider tapping into the unconscious mind of the prospective customer or client.

References

Books

Ambler, T (1996) *Marketing from Advertising to Zen*, FT Pitman Publishing
Fisk, P (2009) *Customer Genius*, Capstone Publishing
Goldstein, N, Martin, S and Cialdini, R (1997) *Yes! 50 secrets from the science of persuasion*, Profile Books
Maslow, A (2011) *Toward a Psychology of Being*, Wilder Publications
Scott, DM and Halligan, B (2010) *Marketing Lessons from the Grateful Dead*, Wiley

Websites

Institute of Customer Service article on my keynote at the National Business Awards 2010: http://www.instituteofcustomerservice.com/3812-6009/Death-of-the-average-customer.html (accessed 18 June 2011)
Threadless: http://www.threadless.com (accessed 18 June 2011)
Wikipedia definition of selling: http://en.wikipedia.org/wiki/Selling (accessed 16 June 2011)

"I've got it. We can double our quarterly sales! From now on, each quarter will last six months..."

The sales pipeline and how to ensure it's realistic

Introduction

When salespeople talk about the 'sales pipeline', what they're really referring to is an imaginary giant funnel somewhere above their head where at the top are gathered a large number of individual 'prospects' of different shapes and sizes (defined by the *Oxford English Dictionary* as 'a person regarded as a potential customer') and at the bottom are gathered a smaller pool of happy, smiling customers or clients to whom you've sold your products or services and who appear to have a lot in common.

In business, your dream sale in fact doesn't involve any selling whatsoever! 'I'm interested! I'll take it! I'll love it!' We all want confident, responsive customers and clients, the right product or service at the right price, and an inevitable sale. Job done!

However, for most of us the reality looks very different. More often than not 'selling' isn't always that easy. It's hard work.

Trying to convince people to change their behaviour in a way they may or may not want to do is a challenge. That's what 'selling' usually feels like – convincing, cajoling, and struggling to be heard against a lot of background noise and distraction – and as a result it isn't always successful.

So what's the shortest distance between 'selling' and landing the 'dream sale', and where do you find those responsive, confident customers or clients who instantly recognize the value of your products and services and don't need to be sold to? Will they come flocking to your three-star Michelin restaurant and not worry about being on a six-month waiting list or indeed be concerned that the bill for the meal could have bought the groceries for a family of four for a month?

The starting point is to rewire our thinking about 'selling'. In fact, we need to stop 'selling' in the traditional sense!

Selling, by definition, is about the seller. It focuses on you and what you need. It's an internalized perspective, and if you're thinking about what you need to do to make the sale you won't be focusing on your customer or client and will end up losing the sale.

When you make a sale, you don't always create a customer. Think about it. Selling tends to have a short horizon and tends to focus on a single transaction, but a customer isn't a one-night stand – well, at least the customer you want to do business with in the future!

Depending on the nature of your business, contact with your customer or client may be fleeting or sustained, daily or infrequent, but when customers have a need for a product or service you want them to come to you and only you. The reason they do is because they need help in making the right purchasing decision and fundamentally trust you to provide this to them. It's your job to make them believers. Convert their interest and hope into the conviction that you can give them what they need and desire.

This chapter is all about focusing on the customer and client, and how they'll value your business and its products or services through their own perceptions and their own sense of reality. Increasingly this is a collaborative rather than one-way process. The sales pipeline you're therefore looking to build is all about 'lead conversion' because it recognizes your prospects' willingness to become paying customers or clients if you can give them what they need and desire. You need their custom and loyalty to grow your business, and they need your products or services and a relationship that's gratifying and valuable for them. This is the sales pipeline or, put another way, the 'customer pipeline' that needs to be built.

When you stop being manic about doing everything humanly possible to land a sale and instead start to look for ways in which you can satisfy your customers' needs, then the sale – when it comes – will be the natural consequence of giving your customers or clients what they want in order to make that purchase decision. And that means you won't have to 'sell' to them! Phew! Well, I only wish it were that easy! Better read on.

Effective market and customer segmentation will provide you with some of the insights you'll need in order to construct an effective prospective customer or client pipeline, and this is discussed in detail in Guru in a Bottle®'s *High Impact Marketing That Gets Results*. In this chapter, we're assuming that you've carried out this segmentation process and now have to manage the pipeline of prospects effectively in order to drive sales of your products or services.

Few would argue that the nature of communication, information and the global economy has transformed the way we now communicate and prospect for customers and clients. In many respects, the strategies that are often employed to predict and manage customers' or clients' purchasing behaviour have been spurred on by the growth of online information, which in itself has its challenges for the sales and marketing professional.

More information about the legal use of such data about your prospective customers and clients can be found in Guru in a Bottle®'s *Essential Law for Marketers* (2nd edition). What started life within the airline and hotel market segments has rapidly been adopted across other market segments, and now database and online strategies proliferate in sales pipeline management thinking.

Implementation of these techniques often requires a sophisticated mix of tools with equally sophisticated statistical methods to help manage and track the frequency and timing of purchase, repeat purchase behaviour, market share and other indicators of commercial success including cost of sales, profit data and return on equity. The approach taken in this chapter is to strip this stuff to the basic level and keep it straightforward without getting lost in the undergrowth of complicated mathematics!

Doing business on customers' terms

As sales and marketing professionals, we feel we've been trained to do things a certain way, and to think in a certain way that distinguishes us from our colleagues in other parts of the business or organization, such as operations, logistics, HR and finance. Yet this distinction that lives in our own minds may in fact inhibit our ability to become successful at sales pipeline management. At one level, we have much more in common with these people than we may first believe!

The point here is that away from the office we all behave very similarly. We'll often hold differing and conflicting points of view contemporaneously. We'll often make compromises and customer sacrifices if we can't get exactly what we want. In essence, the way we behave as consumers has also started to seep into our roles as businesspeople. British sales and marketing guru Peter Fisk observes:

Customers are more different and individual, more discerning and demanding than ever. Whilst 100 years ago a new car buyer would be more than happy to buy a Ford Model T, a model that hardly changed in decades, in 'any colour as long as it's black', today customers are intelligent, expectant and pedantic. Their stated needs may well be true, but their unstated needs and wants often matter even more.

A recent survey by Jupiter Research in the UK showed that 70 per cent of the respondents found online research and review to be extremely helpful in making a purchase decision, and 97 per cent of them also trusted online reviews (both negative and positive) five times more than they trusted information in a TV commercial or newspaper advertisement.

British media entrepreneur Mark Palmer adds: 'I see a fundamental shift in power to the consumer, to the people. That requires us to engage, to create and connect with consumers on a scale that we've never seen before.' And this is regardless of whether they are in the home or at the office.

Along with access to the instant knowledge base called the internet comes every sales and consumer dissatisfaction horror story ever told! Yikes! Let's hope you don't end up in the Hall of Shame!

Every consumer today has either heard of or knows someone who's been on the wrong side of a sales transaction that's gone badly wrong. Today, it's colleagues, friends, family and peers that your customers and clients will want to listen to, and it's this group who increasingly have a stronger influence on the ultimate purchase decision that's being made (Figure 2.1). What Figure 2.1 clearly demonstrates is that the balance of power has fundamentally shifted from sellers to customers and clients.

In markets of infinite choice and oversupply, it's customers who are in control. They expect companies to do business where, when and how they want and they don't appreciate the pursuit of profit being placed in front of their own needs and requirements!

Today, building a sales pipeline isn't that straightforward and will require you to start from the 'outside in' and then respond 'inside out' in a more enlightened and focused way in order to do business.

Irrespective of the market segment you're in, customers and clients will resist being stereotyped:

- They value products less than ever before; instead how they engage with brands through service and support is now far more important.
- They respect youth more than age and aspire to be youthful at every age, rather than automatically respecting elders.
- They now value life more than money, preferring to deal in currencies such as knowledge, friendship or well-being rather than hard cash, and so are less transaction-orientated than their predecessors.
- They seek to enhance the things they enjoy or value and to minimize the things that they don't enjoy or that aren't important to them.

Figure 2.1   The intelligent customer and client

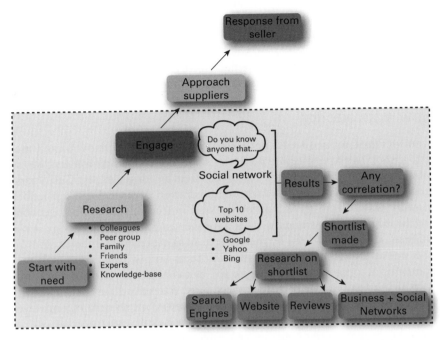

Source: McPheat (2008) *The Sales Person's Crisis* http://www.mtdsalestraining.com

'The challenge is as it always has been – to understand customers, to develop solutions to their needs and connect with them in appropriate ways that result in their satisfaction, maybe even their loyalty and advocacy, and deliver a profit for the business. It's just a million times more complicated than it was for Henry Ford', reflects Peter Fisk.

A further complicating factor in building a realistic sales pipeline is the unstable nature of markets and the inability of politicians to manage economies without recourse to eye-watering amounts of debt. For example, in August 2011, turmoil in financial global markets wiped US$200 billion off the value of equities on the London Stock Exchange given the wobbles within the Eurozone and the question mark that continues to hang over the US handling of its national debt, now standing in excess of US$14.5 trillion – something my calculator isn't able to cope with!

In an editorial, 'Markets have lost faith in the politicians', published in the *Evening Standard* (London), 5 August 2011, seasoned city commentator Anthony Hilton argued that consumers in the West have been insulated from the effects of such seismic shifts in market confidence because it's yet to hurt them directly in their pockets. 'The imbalances of world trade and growth over the last decade have been hidden from the average voter by the ability of the West to borrow. This has allowed consumers and governments in Europe and America to maintain their living standards and neither recognizes nor adjusts to the fact that the economic tide has turned against us.'

In the UK, the Centre for Economic and Business Research predicts that living standards could fall by as much as 25 per cent over the next quarter-century as consumers adjust to the pressure not only from much cheaper Asian labour markets but also from far greater competition for share of scarce resources.

It's against this backdrop that we must rewire our approach in constructing a realistic sales pipeline that takes account of these forces for change.

New approaches

Sean McPheat, a British sales guru, emphatically declares that you can't use 'old-school' sales prospecting tactics in search of today's customers. 'Most sales training is developed for a prospect that no longer exists! Customers have responded with a worldwide demonstration of sincere dissatisfaction in every way – from mere indifference and indecision to flat-out rejection and hostility against standard sales approaches. The customer today is so frustrated, bored and tired by the old-school salesperson and their tactics.'

It's clear today that our dealings with others both within and outside the company or organization we work for has changed in two fundamental ways that affect how we persuade others. First, widespread use of the internet in home life and in almost every aspect of business has resulted in a massive shift in how we communicate with others on a daily basis. Second, we're more likely than ever to encounter people in our work environments and our business interactions who come from a variety of cultures and backgrounds vastly different from our own.

An important challenge that we all face is in understanding how electronic communications have affected our ability to persuade. For example, how might a process like negotiation be affected, whether it takes place online or face to face?

Gone are the days when negotiations were conducted exclusively in person or over the phone. Today, more and more negotiations are being conducted online, with the stakes ranging from important terms in multibillion-dollar deals to the sandwich order for the internal office meeting. Sean McPheat warns:

> In the traditional world of sales, you start with prospecting; you set up an appointment, get a meeting, make a proposal and then play the game of back and forth until you finally close the deal. Depending on the typical sales cycle for your product combined with client business factors over which you have no control, this could take days, weeks, months or even years! Meanwhile, you're forced to do a lot of work to keep the opportunity warm and you risk triggering the 'pest alarm' and being squelched out of your prospect's mind.

He argues that sales pipeline management today is aided by our online presence and through our ability to keep in touch with prospects via social networks and other online engagement activities. 'By the time of your first meeting, your prospect has been able to review a lot of information about your solutions and also about you', he says.

Although the internet has often been referred to as the information super-highway, research has shown that the lack of personal contact between negotiating parties can be more of a road block than a route to a successful sales outcome.

Typically, negotiating through e-mail can make it less likely that negotiators exchange the kind of personal information that typically helps establish better rapport and as a result could ultimately result in poorer outcomes.

An experiment in the United States amongst pairs of MBA students from two leading business schools – some of whom shared personalized information and some of whom didn't – found that, where negotiators engaged in some form of self-disclosure, such as providing a photograph or some biographical information and interests, 65 per cent were able to agree on a deal, with only 6 per cent of the 'personalized pairs' arriving at an impasse and unable to negotiate a deal.

Using another measure of success, the researchers also found that, when the pairs involved in the experiment were able to come to a mutually agreeable negotiated solution, the joint outcome of the settlement – the sum of what each participant walked away with – was 18 per cent higher in the personalized groups compared with the non-personalized groups. Remember, all of this interaction happened remotely.

There are other issues that total dependence on electronic communications can create, such as miscommunication, which is more likely to occur than with traditional face-to-face communication, which may not be possible to conduct in every situation, however desirable it might be.

Cultural differences

In another US study, published a few years ago in the *Journal of Experimental Social Psychology*, there was a fascinating study that explored the differences between US and Japanese culture when it came to leaving voicemail! Unbelievable but true!

The researchers suspected that, because people from the Japanese culture tend to be collectivistic in their behaviours and more focused on forming and maintaining relationships with others, they would have a much harder time making somewhat complex requests left on voicemail. The researchers reasoned that, if Japanese people care more about how their communications affect their relationships with recipients compared with the approach taken by Americans, then conveying a message in which the Japanese participant receives no feedback as to how it's being received should cause them more stress.

To test this hypothesis, the researchers asked a group of American and Japanese participants to leave a somewhat detailed voicemail request for help in their native language. The American participants tended to cut straight to the chase with what they wanted, whereas their Japanese counterparts took much longer to leave their voicemails, seemingly more concerned about how their messages would affect their relationship with the recipients.

Further differences emerged from the study that illuminated the need for face-to-face communication rather than total dependence on remote communications. The American participants reported hanging up around 50 per cent of the time when hearing the recorded message of the person who wasn't available to take the call, whilst the Japanese hung up an astonishing 85 per cent of the time without leaving any message.

Part of the reason for such a difference in behaviour was that Japanese respondents found it more difficult to sound personal when leaving a message compared with the American participants.

The conclusions to be drawn from this US study are that relationships are a key part of the persuasion process, both within and outside the workplace, and this is especially true of people from collectivistic cultures.

Power of the personal brand

Sean McPheat adds that, in order to turn prospects into customers, sellers need to invest in their 'personal brand':

> *Your personal brand is who you are, but if you're like most people you may not have given a lot of thought to that. Before you start writing blog posts, recording videos or engaging with others through LinkedIn, Facebook or Twitter, give some thought to how you want to 'show up' online. Emotion is always muted through online interaction, so the goal isn't to adopt a false persona. Instead, aim to emphasize the qualities you want to put on display to the public.*

Where certain salespeople score so well is when their 'personal brand' is a mirror image of that of the buyer, which in neurolinguistic programming (NLP) speak is known as 'mirror and matching' (Figure 2.2).

No matter what market segment you're in, you're no longer the gate-keeper for information about your products and services. That's the scary part. More often than not your clients and prospects will know as much as you do about your business by the time you agree to meet them! On top of that, your clients and prospects have checked up on you and have formed opinions of you based on whatever came up on Google and Bing and other search engines as well as your profile on business networking sites such as LinkedIn. There's no hiding place and there's no longer any element of surprise left in the process of matching buyers and sellers. It must be meticulously planned and well executed, leaving nothing to chance.

Treating consumers whom you want to do business with as individuals first and foremost was at the centre of the phenomenal database and then online sales strategies adopted by iconic US rock band the Grateful Dead, as discussed in Chapter 1.

Figure 2.2 The 'personal brand' of buyers and sellers – 'mirror and matching'

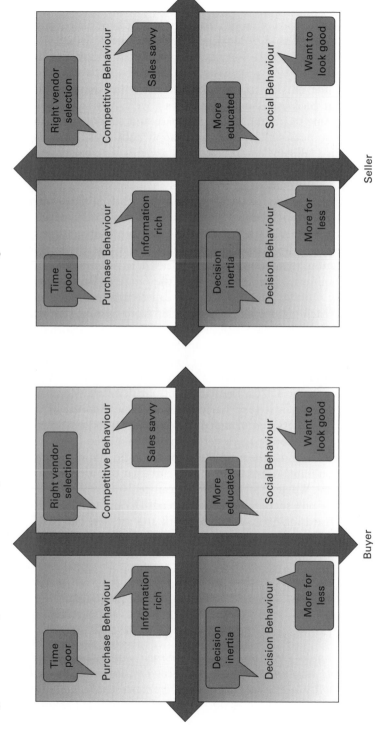

Building a fan base the Grateful Dead way!

Back in 1965, word of mouth was very important in increasing the Grateful Dead fan base. Friends told friends, who told friends, which spread the word and swelled the fan base, but all done without Facebook, YouTube, MySpace and Twitter!

'From the outside, the Grateful Dead looked like they didn't have a clue about business, but in reality they were forward-looking, especially when it came to building their database and connecting with their fans – a lesson companies today can readily apply', observes David Meerman Scott and Brian Halligan, co-authors of *Marketing Lessons from the Grateful Dead*.

Early direct marketing techniques included notices for 'Dead Freaks Unite!' tucked inside the sleeves of the band's early albums, and encouraging fans to sign up for updates about the band and forthcoming tours, which became the early days of the Grateful Dead Fan Club and the beginnings of the burgeoning direct mail list. Back in 1971, it was a radical idea to add a 'call to action' to an album a band released, as this appeared to be an overt way of building a mailing list – but the Grateful Dead were no ordinary band! Six months after running the call to action, the band had 10,257 names on their mailing list, including 885 from Europe. Five years later, that list stood at 63,147 names in the United States alone – sorted by name and zip code without the aid of a computer!

'The band not only reached out to fans, but fans reached out to the band by sending in letters, postcards and artwork', write the authors.

Starting in the 1970s, the band sent out newsletters and other mailings two to three times a year. Early newsletters were typed by hand on IBM electric typewriters and included personal letters to fans. In May 1974, the band sent fans a one-page letter alerting them to the *From the Mars Hotel* album release and exhorting them to call radio stations: 'We know you'll enjoy our album, and if you get real enthused call a radio station or tell a record store. We need all the help we can get.'

As the band's success went from strength to strength, the newsletters also evolved, featuring hand-drawn artwork and articles. The band intrinsically understood their fan base and fed the voracious appetite for any news as well as information about new releases and forthcoming gigs.

When the internet finally caught up with the band they were quick to launch a user net group, 'Dead Flames', as well as an official website and e-mail newsletter that helped to drive sales of albums and merchandise whilst most other rock bands were still stuck in the dark ages hoping to sell branded T-shirts at gigs in order to supplement ticket sales. The authors say:

The Grateful Dead understood that their mailing list was a highly valuable asset and they used it to keep fans informed, to build a community and to let fans know their concert schedule. Building a following today requires much more than simply collecting names and e-mail addresses. You need to collect telephone numbers, SMS, Twitter followers, Facebook fan page followers and LinkedIn group members. You build this following by creating lots of remarkable content that pulls people in – content that's personal, relevant and interesting to your followers.

The sky's the limit

Today, we have a global population of about 6 billion and, with a vast proportion of that being able to consume products and services, it's never been a better time to sell, given the internet and cheap phone calls. Advances in manufacturing, IT and service delivery make it possible to create products and services and compete in markets just about anywhere on the planet. So why then does it seem that the actual process of converting leads into customers has become so difficult when it's obvious that there are people out there who'd really benefit from your product or service?

Sean McPheat offers his own explanation:

In today's world of sales, just about everything has become that little bit more difficult. It seems that the problem isn't one of supply and demand but rather a growing rift between how people want to buy and how some salespeople continue to sell. It's been long said that people hate to be sold to but they love to buy. This is true even in murky economic times. Just look at the sales for plasma TVs and other consumer items like smartphones, tablet PCs, online music, broadband internet and hybrid cars.

What's changed is how we're able to interact, the nature and frequency of those interactions and how customers and clients now have unprecedented access to information. This in turn has led to changes in the way that we make our purchasing decisions. According to Chris Anderson, author of *The Long Tail: Why the future of business is selling less of more*, fewer products and services are now overwhelmingly sold in large quantities versus many more products that are now sold in lower quantities (Figure 2.3), hence the so-called 'long tail'.

When traditional limitations of distribution and shelf space are removed or managed for the benefit of making it easier to shop, then products like the Grateful Dead's back catalogue continue to sell for years to come, well after the band ceased to exist and Jerry Garcia had passed away.

Take Apple's iTunes. Music lovers can now trawl through the back catalogues of hundreds of bands, and there's also a new generation of fans who will discover this music for the first time, creating new sales opportunities and a 'long tail' for these products. In this way, iTunes helps connect fans with bands and artists whom otherwise they'd never have thought of following, making 'listening for leads' based on iTunes users' musical preferences and tastes a highly profitable enterprise.

Figure 2.3 The dynamics of the 21st-century marketplace

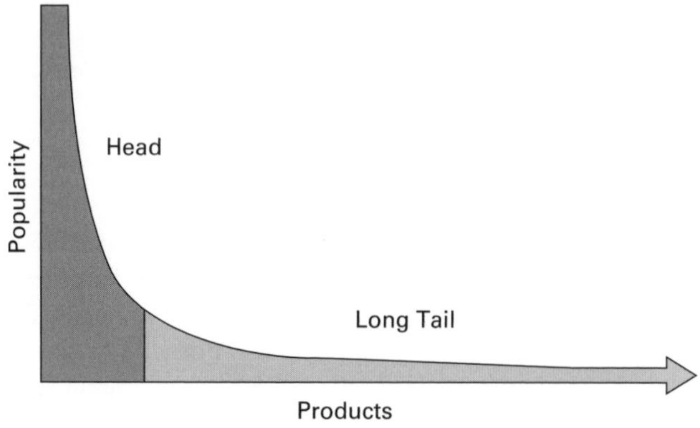

Source: Anderson (2006)

The lead conversion process

The first thing to say is that you need to manage your expectations! Even if you do everything written in this chapter and build yourself the best, most shiny 'lead conversion machine' ever, you may still be driving around in your second-hand car a year from now! Only kidding, but I hope you get the point!

There are no guarantees that any lead conversion system is foolproof – all the so-called sales experts on the web and YouTube believe that only they've the answer to turn you into a multimillionaire overnight if you buy their sales training programme and subscribe to a small library of CDs and books, at a special, discounted price, of course! If it's too good to be true, then it's likely it isn't true. The business world is littered with failed customer relationship management (CRM) systems that promised the earth but ended up failing because they were too complicated, salespeople didn't use them properly, or quite simply they were useless for the job they were designed to do!

There's no substitute for knowing as much as you can about your prospective customers or clients and understanding what drives their needs and requirements – what keeps them awake at night and how your product or service can make a difference. If you can crack this, you'll be successful.

It can be a small but important difference that you seek to make, such as keeping your customer warm or dry. It can be a medium kind of difference that you seek to make, such as getting your customer to a destination as safely and as quickly as possible. Alternatively, it can be a massive difference that you want to make for your client – such as delivering an outsourced middle- or back-office function with a fixed cost that guarantees a bottom-line cost saving of millions a year.

In essence, a lead conversion is a process through which your company or organization 'converts' a revenue opportunity into actual revenue. That means that every contact made by a prospective, new, existing or long-established customer is a 'cold', 'warm' or 'hot' lead that can be converted!

As discussed in Chapter 1, the starting point must be your prospective customer or client's point of view (POV).

Champion salespeople see things through their prospects' eyes. Can there be any other way? These top-performing salespeople know that their products and services offer many features and benefits but only talk about the benefits that their prospects really want to own. Think about it. What's the point of wasting your time and talking to prospects about stuff they aren't vaguely interested in that won't motivate their behaviour? Yet poor salespeople stick to 'the script' as if it's foolproof. Well, scripts don't work where prospects are knowledgeable, savvy and suspicious.

Successful salespeople don't sell what they want to sell. They sell what their customers or clients want to own.

Some of the most successful sales strategies are evidenced-based. This involves stripping away anything you feel emotionally about your product or service in the first instance and focusing on the hard, verifiable facts backed up wherever possible with compelling third-party endorsement. This is why case studies within B2B markets are so important. That may sound rational, and of course it is.

The really clever bit is reading the body language and non-verbal communication of the recipient of the 'pitch', as well as packaging the sales proposition using emotional cues as well as enthusiasm, remembering always to keep in mind the unasked question 'What's in it for me?' If you're able to answer this in a compelling way, you're on your way to closing the sale (see Chapter 10).

Check that your sales radar is working

A prospect or sales lead can come from just about anywhere on the planet given that we are all virtually linked in a wired world through a myriad of electronic, digital and mobile devices. A sales lead could come from family, friends, acquaintances, business colleagues and contacts, existing customers or clients, former or existing employers and even other competitors for whom the business is too small to make it worthwhile (Figure 2.4). In each of these interactions there's an opportunity to sell either face to face or remotely, by telephone, e-mail, mobile and online.

Your lead conversion process should be designed to create customers or clients and not 'sales' because, as we discussed earlier in this chapter and elsewhere, the sale is a natural consequence of having the right product for the right prospect in a selling process that recognizes customer purchase decisions as the driving force (Figure 2.5).

Figure 2.4 The sales radar

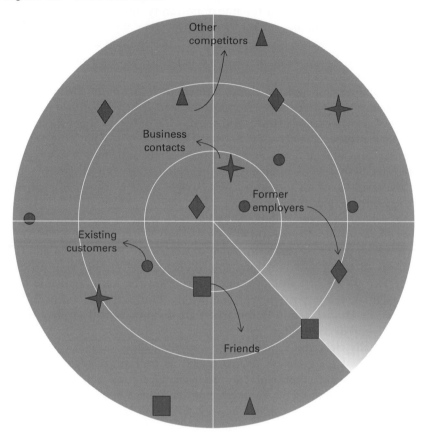

Nine phases of customer or client behaviour

Prospects and customers generally go through nine predictable phases:

1 *Identifying needs* – out in the global marketplace, a certain customer segment will recognize the need or desire for a product or service that's available.

2 *Awareness* – those with a recognized need become aware that the company or organization has products or services that could fulfil the need.

3 *Learning* – potential customers or clients seek information about the company or organization's products and services as well as how it does its business.

4 *Consideration* – the prospect considers whether or not to make the purchase.

Figure 2.5   Typical lead conversion process

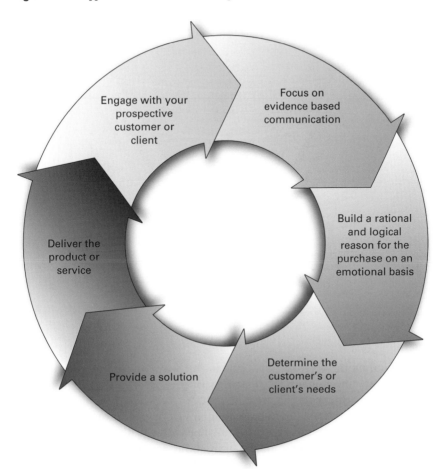

5 *Evaluation* – the customer compares available products or services from various sources to select one that is preferred or best suits needs and requirements.

6 *Acquisition* – the customer or client takes action to acquire the product or service.

7 *Use* – the customer uses the product or service during its lifespan. It's during the use stage that a company or organization has the greatest ability to influence customer satisfaction through positively fulfilling the customer's expectations for the product or service.

8 *Re-entry* – as the product or service reaches or nears the end of its lifespan, the customer may identify a need or desire for the same or a different product or service and will then re-enter the cycle.

9 *Transaction processing* – gathering information about the customer in order to maintain communication, provide services and involve the customer in selling to new prospects.

Figure 2.6   The typical sales pipeline

Understanding the customer life cycle in this way can lead to ensuring that the sales pipeline remains populated with prospects, leads, opportunities and customers or clients (Figure 2.6).

If you work in a medium to large company or organization, then it's likely that the sales and marketing department will have created goals, strategies and a framework for collecting information about actual customers or clients, potential customers or clients and desired customer or client segments and documented these in a customer life cycle management plan.

Methods for collecting information include:

● surveys and questionnaires (including web forms);
● focus groups;
● customer or client post-purchase, postage-paid warranty and response cards;
● sales, customer service, and order entry interviews and discussions; and
● contracting with market research companies.

It is usual that companies or organizations set conversion rate goals for each section of the sales pipeline:

● the success rate for capturing return sales;
● prospect awareness;

- customer or client satisfaction; and
- quality and quantity of prospect and customer or client information collected.

Surveys are a useful way of collecting information about market and customer segments:

- level of awareness about the company or organization and its products and services among those in prospect and customer/client demographics;
- where customers or clients first learnt about the company and its products or services;
- which attributes of the company or organization's products or services persuade them to purchase, eg price, features, design, quality, availability, delivery, service, reliability, reputation, convenience, ease of purchase, or knowledge of the salesperson;
- when was the last time this product or service was purchased, what particular brand or make was purchased and where and how the purchase was made;
- the level of satisfaction with using the product or service;
- the level of satisfaction with the company or organization in providing information and/or support;
- likelihood of repurchasing this product or service from the company or organization;
- whether they would consider other products or services; and
- whether they would recommend the product or service to others.

Typically, this information collected from customer or client surveys is used to create interface strategies with prospects in the pre-purchase stages of the customer or client life cycle, media (online and offline) to use for advertising, and messages to promote in advertising, such as price, performance, reliability, reputation, fun and other attributes. An example of a customer life cycle management plan is provided in Table 2.1.

In addition to the customer life cycle management plan, the company or organization you work for is likely to have a clear and thoroughly developed plan for setting sales goals and for creating and implementing a strategy for achieving these goals (Table 2.2).

US sales guru Michael Gerber adds:

The specific needs of individual customers or clients will depend on their perception of the impact the purchase of the goods or services will have on them and the confidence they feel in making the decision to buy. Your job is to satisfy those needs so they can find the rational and logical support for the emotional decision to buy that brought them to you.

Table 2.1   Customer or client life cycle management plan

PART 1: INFORMATION GATHERING		
Methodology	Objectives	Results
Surveys and focus groups	1 Survey goal:	
	Survey segment (ie prospect or customer/client):	
	Frequency (dates):	
	Distribution/sample response goals:	
	Key measurements:	
	Open questions:	
	2 Survey goal:	
	Survey segment (ie prospect or customer/client):	
	Frequency (dates):	
	Distribution/sample response goals:	
	Key measurements:	
	Open questions:	
	3 Survey goal:	
	Survey segment (ie prospect or customer/client):	
	Frequency (dates):	
	Distribution/sample response goals:	
	Key measurements:	
	Open questions:	
	4 Survey goal:	
	Survey segment (ie prospect or customer/client):	
	Frequency (dates):	
	Distribution/sample response goals:	
	Key measurements:	
	Open questions:	
	Focus group plan:	

Table 2.1 *continued*

PART 1: INFORMATION GATHERING		
Methodology	Objectives	Results
Collecting customer/client information	Methods of collecting customer information (other than surveys):	
	Key customer life cycle information to be entered	
	Customer information collection training plans for sales, customer service, technical service	
PART 2: USING INFORMATION		
Methodology	Objectives	Results
Quantitative and qualitative research	1(a) The most common sources of customer awareness:	
	1(b) Impact on marketing strategy/methods:	
	1(c) Impact on sales strategy/methods:	
	2(a) Key criteria influencing purchase:	
	2(b) Impact on marketing strategy/methods:	
	2(c) Impact on sales strategy/methods:	
	3(a) Most positive feature/attribute identified by customers/clients:	
	3(b) Impact on marketing strategy/methods:	
	3(c) Impact on sales strategy/methods:	
	4(a) Least favourable feature/attribute identified by customers/clients:	
	4(b) Impact on marketing strategy/methods:	

Table 2.1 *continued*

PART 2: USING INFORMATION		
Methodology	Objectives	Results
	4(c) Impact on sales strategy/methods:	
	5(a) Customer satisfaction level with product/service purchased:	
	5(b) Strategy for improving satisfaction level	
	6(a) Customer satisfaction level with company/organization personnel interactions (sales force, customer service):	
	6(b) Strategy for improving customer satisfaction level with company/organization personnel interactions:	
	7(a) Customer satisfaction with miscellaneous company touch points (web, commercial documentation, PR, customer service):	
	7(b) Strategy for improving customer satisfaction level with miscellaneous company touch points:	
	8 Customer retention actions (and responsible department):	

Table 2.1 *continued*

PART 3: CUSTOMER PROFILE		
Individual profiles	Age:	
	Income:	
	Gender:	
	Profession:	
	Education:	
	Family size:	
	Home owner:	
	Marital status:	
	Hobbies:	
Business profiles	Company/organization size:	
	Annual revenues:	
	Location:	
	Branch locations:	
	Number of employees:	
	Industry and products	
	Years in business	
PART 4: COMMENTS AND APPROVAL		
	Comments:	
	Prepared by:	Date:
	Approval:	Date:

Table 2.2 Typical sales management plan

PART 1: SALES CYCLE	GOAL	ACTUAL
Time from prospect to qualifying lead		
Time from qualifying lead to sales appointment date		
Time from first sales appointment date to closing the sale		
Typical number of sales calls required to close the sale		
Total sales cycle time		
PART 2: SALES PIPELINE GOALS		
a: Number of prospects from marketing department: (daily/weekly/monthly/quarterly/yearly)	Actual	
b: Number of qualified leads: (daily/weekly/monthly/quarterly/yearly)	Actual	
c: Prospect to qualified lead conversion rate goal:	Percentage	
d: Number of sales call appointments goal: (daily/weekly/monthly/quarterly/yearly)	Actual	
e: Qualified lead to sales call appointments: (daily/weekly/monthly/quarterly/yearly)	Percentage	
f: Number of sales call appointments: (daily/weekly/monthly/quarterly/yearly)	Actual	
g: Number of closed sales: (daily/weekly/monthly/quarterly/yearly)	Actual calls Actual units Actual value (money)	
h: Sales call appointment to close sale conversion rate:	Percentage	
PART 3: SALES STRATEGY		
a: Information and strategies used to qualify leads:		
b: Strategy to set sales appointments:		
c: Strategy to propose/quote:		
d: Strategy to close sales:		

Table 2.2 *continued*

PART 4: SALES EMPLOYEES' REQUIREMENTS		
a: Required number of professional sales employees:		
b: Required number of sales administrators/assistants:		
c: Sales territories staffing requirements:		

Territory	Professional sales staff	Sales administrators
1)		
2)		
3)		
4)		
5)		
6)		
7)		

d: Sales training requirements:	
Product training	
Company sales training	
General sales training	
Other training	

PART 5: REGULAR SALES DEPARTMENT MEETINGS	
Daily meetings	Time
Attendees:	
Materials:	
Agenda:	
Weekly meetings	Time
Attendees:	
Materials:	
Agenda:	
Monthly meetings	Time
Attendees:	
Materials:	
Agenda:	

Table 2.2 *continued*

PART 6: REPORTS	
Daily reports to sales manager	From:
Report name:	
Content:	
Action points:	
Weekly reports to sales manager	From:
Report name:	
Content:	
Action points:	
Monthly reports to sales manager	From:
Report name:	
Content:	
Action points:	
Quarterly reports to sales manager	From:
Report name:	
Content:	
Action points:	
Yearly reports to sales manager	From:
Report name:	
Content:	
Action points:	
Daily reports from sales manager	To:
Report name:	
Content:	
Action points:	

Table 2.2 *continued*

PART 6: REPORTS	
Weekly reports from sales manager	To:
Report name:	
Content:	
Action points:	
Monthly reports from sales manager	To:
Report name:	
Content:	
Action points:	
Quarterly reports from sales manager	To:
Report name:	
Content:	
Action points:	
Yearly reports from sales manager	To:
Report name:	
Content:	
Action points:	
PART 7: COST OF LEADS/SALES	
Cost of marketing/advertising:	Actual value (money)
Number of qualified leads:	Actual
Cost per qualified lead:	Actual value (money)
Cost of sales:	Actual value (money)
Number of sales:	Actual
Cost per sale:	Actual value (money)

Table 2.2 *continued*

PART 8: COMMENTS		
	Comments:	
	Prepared by:	Date:
	Approval:	Date:

There are two essential elements of the lead conversion infrastructure that will affect how you structure your selling process: people and pathways. These are the ways you manage the sales process and the channels you choose for selling your product or service.

The typical sales force configurations are:

- order taking;
- own sales force or outsourced sales team;
- conventional selling;
- consultative selling; and
- remote selling.

A general rule of thumb in selecting the selling mode is that the more selling functions your customer or client requires for the purchase decision, the more important the relationship-building qualities in your sales method.

Real and virtual worlds of prospecting for customers or clients

Prospecting for customers and clients can be a tedious process, and actually most of us aren't natural at doing it well, so we may consider turning to external support for this part of the selling process. If you're new to sales – an assumption made in writing this book – then your company or organization may have partnered you with one of its more experienced salespeople as a mentor or to provide you with on-the-job sales training. Alternatively if you run your own business and recognize that prospecting for customers or clients isn't your bag, then you may decide to outsource this to a third party.

Many small to medium-size businesses of all shapes and sizes often hire a telemarketing agency to make outbound calls on their behalf.

From the recipient's perspective, it's not apparent that it's an outsourced agency making the call. Often these agencies are hired to source leads and even book appointments, but costs can rack up fast without any tangible evidence of actual sales having been closed over a short period of time. Avoid paying an agency on an hourly- or daily-rate basis, but only when they've booked a sales appointment with a qualified lead where the chances of closing a sale are at least greater than 50 per cent.

Usually, using this type of service isn't recommended, particularly if you haven't attempted to put into practice the methods contained in this book and learn how to do this for yourself. After all, no one's better qualified to talk about your products and services than you are, and prospecting for customers or clients is something that you need to consider doing by focusing on the customer and client needs and requirements. This should be integral to the way you conduct your business.

Tools for prospecting

The vast majority of sales professionals use a combination of phone, mail, e-mail, web and face-to-face communications to work for them in helping to prospect for customers or clients. In the past 20 years, sales communication has swung from face-to-face to mass e-mail marketing and also mobile push marketing.

Telemarketing

These are sometimes the most annoying and intrusive forms of prospecting for customers and clients known! You can often hear the rustling of the script or the laboured delivery of the cold caller, which frankly is the biggest turn-off imaginable. The art of cold calling is discussed in detail in Chapter 3. The fact remains that telemarketing can potentially reach more potential users of a company's products or services in one hour than most salespeople working face to face can meet in a week.

This form of prospecting is still extremely popular, but is also governed by laws and regulations, as explained in detail in Guru in a Bottle®'s *Essential Law for Marketers* (2nd edition).

Telemarketing, whilst effective, can also damage your reputation if it isn't done well. In order to make telemarketing effective, it usually helps to combine a phone call with a flyer or an e-mail and where appropriate a face-to-face meeting.

In many respects, we all use telemarketing techniques even if we aren't aware that we are in fact doing so! For example, in public relations, 'selling' a story to a journalist over the phone where you have just a few precious minutes to get your points across is telemarketing!

There are a number of strategies that you should consider adopting when using this sales prospecting technique:

- Always ask whether the recipient of the call is in the middle of something or if it's OK to talk. This is not just polite and professional but also respectful in the way you want to handle the interaction. So many of us have the experience of being on the receiving end of an obvious cold call and the other person has simply launched into the script on the computer screen without so much as asking whether this is a convenient time to have a conversation! Doh!

- Never spend more than a few minutes speaking – you get someone to buy your product or service by listening!

- Ask questions that are relevant and not irritating. If it's clearly a clumsy effort to get your sales message across, that's just plain annoying.

- Be honest – we've all been on the end of the call where someone who doesn't know us from Adam speaks to us as if we've known each other for a lifetime! If you've never spoken before, why not say so? After all, honesty is something that a prospective customer or client is looking for.

- When asking questions, why not use an NLP technique called 'chunking'? Chunking means breaking things into bits. For you to process information, it needs to be in chunks of the right size – tiny details or the bigger picture, whatever is appropriate for the person you're speaking to.

- Keep in mind what outcome you want to achieve from the telemarketing call, such as a face-to-face meeting or permission to send further information to the prospect.

Direct mail

In the UK, the Direct Marketing Association, which has over 800 members including BT, M&S, Lloyds TSB and the AA, has been campaigning for raising standards within the industry in order to shake off the label of junk mail and bring respectability for this long-standing and proven method of acquiring prospects, particularly for local businesses.

If you choose direct mail as the primary method of prospecting for customers and clients then you should choose the recipients very carefully.

This form of prospecting is also extremely popular but is also governed by laws and regulations, as explained in detail in Guru in a Bottle®'s *Essential Law for Marketers* (2nd edition).

Mail sent to the wrong prospect is junk and a waste of time and resources. It can also have the effect of damaging the reputation of the business, particularly if the person receiving this mail had opted out of being on such lists via the Mailing Preference Service operating in the UK. Some experts advise that this form of prospecting works best when it is short and indicates that you'll be following up on a certain day at a certain time. It should also go to those whom you know. Redemption coupons and free trials of products such as sachets of shampoo or coffee are likely to get noticed and engage the prospect given the perceived value of communication. The piece of direct mail should also, ideally, have some call to action of the kind adopted by the Grateful Dead when they sent out notices with copies of their latest albums.

E-mail

Over recent years this has become de facto the way in which most prospecting for customers or clients is carried out by the vast majority of companies and organizations.

This form of prospecting is governed by privacy and strict data protection laws and regulations, as explained in detail in Guru in a Bottle®'s *Essential Law for Marketers* (2nd edition).

E-mail prospecting generally comes in two flavours: 1) use of an opt-in list from a list broker to push e-mail to a group of people who've expressed an interest in receiving information about your type of products and services; and 2) searching out the e-mail addresses of a consumer or purchasing agent and mailing a very specific, customized e-mail. Spamming isn't permissible, and this tends to work only where there's an existing business relationship. Sending an e-mail that resembles an advertisement isn't likely to lead to a sale, unless of course you have an existing relationship with the customers or clients and want to attract their attention with a special offer or other inducement.

Web

Social networking has possibly become the single most important sales tool outside of face-to-face selling in the world today, as its growth and penetration in just about every conceivable market and customer segment have been phenomenal.

Research on the power of social networking published in 2011 by Edison Research in the United States reveals that:

- 57 million adult Americans read and follow blogs and 12 million maintain one;
- 92 per cent of Americans are familiar with Twitter, although only 8 per cent of those aged 12 or over use Twitter;
- approximately 20,000 US users contribute more than half of all Twitter content, which is 0.01 per cent of total users;
- 93 per cent of adult Americans are familiar with Facebook and nearly a quarter of adult social network users surveyed indicated that Facebook is the social site or service that most influences their buying decisions;
- location-based sites and services, such as Foursquare and Facebook Places, are familiar to 30 per cent of Americans aged 12 and older and used by 4 per cent of Americans aged 12 and older;

- on average, 22 per cent of Facebook users comment on another's post or status, 20 per cent on photos, and 26 per cent 'like' another's content;

- nearly twice as many men as women use LinkedIn (63 per cent compared with 37 per cent of women), but all other social networking sites have significantly more female users than male users;

- from 2008 to 2010 the percentage of people using social networking sites fell among 18- to 22-year-olds by 12 per cent (from 28 per cent in 2008 to 16 per cent in 2010) and among 23- to 35-year-olds by 8 per cent (from 40 per cent in 2008 to 32 per cent in 2010); and meanwhile

- social networking use increased among 36- to 49-year-olds by 4 per cent (from 22 per cent in 2008 to 26 per cent in 2010) and among 50- to 65-year-olds by 11 per cent.

From a sales prospecting perspective, it's extremely important to know which social networking sites it is worth investing time in, to cultivate a presence, and those that won't actually assist you achieve your business purpose.

US marketing and social network guru Malcolm Gladwell adds: 'Merely by manipulating the size of a group, we can dramatically improve its receptivity to new ideas. By tinkering with the presentation of information, we can significantly improve its stickiness. Simply by finding and reaching those few special people who hold so much social power, we can shape the course of social epidemics.'

In many traditional markets, such as global insurance, there's a reticence about using social or business networks for prospecting for clients where the 'gentlemen's or old boys' network' still exists. But it's only a matter of time before these old-fashioned networks lose their impetus to the power of global electronic networks that can instantly open the door to thousands of like-minded professional people with a single click of a mouse. As Malcolm Gladwell argues, 'In the end, Tipping Points are a reaffirmation of the potential for change and the power of intelligent action. Look at the world around you. It may seem like an immovable, implacable place. It is not. With the slightest push – in just the right place – it can be tipped.'

The distinction between B2C and B2B is rapidly evaporating in this space, and social networking provides a way to connect people of similar backgrounds and interests, irrespective of geography, instantaneously. A wide range of social and business networking sites provide useful tools for individuals for both private and business use (Table 2.3).

Table 2.3   Useful social networking sites

Site	Website address	User profile	Number of users
Bebo	http://www.bebo.com	Mainly personal rather than B2B. Described as 'MySpace meets Facebook, with video-sharing and built-in Skype'	117 million
Facebook	http://facebook.com	Mainly personal rather than B2B, but an increasing number of companies and organizations are creating 'pages' for branding and sales and marketing. Less than one-third students; fastest-growing demographic is 35-year-olds and over	640 million
Flickr	http://www.flickr.com	Online photo management and sharing application	32 million
Hi5	http://www.hi5.com	One of the largest social entertainment sites in the world; 43 per cent of users are 15- to 24-year-olds	80 million
LinkedIn	http://www.linkedin.com	B2B focus aimed at professionals, representing 170 business sectors in 200 countries	100 million
MySpace	http://www.myspace.com	Mainly personal rather than B2B; 30 per cent of users are 15- to 24-year-olds	100 million
Plaxo Pulse	http://www.plaxo.com	Online address book with social networking	15 million
SlideShare	http://www.slideshare.com	Allows uploading and sharing of presentations in a variety of formats. Users are highly educated (62 per cent college degree, 19 per cent Master's degree or higher), affluent (25 per cent earn $100,000-plus) and adult (64 per cent are 35 years old or over)	100 million

Table 2.3 *continued*

Site	Website address	User profile	Number of users
Twitter	http://www.twitter.com	Mix of personal and B2B; micro-blogging site restricted to 140 characters; useful as a signpost to blogs on websites and other content	200 million
Xing	http://www.xing.com	Alternative to LinkedIn in Germany	8 million
YouTube	http://www.youtube.com	World's second-largest search engine after Google; video-sharing website with a very broad user base (18- to 55-year-olds)	1.2 billion

Source: Wikipedia, 2011

Face-to-face

In many respects all the other prospecting techniques are alternatives to face-to-face, which remains the most powerful but also the hardest way of prospecting for a customer or client given that it takes time and money and there's no guarantee of success at the end of the process. That said, it may dramatically increase the opportunity of closing the sale, and certainly where large or complicated purchases are involved it's essential.

Typically, if prospecting face-to-face you can expect one of four outcomes:

- You may be asked to follow up with a proposal and a detailed costing of what you propose.
- You may be required to attend a meeting where other decision makers and budget holders are involved.
- You will be asked to leave information or literature behind about your product or service.
- You have the opportunity to demonstrate the product or service that you wish to sell to the prospective customer or client.

In the past, this type of prospecting was called getting a 'foot in the door', as it tended to be used by door-to-door double-glazing salesmen or traders who might have appeared to be a bit dodgy!

That of course belies the very powerful nature of face-to-face selling, which has become highly sophisticated within many business sectors, such as law, accountancy, management consultancy, public relations, marketing and financial services.

Monitoring the performance of your prospecting efforts

Microsoft founder Bill Gates once said 'If you don't measure it you can't manage it', and so it makes good sense to audit the performance of all sales prospecting activities on a regular basis as well as learn from them as an important part of improving the sales pipeline management process.

In the last part of this chapter, we've divided the metrics you need to watch into three key areas of sales and business performance (Figure 2.7).

Figure 2.7   Key sales performance metrics

Profitability

Gross profit

Typically, a high gross profit suggests that a company or organization is efficient and well managed and has a handle on its costs. Operational costs are controlled through internal programmes designed to ensure they remain within certain limits. Sales and marketing costs are more difficult to control since the expenditures usually go towards sales and marketing programmes and communications that have a longer-term impact.

Sales professionals may be tempted to increase market share through lowering prices for products and services that drive revenues, but profitability will be sacrificed as a result, so this should be avoided. Sales professionals have a responsibility to know whether their efforts contribute to the bottom line (gross profit).

Gross profit is a company's or organization's total revenue less the costs incurred when delivering the product or service that generates the revenue. In ordinary language, it's the total of sales less total costs – sometimes referred to as the cost of goods sold (COGS).

The calculation for determining gross revenue is:

$$GP = R - C$$

where:

GP = gross profit
R = revenue
C = costs

By itself gross profit doesn't tell salespeople much about the overall performance of their company or organization's products or service except to indicate whether the performance is generally positive or a cause for concern. Typically, gross profit is calculated before accounting for operating expenses, which include general and administrative, research and development and non-recurring or one-off expenses, such as registration of the company and its intellectual property rights (IPRs). It's possible that a company has a positive performance trend with gross profit increasing each year, but the operating expenses might have increased substantially during that time, which could severely affect net profit or net income.

Net profit

Typically, this figure is the final profit of the company or organization after taxes, cost of sales, general administrative expenses, research and development, non-recurring expenses and other charges on income:

$$NP = (V \times Mc) - Em - Eo - It$$

where:

NP = net profit (in money)
V = customer or client volume (in units sold)
Mc = margin per customer (in money)
Em = marketing expenses (in money)
Eo = operating expenses (in money)
It = bank interest and taxes (in money)

Margin per customer is calculated by the simple formula:

$$Mc = Rc - Cv$$

where:

Mc = margin per customer
Rc = revenue per customer
Cv = variable cost per customer

Customer volume is calculated as follows:

$$Vc = MD \times MS$$

where:

Vc = customer volume
MD = market demand
MS = market share

To use a hypothetical example, our publisher markets the Guru in a Bottle® Series to ambitious sales and marketing executives. It has the following statistics:

$V = 400,000$
$Mc = \$50$
$Em = \$1,500,000$
$Eo = \$500,000$
$It = \$6,500,000$
$NP = (Cv \times Mc) - Em - Eo - It$
$NP = (400,000 \times \$50) - \$1,500,000 - \$500,000 - \$6,500,000$
$\quad = \$11,500,000$

So the $11.5 million profit appears to be quite healthy!

Net profit helps sales managers understand how profitable their company is after accounting for additional, below-the-line expenses resulting from their business development activities, including marketing. It's a good measure for determining how effective a company or organization is with turning revenues into real profits while keeping costs under control. Internally, you may need to check what cross-charges may be levied to each department or strategic business unit (SBU) automatically.

A key challenge is determining the customer-volume and customer-margin figures reasonably accurately. This will require a detailed understanding of the actual customer or client base, the customer's purchasing specifics (to help determine the average margin) and a good description of the operating expenses associated with this effort.

As a rule of thumb, an increasing net profit is good in that it may be indicative that the company's products or services are making more profit per money unit of sales than in the past.

The reasons for this may include greater operational efficiencies that have helped to reduce costs as a percentage of sales. Alternatively, it could reflect a more favourable tax situation. Increasing net profit can also indicate that customers or clients perceive the price–value relationship for the company's products favourably and therefore it's able to command a price premium over the competition. Increasing net profits may also highlight management strengths, since good managers are usually more effective at leveraging the budgets and investments they oversee and they know where to deploy resources in order to maximize returns. The converse is likely to be the case for a declining net profit, for example the company's handle on costs is not good, as this may be rising faster than sales.

Return on sales

All companies and commercial organizations must have sales in order to survive and profits in order to grow the business.

In order to have a bright future, the quality of sales must be understood by sales and marketing professionals, so an important consideration is the amount of profit generated relative to each money unit of sales.

Return on sales (ROS) is a measure of a company's ability to generate profits from sales. It's effectively the profit resulting from each money unit of sales and is based on net profit before tax and total sales:

$$\text{ROS} = \frac{\text{Pnbt}}{\text{S}}$$

where:

ROS = return on sales
Pnbt = net profit before tax
S = sales

Going back to the hypothetical example, the publishing company is quite successful. Its business generated $300 million in sales, and from the previous profit calculation it generated $11.5 million in profits. Calculating the return on sales is as follows:

$$\text{ROS} = \frac{\$11,500,000}{\$300,000,000} = 3.8 \text{ per cent}$$

This may indicate that the company (in this case the publisher of the Guru in a Bottle® Series) needs to improve its profit margins, but this needs to be seen in light of the industry average for profit margins in order to make such a determination. ROS is a practical indicator of the profitability of your sales and marketing efforts and is most effective if reviewed over time. ROS measures the financial efficiency of a company's recent sales efforts, particularly in comparison with other companies in the same market segment.

Sales force performance

As a company's business grows, successfully servicing existing and new customers is an important consideration for the sales team. Each company and organization is different in the way it shapes its sales planning based on sales objectives and market conditions. Typically, sales managers design their go-to-market plans around maximizing the potential financial returns from their targeted customer base.

Breakdown approach

Sales managers must determine how many salespeople are required to service existing customers and also to attract new customers. Given these factors, companies need to determine sales force size, and the breakdown approach is useful when the primary information available to a company's decision makers, aside from its own baseline sales, is market growth.

To determine the size of the sales force using the breakdown approach, sales managers must know the previous year's sales history, projections of their own new sales for the forthcoming year and market forecasts:

$$SFS = \frac{FS}{SPP}$$

where:

SFS = sales force size
FS = forecasted sales
SPP = average sales per person

Although the breakdown approach is useful for determining sales force size, sales professionals mustn't over-rely on last year's average sales per person as a benchmark for future sales needs.

Workload approach

Sales plans usually include a projection of the total work required to achieve a goal. The challenge lies in the cost of reaching the goal – a sales force can be expensive! The management team will want to keep costs low in order to maximize profits whilst also maintaining good relations with customers and clients. The workload approach organizes customers into common segments usually based on account size.

It's the job of the sales manager to determine how many salespeople are required to call on the various customer groups:

$$SFS = \frac{SE}{SEaps}$$

where:

SFS = sales force size
SE = total selling effort needed (total calls to be made, for example)
SEaps = average selling effort per salesperson (average total calls made per salesperson)

An alternative workload method is known as reach frequency:

$$FTE = \frac{reach \times frequency}{capacity}$$

where:

FTE = full-time employees
reach = how many customers need to be reached
frequency = customer visits during the sales period
capacity = total number of calls per sales representative per time period

The workload approach is useful, particularly with less complex, higher-volume products such as consumer goods, since established practices and expectations exist between product manufacturers, sales reps and customers. However, the workload approach becomes more challenging with more complex products, since achieving sales objectives depends on qualitative factors such as the depth of the relationship with customers and the amount of customization required to close a sale.

Sales performance quotas

Typically, a sales manager will set a sales quota for each person in the sales team, and these are likely to include one or more of the following objectives: geographic territories, product sales and/or number of customers or clients measured in units or money units. Sales volume quotas are a common tool for companies and organizations because they guide salespeople in where to apply the most effort as well as motivate them to perform, and they serve as benchmarks for performance evaluation.

The following are useful guides for establishing sales volume quotas:

● previous year's territory sales numbers by product/service or customer/client;

● previous year's salesperson's sales numbers by product/service or customer/client;

- sales costs times a multiplier (× 3, for example);
- corporate administrative costs plus gross margin;
- total of the sales team's goals (by territory, product or customer) divided by the number of salespeople; and
- estimated income potential provided to the salesperson on achieving 100 per cent of his or her quota.

The sales management plan flows directly from the corporate strategic plan and key marketing objectives.

For example, the corporate strategic plan may set product innovation as the primary objective. Marketing would develop its customer development plans based on the corporate objective. In this case, marketing would only target early adopter customers who find innovative products appealing. Sales would then identify specific customers who are the closest fit to the corporate and marketing profiles. When the targets are achieved, sales representatives receive compensation above and beyond their base salary. Sales quotas are most effective when salespeople are directly involved with sales management in their own goal development. Setting goals with the sales manager allows salespeople to provide and receive direct feedback on their past performances and provide their insights to sales management about unique characteristics of their territory.

Average sales per call

A sales manager will want to know how much each salesperson generates in money units per call.

Typically, the average sales per call measures the value in money sales arising from each sales call:

$$SPCavg = \frac{Tsalest}{Tcallst} \times 100$$

where:

SPCavg = average sales per call
Tsalest = total sales in time period t
Tcallst = total calls in time period t

In a hypothetical example, a sales team consisting of two people is responsible for 10 properties on the real estate agent's books. The average number of cold calls in a five-day working week is 75, and the average total group sales per sales rep per week is $1,200,000. Therefore the average sales per call is $16,000.

As a stand-alone measure, average sales per call is less revealing than if it's applied in conjunction with other productivity measures based on a company or organization's strategic business goals.

Sales productivity

Typically, sales productivity can be measured in the following ways:

- sales (revenues) per person (money);
- profits per person (money);
- volume sold per person (units).

Most sales productivity measures focus on revenues per person:

$$SP = \frac{\Sigma St}{\Sigma Sp}$$

where:

SP = sales productivity
ΣSt = sum of total sales for all salespeople
ΣSp = total number of salespeople

A sales manager will use productivity to understand a sales representative's individual performance compared with the representative's colleagues or competitors. Marketers can use these results to advise underperformers on more effective segmentation or new segment opportunities. A sales manager could also use the results to coach sales representatives in better account selection, time management and selling strategies for each customer and also a step-by-step plan for improved individual performance.

A sales manager must be careful not to misinterpret sales productivity data! A handful of top performers may mask the underperformance of the rest of the team. As a result, sales productivity data must be viewed across the sales force and at the individual salesperson level.

High performers will certainly generate substantial revenues, but if those results were partly secured by offering customers generous, low-cost support contracts, for example, then the impact on the rest of the company or organization could be severe. Alternatively, high performers might have generated strong sales but also had higher returns because of a less strategic selling effort.

Web analytics

Website traffic metrics

There are five different components to 'traffic' for a website:

- *Sessions* – these are also known as visits. A session is any one person visiting the website at any one time. If a visitor visits the Kogan Page website 10 times a week, then those visits count as 10 sessions, whether the person stayed for one hour or one minute.
- *Unique visitors* – this is any one person visiting the website any number of times during a defined period. If a person visits the Kogan Page

website 10 times in a week, that person still counts only as one unique visitor.

- *Page views* – this is any one visitor viewing one page on the website, at one time. A page must have a unique address or URL. If a visitor visits the Kogan Page home page but then clicks a link and jumps to the 'Contact Us' page, this counts as two page views.

- *Time on site* – total amount of time a visitor spends on the website in the course of a single session. The average time on a site is an invaluable measure of visit quality and visitor interest as well as demonstrating how 'sticky' the site is from a content perspective.

- *Referrers* – if a visitor clicks a link on the Google site and lands on the Kogan Page website, then Google is a referrer.

Defining conversion goals

A conversion occurs any time a visitor to the company or organization website changes from a visitor to a customer (sale) or potential customer (lead). Conversions can also occur when a visitor takes a significant step toward exchanging value with the business.

The typical currency of measurement on the web is key performance indicators (KPIs), and these track the health of the sales and marketing efforts (success KPIs) and underperformance (warning KPIs).

KPIs are a general measure of success, whereas a conversion is a specific online event.

KPIs are an expression of conversion of goals, such as sales (Table 2.4).

Table 2.4 Success KPIs and conversion goals

KPIs	Conversion goals
Number of sales	A sale
Number of leads	A lead
Number of 'e-mail a friend' submissions	An e-mail sign-up
Number of white paper and other downloads	A download of a specific white paper

Warning KPIs, on the other hand, could mean that something is wrong, and these may include:

- cost per sale;
- cost per lead;
- form of abandonment rate;
- complaint frequency; and
- bounce rate.

Maintaining consistency in goal setting is critical. For example, if you start to track sales conversions based on views of the final checkout page on your website and then at some point decide to track the final order confirmation page completion, this will distort the numbers and make it impossible to track performance over time.

The goal page almost always marks the end of the goal process. In other words, it marks a conversion. The visitor has become a customer, a lead or a subscriber. And the goal page usually says 'Thank you!'

A goal can take many shapes and sizes and could include:

- a download of a piece of content;
- a page view;
- a video;
- a 'forward to a friend' link; and
- a re-tweet.

An e-commerce conversion is relatively straightforward:

$$\text{e-commerce value} = \text{sale amount} - (\text{shipping} + \text{handling} + \text{other costs})$$

Attaching a financial value to a lead is trickier. In these situations, someone fills out 'Please send me more info'-type forms, and it doesn't immediately translate into value for the company or organization.

One way of calculating the value of the lead is:

$$\text{Lead value} = (\text{lead to customer conversion rate}) \times (\text{average customer value})$$

In a hypothetical example, if the Kogan Page website generates 2,000 leads per year and of these leads 10 per cent become customers and the average customer pays $100, then:

10 per cent $\times$ $200 = $20, so the average lead value is $20.

Still trickier is calculating the value of a download of a white paper, for example. These are known as 'soft goals'.

$$\text{Soft goal value} = \% \text{ goal} \times \% \text{ conversions} \times \text{average value}$$

In a hypothetical example:

- Kogan Page website gets 10,000 total unique visitors per year.
- Ten per cent of those visitors (1,000 people) download the white paper (percentage goal).

- Kogan Page keeps track of their names, so it knows that 10 per cent of the white paper readers become customers (percentage conversions).
- Kogan Page also knows that in one year it gets $200,000 in sales from 20,000 customers, or an average value of $10/customer (average value).

So the value of one white paper download to Kogan Page is:

$$1,000 \times 10\% \times \$10 = \$1,000$$

Setting up the goal tracking is also straightforward, provided you know the goal page.

Many people use Google Analytics and provided you identify the goal page:

- Log on to Google Analytics.
- Click Edit next to the website for which you want to track the goal.
- Under conversion goals and funnel, click Edit next to any goal that's not configured.
- Open a new browser window and go to your website.
- 'Complete the form', 'check out' or other process you want to track (goal page).
- Copy the address into the final page in the process – it'll usually be 'Thank you.'
- Paste that address into the goal URL field.
- Name the goal, leave the other settings alone and then click Finish.

After your goal is configured, Google Analytics reports all goal completions. You can then compare paid search keywords, organic search keywords, advertising, e-mail campaigns and most other aspects of site traffic in the context of goal conversion.

In summary, key points to remember are:

- Start with robust customer or client segmentation.
- Frame your prospecting approach to take account of social behaviour, customers and the culture of prospects.
- Use verbal and non-verbal communication and package the sales proposition using emotional cues to get the prospect to buy your product or service on a rational and logical basis.
- Keep an open mind about where sales leads can come from.
- Use telemarketing, direct mail, e-mail and the web in an appropriate way, having due regard to legal and regulatory constraints, in order to reach desired customer and client segments.
- Where it makes sense, try to prospect for customers and clients face-to-face.

- Monitor and evaluate the effectiveness of the customer pipeline by applying the following mix of measures:
  - gross profit;
  - net profit;
  - return on sales;
  - breakdown approach;
  - workload approach;
  - sales performance quotas;
  - average sales per call;
  - sales productivity;
  - website traffic metrics; and
  - defining conversion goals.

References

Books

Anderson, C (2006) *The Long Tail: Why the future of business is selling less of more*, Hyperion Books

Anderson, C, Flick, S and Reed, D (2008) *Sales and Marketing Policies, Procedures and Forms*, Bizmanualz

Gerber, M (2005) *E Myth Mastery*, Collins

Gladwell, M (2000) *The Tipping Point*, Little, Brown

Goldstein, N, Martin, S and Cialdini, R (2007) *Yes! 50 secrets from the science of persuasion*, Profile Books

Hanlon, A and Akins, J (2009) *Digital Marketing*, Oak Tree Press

Kolah, A (2013) *Essential Law for Marketers*, 2nd edn, Guru in a Bottle®, Kogan Page

Kolah, A (2013) *High Impact Marketing that Gets Results*, Guru in a Bottle®, Kogan Page

McPheat, S (2008) *The Sales Person's Crisis*, MTD Sales Training

McPheat, S (2011) *eselling*, Matador

Scott, DM and Halligan, B (2010) *Marketing Lessons from the Grateful Dead*, Wiley

Thompson, L (2008) *The Truth about Negotiations*, Pearson

Article

Miyamoto, Y and Schwartz, N (2006) When conveying a message may hurt the relationship: cultural differences in the difficulty of using an answering machine, *Journal of Experimental Social Psychology*, **42**, pp 540–47

Website

Edison Research: http://www.edisonresearch.com/home/archives/2011/05/the_social_habit_2011.php (accessed 14 August 2011)

"It's a telemarketer. She says if you're not busy,
she'll call back when you are."

Up-selling, cross-selling, cold calling and warm calling

Introduction

It's been said that great salespeople are flexible enough to adapt to new sales techniques and aren't slaves to an overfamiliar sales pitch. In many respects, all salespeople need to have the same degree of flexibility in order to be successful at selling. One reason is that the competitive landscape has changed beyond all recognition, and so too has the behaviour of customers and prospects. Nothing can be left to chance. The well-rehearsed sales pitch that worked six months ago may not work today.

Well-known brands and companies are finding it very difficult to sell their goods and services despite their sales and marketing muscle or even market dominance, which used to be a significant competitive advantage. Not any more. Purchasing behaviour has changed as a result of turbulence in just about every business-to-consumer (B2C) and business-to-business (B2B) market imaginable. Salespeople don't just need to work harder to achieve their sales targets. They need to work much smarter.

As discussed in Chapter 2, it's important to be able to segment your customer or client base in order to adjust what you say to them, whether that's face to face, on the phone, by e-mail or online. But that doesn't mean to say that routine hasn't a part to play in the selling process. Sales techniques such as up-selling, cross-selling, cold calling and warm calling are some of the most tried and tested sales techniques, which have stood the test of time and in the right hands will drive more sales. The key is how to employ their use at the right time and within the right context.

Where cost is an issue for almost every business, precision in the sales effort is essential.

One of the most successful corporate sales trainers in the United States, Stephan Schiffman, observes: 'Great salespeople know the importance of the sales process – and their goals are always to get to the next step.'

In this chapter, we put each of these techniques under the microscope and examine how best they can be deployed to convert a prospect into a paying customer or client.

But first, let's dispel some common myths about selling.

The myths about selling

There are many myths about the sales techniques examined in this chapter:

- *Myth 1: Selling is a numbers game.* Well, it's a numbers game if you decide to treat every prospect in exactly the same way! Not a great idea, as it's unlikely to work, and even calling the same customers over and over again in the forlorn hope of converting them into paying customers when they answer the phone is highly improbable.

- *Myth 2: All successful salespeople have a script in order to sell.* There's no doubt that being well prepared before engaging with a prospect is essential, but that's not the same as reading from a prepared script. As we've said many times in this book, you may be ready to sell, but is the customer or client ready to buy? Putting prospects under pressure to buy yields two responses: flight or fight. Neither is desirable or bankable.

- *Myth 3: All successful salespeople focus on closing the sale.* As discussed in Chapter 10, in an ideal world, quantifying and closing a sale should be a seamless process. It's often observed that good salespeople begin by making a series of small closes and do not focus on getting the customer to part with hard-earned cash at the earliest opportunity. Instead, the successful salesperson focuses on building a dialogue and earning the trust of the customer well before rushing to the cash till.

- *Myth 4: Rejection is always part of the sales process.* Ever met a professional salesperson who suffered from being rejected every time he or she tried to make a sale? Again, rejection isn't bankable. Rejection is often triggered by certain things that are said in the 'heat of the chase' to the customer or prospect that could've been unintentional or unintended and then it's too late to withdraw and the opportunity for closing the sale has evaporated.

Asking the right questions

In many sales situations asking a pertinent question rather than tripping out a stock answer is preferable. Asking the right question often provides a level of insight that couldn't have been achieved in any other way. It's also a fantastic way to build a dialogue and create rapport, and this can very rapidly help to build trust.

The danger with having stock answers is rather like that faced by the stand-up comedian faced with a heckler – the stand-up may have a well-prepared retort that may get a laugh or dig a bigger hole into which to fall. It depends.

There aren't any right or wrong questions to ask, only different ones. It's important that we aren't judgemental of customers or prospects either, as there are no right or wrong answers.

The right question to ask will often go to the nub of an issue faced by the customer or client, and in a sales situation you hope this will have a positive effect in the shortest possible time. The 'wrong' type of question is the one that can send you off course, meandering down a cul-de-sac, where you may gather interesting but irrelevant information that makes no impact on the chances of closing the sale.

It's not just the question you ask but, where this is face to face, also the verbal and non-verbal language you use that can also make all the difference.

For further discussion on verbal and non-verbal communication, see Chapter 6.

Have you ever wondered how many questions you ask make assumptions based on what you want to hear rather than what the other person wants to tell you? Asking questions in the hope of receiving the answers you want to hear is based on what your map of reality looks like, rather than the map of reality of the customer or client. Did you ever stop to think what the customer wanted?

As humans, it's very hard not to project our own thoughts, feelings, ideas, needs, wants and enthusiasm on to others. In fact, in some instances it may be appropriate to do so, for example when we give a product demonstration. But behaving in such a way isn't appropriate in every case.

Our desire to influence people around us means that when we ask questions most of the time they are 'loaded' – in other words they assume something. In such a situation we aren't listening at all. Rather, we are in 'transmit mode' rather than opening ourselves to be in 'receive mode'.

Successful salespeople have a highly tuned 'receive mode' – they are respectful of the other person's point of view (POV) and as a result avoid telling that person what to do based on what they would do themselves.

As a professional salesperson you should be self-aware of what you say, and if you hear yourself issuing instructions to customers or prospects that begin with 'You really must...' or 'If I were you I would...' then it's time to stop directing and imposing your stance on them, as it's not effective in influencing them to buy from you.

The art of influencing and selling is to demonstrate the behaviour you want by doing this yourself. So, for example, if you want a prospect to be curious about your product, then you need to demonstrate curiosity about the prospect's needs for that product.

The way you are with other people will determine how they are with you. Asking the right question also means giving the other person enough time to answer it!

Waiting and allowing the other person time to think

Don't be shy to press the 'pause button' and allow the other person to know that you're really listening. Your body language will let the person know whether you really are. Using the 'pause button' is particularly important when the other person is on the end of a phone – it's all too easy to misread silence as an invitation to jump in and fill the void. You must resist doing this at all costs. Take your time. This also applies when you need to respond to something that you've been told. Don't do this in some knee-jerk way. That just gives the impression to the customer or prospect that you've not listened or indeed don't care about what you've heard in the first place. Listening to others is a generous and unselfish act and an undervalued skill.

For the psychology of selling, see Chapter 1.

How to build rapport

This is one of the most important rules of communication and it also applies to selling: don't expect someone to buy from you unless you've established rapport. It's a fallacy to think that you need to like someone in order to build rapport with them. As we've discussed, rapport is about having mutual respect for the other person's point of view, and you don't have to like them personally – although sometimes it helps!

Rapport is built on an instinctive sense of trust and integrity. It's the close and harmonious relationship in which there's common understanding. Very importantly, it has to be two-way; otherwise there's no rapport. It's about making customers or clients feel that they are being listened to. It's about appreciating and working with their differences. And of course there are different levels of rapport as well as bad rapport.

All of us can usually tell whether we are going to get on really well with people, particularly work colleagues, and build a strong rapport with them if we feel they're 'energy givers'. Conversely, salespeople don't tend to get on well or work well with those colleagues who are 'energy takers'. With the latter, you end up expending all your energy but never feel that it's being reciprocated. It's the same with friends. Those that don't make an effort tend not to end up on the Christmas card list.

As you'll no doubt appreciate, it's extremely hard to build trust and understanding where the other person's unwilling to participate.

There are about eight proven ways to build rapport with a customer, client or prospect:

1 Remember the name of the person with whom you're conversing, and remember to use that person's correct name.

2 Be yourself and don't pretend to be something you're not. Adopt an open communication style.

3 Listen – get to understand the customer, client or prospect's point of view. The more genuinely interested you appear, the more the person will want to talk to you.

4 Where you're face to face, use body language, facial expressions and gestures – this accounts for about 55 per cent of all communication – as well as tone of voice (also applies to speaking on the phone), which accounts for 38 per cent of communication (surprisingly, actual words account for just 7 per cent).

5 Respect other people's time – ask whether it's convenient to speak or whether they are in the middle of something. Be mindful of their situation, particularly where you can't physically see them.

6 Notice how customers or clients like to handle information. For example, do they like big picture or loads of details? When answering them, provide information in a way they feel comfortable with.

7 Don't try too hard or be too needy. Remember, you're in 'buying mode' – the customers should want to buy from you – rather than in 'selling mode' and desperate to push a sale. You can't force rapport – it needs oxygen to develop.

8 Be aware of other people's culture or ways they prefer to do business. For example, Asians tend to place a lot of emphasis on showing respect as well as the need to get to know you as a prequel to doing business with you.

Building rapport in a virtual environment where there's no face-to-face contact can be even more challenging. Remember to slow down and speak more precisely and listen for the style of language that's preferred.

It's also important to know when to break rapport, for example when the other person's showing signs of fatigue and you need to give him or her space to reflect on the subject of the conversation. Be confident in picking up the conversation at another date and time (if appropriate), as this shows your consideration for them too.

How to apply outcome thinking

In many respects, successful salespeople are experts in outcome thinking. They have SMART goals that are specific, measurable, achievable, realistic and timed.

There are a number of questions that need to be answered in relation to goal setting in order to achieve a well-formed outcome process (Table 3.1).

Table 3.1 Outcome process

Questions about your goals	Questions that clarify the outcome
Is the goal framed in the positive?	What do you want? What would you rather have?
Is the goal self-initiated or in your control?	Are you doing this for yourself? Does the outcome rely on you?
Does the goal describe the evidence procedure?	How will you know that you're achieving the outcome? What will you see, hear and feel when you have it?
Does the goal identify the resources required?	What resources are available now? What resources need to be acquired? Is there evidence of achieving this in the past? What would happen if you acted as if you had the resources?
Does the goal fit within all aspects of your agenda?	What is the real purpose why you want this? What will you lose or gain if you have it? What will happen if you get it? What won't happen if you get it? What will happen if you don't get it? What won't happen if you don't get it?

By following this process, you'll begin to understand the true motives of wanting to achieve your goals and be able to weigh up the pros and cons of success versus failure in achieving those goals:

- Know your outcome – it's important to frame precisely what it is that you want.
- Take action – the first step is sometimes the most important.
- Have sensory awareness – have the awareness to see, hear and feel what isn't working and modify your sales behaviour to help steer you towards the desired outcome(s).
- Have flexibility in your behaviour – in sales interactions, the person with the most flexibility of behaviour can control the interaction.

The art of up-selling

According to US sales trainer Stephan Schiffman:

one of the most neglected truths about up-selling is that the very best strategy is sometimes to recognize that there's no possibility to expand a relationship with a customer. The trick is to align yourself so well with the interests of your prospects that you learn to develop a sense for whether or not the possibility really exists to expand your relationship in a way that benefits both parties.

Up-selling is a deliberate act on the part of the professional salesperson to seek that win–win that Stephan Schiffman describes and get the purchaser to buy more of the product or to purchase a different product – whether face to face or online.

Think about walking into a store to purchase a torch that comes with two cells in the packaging. The sales assistant at the checkout should suggest that the pack of batteries by the till would work in the torch you've just bought as well as other appliances you may have in the home. These might be on special offer, so inviting you to enter the conversation and consider that you can reach the point of up-sell all by yourself is worth the effort.

But how often are we faced with dealing with a disinterested salesperson at the checkout? All it would take in the above example would be to drop into the conversation that batteries always seem to run out at a time when you need them most, for example when you need to change a fuse in the fuse box so the lights work. It's precisely why having a torch is essential, but it's not much use if the batteries are exhausted, so it's always a good idea to have spares!

In B2B selling, the up-sell conversation could be around the success of the previous project that was delivered on time and on budget and what's next to be tackled within the business.

The commercial rationale for trying to up-sell to a customer or a client is extremely compelling – it usually costs at least seven times more to acquire a new customer than to sell products or services to an existing one – so up-selling is also highly profitable.

As we've discussed in this chapter, in order to be successful you need to be able to influence the customer or prospect to behave in a way that results in an up-sell. So, at its simplest, up-selling is a conversation. Without additional information that goes beyond the most immediate needs of the customer or client, it's virtually impossible to up-sell, so information is key. It's only by talking about customers' needs and challenges, wants and desires that the licence to up-sell without the appearance of up-selling will take place. The concept of 'closing a sale' will therefore require you to make an assessment that there's no chance that you can up-sell to customers or clients so that they buy something else in addition to the main item or service.

Walking into a clothes shop to buy a suit that doesn't come with a belt or braces could be an occasion for an incremental sale, but it needn't stop there. A shirt and tie, underpants and socks could look relatively minor incidental expenses in relation to the overall cost of the suit. The total up-sale value of the combined purchase could be double that of the suit, but customers won't feel that they've spent double what they intended. They'll consider these other purchases 'make sense'.

In all of the above examples, we've used stories to make the point. People love stories, and they often base their own decisions about whether to keep buying from us not only on the stories that we share with them but also on the stories that they decide to share with us.

Stephan Schiffman advises: 'Consider it your goal to share your own relevant success stories with each and every up-selling contact on your own world. And to ask the intelligent questions and encourage the lengthy responses that will lead you toward the stories that mark the boundaries of the world of the person to whom you are trying to sell.'

Up-selling by mail

In many ways this is the simplest form of up-selling and yet it's also one that's most often overlooked. Where a sale has been made, it's common practice to give or send a receipt for the purchase to the customer. With respect to online sales, this could be in the form of an e-mail.

Perhaps you could also consider a thank-you message and in return for purchasing the product the customer qualifies for a discount on the reorder of the same product or a percentage discount on a range of other products. Rewarding loyalty in this way very often results in an up-sell as well as repeat purchase. It's a win–win in every sense.

For a discussion on sales copywriting, see Chapter 7.

Up-selling by face to face

This has to be one of the most powerful ways to up-sell, because you're able to read body language and the mood of the person you're dealing with. This is important in 'consultative selling' where a professional service is being sold to the customer or client.

Up-selling efforts don't exist in a vacuum, and a successful up-sell will depend on moving customers or clients through a continuum depending on how valuable they perceive the relationship to be (Figure 3.1).

Figure 3.1   The sales continuum

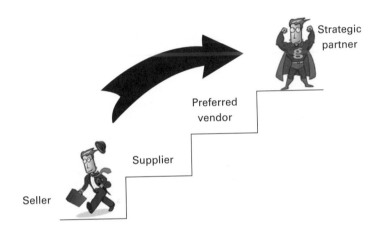

The objective is to move the relationship from where you're perceived as a seller and where the interest in you is based on price to one where you're perceived as a strategic partner, for example in an outsourcing arrangement, and you have a deeper level of commitment that transcends a transactional relationship based on price.

Creating a solution from the 'outside in' is all about focusing on the customer or client's goals rather than bundling products and services together. British sales and marketing guru Peter Fisk explains: 'Customers want to be part of the solution – they understand their problems and can often describe their desired solutions in some detail. Most typically they lack the skills, materials, resources or time to do it themselves. That's why they turn to you.'

The powerful way to achieve this is to involve customers and clients as collaborators in the up-selling process:

- Invite customers or clients to take part in designing or improving products and services.
- Explore their priorities and preferences, working together to design the right solutions.
- Develop the physical solution rapidly, testing and modifying it with customers and clients as you progress.
- Implement the solution as a partnership with customers or clients, helping them to apply it effectively and get the most out of it.
- Capture the learning from individual co-creations to turn it into better standard solutions.

Peter Fisk adds:

> *The starting point is to understand the challenge or problem and identify all the issues and likely causes and possible impact. Although it might seem like a problem of employee motivation in the customer service function, the real issue might lie in the low quality of after-sales support and subsequent complaints back to customer service people. The process helps the customer and consultant to get a feel for the scale and importance of the project in terms of its implications on customers and together to shape a sensible approach.*
>
> *This is up-selling in a consultative context – it's free advice for the customer and an investment for the consultant. However, the collaboration, by having access to the internal information and people, helps the consultant to scope out a potential solution that might be much more significant than at first sight and to access internal commercial data from which they can estimate a financial value at risk. This can then lead to a much more appropriate customer solution as well as bigger and more profitable consulting project.*

Another way to look at this from the perspective of the professional salesperson is as an up-selling pyramid (Figure 3.2).

Strategic partnership

This is where there's an alignment of the vision and purpose, mission and values between the customer and the seller. Positioning yourself here sets you apart from your peer group and makes it extremely difficult for your competitors to woo the customer away from this stable relationship.

However, increasingly, long-term agreements, such as an outsourcing arrangement, will contain clauses where the service delivered will be benchmarked on an annual basis to ensure it continues to meet the objectives of the customer or client and represents good value for money compared with the service delivered by other competitors in the market. These arrangements

Figure 3.2 The up-selling pyramid

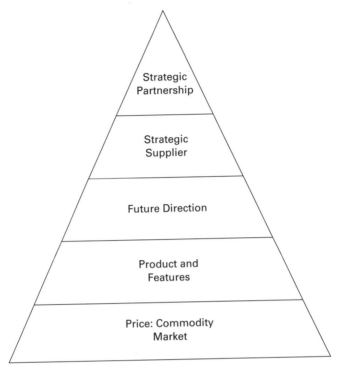

Source: DEI Management Group, 2005

also provide a right to the customer or client to renegotiate or even cancel the service if it falls below this benchmark. Clearly, the service provider must be supremely confident that this will never happen in order to agree to such a term.

For more discussion on contractual agreements, refer to Guru in a Bottle®'s *Essential Law for Marketers* (2nd edition).

Strategic supplier
The proposition here is that you help customers or clients do more business, such as providing sales training or marketing services that can be measured in terms of incremental sales. By helping them to achieve their sales objectives, you begin to differentiate yourself over time.

Future direction
This is where your company emerges as a market leader with a reputation for solid service as well as reliability. Up-selling in this context has a higher chance of succeeding given the small number of competitors that would be considered to be in your peer group by the customer or client.

Product and features

Feature, functionality, service quality and application are key issues, and it's unlikely that up-selling will figure in the mind of the customer or client at this point in the up-selling pyramid. 'Up-selling isn't an issue, nor is it likely. If the prospect's decision is based on nothing higher than price and features, the competition may win this sale from us. If we win this sale, the competition may win the next sale with little difficulty', observes Stephan Schiffman.

Price: commodity market

At the bottom of the up-selling pyramid is price-based commodity competition. It's highly unlikely that this will provide a sufficient foundation for up-selling to take place, particularly in a consultative sales situation.

Up-selling by telephone

In one respect there's a disadvantage of up-selling by phone in that you can't read the customer or client's body language, so in effect you are using two senses to engage – those of speaking and listening.

Telesales is without doubt one of the most difficult things to do successfully. On the other hand, it's quite possibly one of the most efficient channels for up-selling a product or service. The key is to listen.

Stephan Schiffman says:

> *Ultimately, the guiding principle for up-selling and all aspects of person-to-person selling is simply to pay a heck of a lot of attention to the other person. Not 'sales' attention. Real attention. Be absolutely certain that, when you're in a meeting with your contact, interacting with them on the phone or sending an e-mail, you're sending the message that this person really is more important than anything or anyone else on earth. Forget about selling. Just focus on what the other person is doing with incredible focus and attention. If you can follow through on that type of commitment, genuine interest and unapologetic attention, you'll attract interest, you'll build a relationship and you'll be able to sell more to your current customers.*

Telesales is a highly pressurized environment, as there's not much time to get the 'pitch' across before the call has ended. It's also got a stigma attached to it as a result of the way in which it's been abused as a way of up-selling to existing customers.

Not all telesales people are unprofessional, but they do tend to get tarred by the same brush, which of course is unfair but it's a fact of life.

It's also not much fun waiting for the phone to ring. Whereas outbound telesales people make calls to people on a more or less restricted basis, there's a time management challenge that's unique to people whose job is exclusively related to inbound selling, such as direct response on a shopping television channel. In such situations, call volumes tend to fluctuate between peak and non-peak times.

Telesales isn't that well paid compared with other forms of selling activities and is very often outsourced to a third party, as it's more cost-effective to do so. It also suffers from 'selling by script', as well as the high turnover of people who find that they need to make financial targets or find themselves out the door. This is very often the case in the real estate sector.

Against this background, up-selling to a customer or client perhaps is exceptionally difficult but it's not impossible. Training is extremely important.

There are well-established protocols and procedures that many organizations follow in the conduct of outbound and inbound telesales. These include customer contact worksheets, the use of open questions, active listening, building rapport, the sales qualification process that often results in proposals being sent to the customers or prospects, and a post-call worksheet (Figure 3.3).

In terms of outbound telesales activities, Stephan Schiffman advises thinking about the relationship between outbound calls, conversations, appointments and sales:

> The numbers don't operate in a vacuum. And you can't expect your sales manager to track them for you. You have to track them for yourself, because it's your lifestyle that the numbers will determine. You can't set a quota for the final element without setting a quota for the first element. Too many sales managers and salespeople focus only on the result – and not on the cause that will deliver their results.

There are two typical call flows depending on whether it's an inbound call that you receive from the customer or whether it's an outbound call that you need to make.

Outbound sales calls techniques

It's likely that, unless you've made an appointment to call a customer or prospect at a certain time, the outbound call will come as a surprise and more often than not will be met with a negative response.

It's polite to ask whether it's a convenient time to speak or whether it would be more convenient to call back. This does two things: it recognizes that you are entering the space of another person uninvited and that you are mindful that the person may be in the middle of something. It's a major failing of so many outbound telesales callers that they don't stop and think about this before launching into a standard script (and, by the way, it's really easy to tell if someone is reading from a script).

On the assumption that you have permission to continue the call, then getting past the initial negative reaction is the next critical point in the up-sell process.

It's here that there needs to be a conversation and a compelling reason why the call should continue. Asking a question (which could be about

Figure 3.3 Typical post-telesales worksheet

Completed by: _____   Date: _____

Targets:

No. of qualified prospects:	Daily/weekly/monthly: ___	No. of sales calls:	Daily/weekly/monthly: ___
No. of presentations/proposals:	Daily/weekly/monthly: ___	No. of closes:	Daily/weekly/monthly: ___

List of qualified leads:

Contact info (name, company, address, phone, e-mail)	Appointment?	Up-sell?	Date	%	$	P/Q?	Up-sell?	Date	%	$	Close?	Date	$

Percentage (%) prospect conversion rate _____ %

Percentage (%) appointment conversion _____ %

Percentage (%) proposal/quote conversion _____ %

(P/Q=proposal/quote)

a purchase recently made) will provide additional information. This will allow you to verify the information so you can close the presentation. The presentation or plan is the solution or offer you want to propose based on the information given to you by the customer or prospect.

Inbound sales calls techniques

In this scenario, a customer or a prospect is calling you, so it's important to get past the greeting phase and move as quickly as possible to the information-gathering phase. This is a critical part of the inbound call-handling technique.

As in the outbound sales call, the next critical step in the process is the verification phase. This is where we confirm what we've learnt about the caller and try to get the facts straight so that the presentation can be built around this. This presentation can take place at this point or at a subsequent time that's convenient to the customer or prospect.

It's important to remember that, in order to close the sale, you'll need to verify this information. Where a sale is closed for one product on the phone, there may be an opportunity to use the 'by the way' line that could open the door to the up-sell provided it's a natural extension of the conversation. This depends on having built rapport with the caller.

How to cross-sell successfully

As the global economy takes its faltering steps to recovery, many companies are looking for opportunities to claw their way back to pre-global recession sales levels. Companies that fared well want to be sure they keep their customers and clients as the competition intensifies.

Cross-selling is offering customers a product or service related to whatever they're already buying. It can be as simple as a waiter asking if you want a salad to accompany your pizza and garlic bread!

While sales teams have long had goals for up-selling and cross-selling, increasingly more companies are asking their customer service reps to do the same. For example, many high-technology companies now ask their support engineers to become salespeople by recommending product upgrades and to contact customers to renew warranty agreements.

According to research by MarketSoft Corporation, a provider of cross-selling technology in the United States, nearly three-quarters of all businesses surveyed reported they had cross-selling programmes, but as many as 70 per cent of such efforts had failed to increase revenue in any significant way.

Despite advancements in technology to identify sales opportunities through segmentation and behaviour analysis, if customer service professionals who speak with customers don't want to sell or don't introduce the sale in a way that benefits the customer then no sale will take place.

When presented with an up-sell and cross-sell initiative, many customer service professionals run a mile, as they don't see it as their job to sell. That's someone else's department, they'll say. In such instances, training is key. Cross-selling techniques should be built around serving the customer, not just selling more stuff.

It's also important not to overload customers with too many unrelated cross-selling suggestions. For example, you could be successful in cross-selling the entire list of ingredients for a recipe, but the customer is unlikely to be in the frame of mind to purchase an expensive liquidizer at the same time.

Another successful strategy of cross-selling is to bundle products that will appeal to the customer and offer a special price on these bundles. This can work extremely well in clothing, fashion accessories, stationery and food and drink, where multiple purchases can be very appealing as well as help to drive profits. It can also work well in professional services.

Ford Harding, a cross-sales expert who has worked with a wide range of professional services firms in the United States, observes:

> Clients who receive several services tend to be more loyal than those who receive a single service. It becomes harder for the client to totally sever the relationship, should something go wrong. The multiple relationships and values you are providing can help you buy time while you fix the problem. If business in one area drops off, the firm is often able to hang on to business in another. In time, professionals may be able to rebuild the relationship from this alternate position, a task that would be much more difficult if they were no longer working with the client.

However, the ethics of cross-selling should also be considered, as global accountancy firm Arthur Andersen found to its cost when it was fined over US$7 million by the Securities and Exchange Commission (SEC) in the United States in 2001.

Arthur Andersen case (2001)

About a decade ago, the SEC brought its first successful action for fraud against an auditor in more than 20 years.

Arthur Andersen's relationship with Waste Management was both long and broad. The company's accounts had been audited by the accountancy firm for over 30 years, and until 1997 every chief financial officer in Waste Management's history had previously worked as an auditor for the accountancy firm.

In the early 1990s, the Arthur Andersen partner in charge of Waste Management's audit was Robert Allgyer. He was also 'marketing director' for Andersen's Chicago office, in charge of cross-selling other services to audit clients – a job he was good at. Between 1991 and 1997, Waste Management paid Arthur Andersen US$7.5 million in audit fees and US$11.8 million in other fees.

Waste Management's unqualified accounts for the years 1992–96 were subsequently found to have overstated pre-tax income by more than US$1.4 billion. Without admitting or denying the allegations, Arthur Andersen agreed to pay what was the biggest-ever penalty imposed by the SEC on a leading firm of accountants pre-Enron scandal. The case underscored the SEC's concern that the quality of auditing was being compromised by the amount of more lucrative non-audit work that Arthur Andersen was providing to the company.

Cross-selling online

You see it on just about every online shop. 'You may also be interested in these products' or 'Recommended products'. Amazon is the king of the cross-sell!

Cross-selling in the virtual world is about offering related items that customers or prospects have recently searched for.

The compelling argument for investing in a cross-selling system is that it can generate more profit per sale in the same way that up-selling can drive the total value of a sale. Simply placing higher-priced alternative items next to items that a customer has expressed an interest in purchasing is a very efficient way of cross-selling online. It also can create a more personalized shopping experience and utilizes behavioural analytics in order to remove the guesswork from what can be suggested to customers as they browse the website. For example, alongside an expensive pair of leather shoes could also be the product details of a specialist leather care product that will help to keep those shoes in pristine condition.

Online sites are also easier places in which to navigate and search for similar and related items compared to the time it can take in a physical environment, which may not yield the same results, as some products may be out of stock or not available in the store at the time of the visit.

One of the most powerful ways of cross-selling and up-selling is the use of recommendations from other customers. Psychologically, people want to feel they are making 'the right choice', and deep down they may also be seeking recognition in having made this choice as well as earning the 'approval' of their peer group.

How to cold-call without someone hanging up

If you're not doing well, if people aren't returning your calls, if you're not getting appointments, if you're not closing sales – you know something's wrong, don't you? But what should you do about this?

One piece of advice is to stop fearing rejection. According to psychologists, this fear of rejection is deeply ingrained in all of us and is felt by 99 per cent of all young men in just about every global culture in which selection of a mate is allowed.

Cold calling isn't the same as asking someone for a date, but it's not that much different. The point here is that it's attitude that counts. Calling the names in a telephone directory in the vain hope of finding a person to sell to never made anyone rich. As with all the sales techniques discussed in this book, it pays to know who your prospects are – and who you want to chat up. There is no point trying to cold-call a person who has signed up for the Telephone Preference Service (TPS) – several countries including the UK, the United States, Canada and Australia operate similar schemes. Not only has the person elected not to receive the call but you could also face a stiff fine from the regulator for making the call in the first place.

According to British sales trainer Bob Etherington, in any market 85 per cent of the available new business goes to the 5 per cent of salespeople who know the secret of successful cold calling. So that says there's a big opportunity!

Essentially there are four proven ways of ensuring that the person picking up the call at the other end won't hang up:

1 Grab attention (A).
2 Build interest (I).
3 Create desire (D).
4 Encourage the other person to act (A).

'AIDA' is important because cold calling, when done effectively, is one of the best and most economical ways of developing prospects on an ongoing basis.

A common mistake often made by sales professionals is to say that they'll call back in a week's time. The successful sales professional will want to make the appointment to call or visit the prospect as a follow-up when on the first call. It's only by making appointments that prospects can be turned into customers.

According to Stephan Schiffman, it's important to understand the ratio of cold calls that are necessary to generate appointments in order to calculate the chances of closing a sale from the appointments made. In his case, he has to make 15 cold calls a day in order to generate five appointments a week (a ratio of 75:5 or 15:1). However, he may only get through to seven people in any one day, so he needs to convert the caller into an appointment. But it doesn't stop there. Experience shows that three of those appointments will become follow-through appointments. So in fact he manages eight appointments each week, rather than five, as three are carried over to the subsequent week's cold-call activities. His closing ratio is 8:1, so for every eight appointments Stephan Schiffman expects to make a sale, which computes as 50 new accounts a year. In this respect, you reap what you sow.

It may be very tempting to think that there's a magic formula and that it works every time. Well, there isn't; otherwise we'd all be experts at cold-calling.

Many books will go into detail about the 'perfect' script or methodology, but essentially successful cold calling relies on your attitude.

In the opinion of US sales guru Art Sobczak, cold calling is a waste of time. It's smart calling that gets results. He breaks this down into the following components, which are a variation on AIDA:

- Acquire intelligence about people, companies and industries prior to speaking with a decision maker.
- Use that information within a proven prospecting ad sales process, speaking in a conversational, consultative dialogue that puts both you and the prospect at ease.
- Consequently, you help prospects take actions (buying from you) that they feel good about and from which they gain value.
- As a result, you get through to more buyers, more often, since the gatekeepers not only provide you with information but also become part of the process and your sales team.
- Buyers are more receptive initially, in the first 10–20 seconds of the call – the time during which most calls fail.
- Buyers don't view you as a typical salesperson or vendor but rather as someone who has their best interests in mind and can deliver real value and a return on investment.
- You become more comfortable with your calls and confident in what you say – even in difficult situations.
- You'll suffer less from rejection.

This perspective is a million miles from the stereotypical image of cold calling that sees this exercise as a painful grind, depressing, embarrassing, draining, exhausting and just plain horrible. And that's just from the sales professional's perspective! Just think how that experience feels for the caller.

Yet cold calling (or 'smart calling' as Art Sobczak prefers) can be extremely potent and can enable the professional salesperson to:

- supersede existing suppliers;
- pre-empt the competition;
- identify and create huge new business opportunities;
- become indispensable as someone who can make things happen and create new business;
- build personal reputation; and
- establish a much wider circle of contacts and relationships that can endure in the long term.

The eight 'golden rules' of cold calling

Cold calling isn't for the faint-hearted and shouldn't become a robotic exercise. Far from it.

All the sales gurus on both sides of the Atlantic tend to converge on eight 'golden rules' of successful cold calling. There are of course many more and also different ones, but eight is quite enough to be getting on with.

Golden rule 1: preparation

This is the pre-cold-call planning phase, and it's really important. As we've said many times already in this book, you need to start from the point of view of the person you're communicating with. After all, obsession about a customer or client is likely to be more profitable than being obsessed about you or your wonderful product or service. As Art Sobczak observes: 'Get over yourself. When you embrace the all-about-them mindset, you distinguish yourself from the typical self-interested salesperson or cold-caller that everyone tries to avoid. The two fundamentals of sales are that people love to buy but hate to be sold to and they buy for their reasons, not yours.'

The product or service doesn't need to be the most expensive or of the highest quality but must be fit for purpose and must meet the needs and requirements of the person you're trying to influence. Understanding the attitudes, values, beliefs and behaviours of the person that you're calling will make a big difference.

As we've said earlier in this chapter, you need to put yourself into an environment and mood that will work for you and be confident and assertive and not arrogant or defensive. You also need to understand and word the proposition in relation to the recipient's situation.

You must have a good strategic appreciation of the issues and challenges faced by the prospect in relation to your basic opening proposition. This is an absolutely fundamental requirement, and its absence will have a severe impact on the success of a cold call.

Customers or clients will have a very keen sense of what's important to them and what's not – and if you fail to acknowledge this in your opening exchange or, worse, completely ignore their perspective then they will hang up. Also bear in mind that the initial proposition shouldn't make assumptions as to the final offering or product/service specification. In the case of large clients with complex needs and requirements, its definition could be weeks or months away.

Golden rule 2: introduction

You need to have established some key phrases explaining and positioning yourself and the purpose for the call. In other words, you need to have carefully considered why you're calling this particular person rather than randomly plucking a name out of the telephone directory.

Successful sales professionals are clear and concise about who they are and the purpose of the call and have a powerful strategic basis (main reason) for the call – either now or to be rescheduled later, depending on the availability of the other person at the time. Many sales gurus advocate making such calls whilst standing, as the diaphragm is open rather than restricted, smiling when speaking, as this adds a quality to the tone of the voice, and slowing down and not rushing.

Many sales professionals never leave a message when the phone clicks into voicemail. This is a mistake, as an effective voicemail message is almost identical to an interest-creating opening statement. The only difference is that at the end of the message you advise the person you're calling that you'll call back – and leave your contact information as a matter of courtesy. Where possible, it's usually good practice to review the voicemail before it's delivered.

Golden rule 3: questioning
Assuming that you're able to get through, asking good facilitative questions that help the other person to see the purpose of the call and to get that person to a decision point is extremely effective. As discussed earlier in this chapter, asking the right questions pays dividends, as it allows you to gather important and relevant information that will help you sell a product or service. 'You need to move them further into a state of mind where they better understand, see and feel their needs, problems, pains and desires', explains Art Sobczak.

Golden rule 4: objectivity
Remaining objective at all times helps to steer the conversation in the right direction and make it much more of a consultative exercise. Remaining fair and neutral is much more powerful than trying to be a 30-second commercial that could be heard on a radio station and just as quickly forgotten. It's less about 'push' and much more about 'pull'.

People don't want to be 'sold' to but rather want to be guided and assisted by an expert in a field who has credibility.

Golden rule 5: listening and reflecting
As we've discussed earlier in this chapter, listening is one of the most powerful ways of selling. In an interview situation, for example, it's a fallacy to assume that you need to do all the talking – if you reverse the ratio you are more likely to land the job. That's because the interviewer feels you've been listening and have understood what's being said as opposed to wanting to stick to some well-rehearsed script. Experienced interviewers can sniff out when this is happening.

In much the same way, a prospective customer or client can often leave a trail of clues if you are prepared to listen out for them. For example, 'Here's our biggest challenge', 'Our biggest issue is...', 'Where we need to improve performance is...' or 'We have to catch up with the competition' are all valuable aural clues for helping you to sell your product or service.

Poor salespeople often talk themselves out of a sale by not shutting up!

Other common errors include making negative recommendations ('I wouldn't do that'), whereas it's much better to make a positive recommendation and then pause, regardless of how awkward the silence may feel – you need to allow the other person back into the conversation. By adopting such an approach, you will reduce the chances of being seen as 'pushy'.

Golden rule 6: informing and illuminating

This is sometimes referred to as the presentation stage, and at this point in the cold call you are likely to have focused on the headline benefits of the product or service that you feel will meet the needs and requirements of the prospect. Now it is time to dive a bit deeper and to inform and illuminate through listening for vital clues from the prospect in terms of the information he or she requires. Again, the temptation to 'sell' should be strongly resisted – you're using your powers of persuasion to influence the way the prospect is thinking about whether you have something that can help that person achieve his or her goals.

A mistake often made is to try to 'close the appointment'. Ideally, the presentation stage should segue into the closing stage.

It's not a race or a rush to the finishing line. The aim of this part of the cold call is to build understanding and identify whether there's a potential useful fit between what you can offer and what the prospect might need. This should be part of a natural dialogue, and if you skip this bit you could fail to establish yourself as an enabler and relegate yourself to being yet another pushy salesperson.

Golden rule 7: involving and coordinating

At this point of the cold call you are still in conversation and the recipient hasn't hung up – so that's a positive sign. It's important to explore how you can move the conversation to the next stage and what would be helpful from the prospect's point of view.

If the person works for a large organization then there will be procurement and other procedures that will be required depending on the nature of the product or service you're attempting to sell. This needs to be respected and observed, as there's no point in trying to circumvent it.

Golden rule 8: getting commitment for the next action

This last stage of the cold call moves from active involvement to active commitment, which some sales gurus prefer to call the 'close'. However, the word 'closing' implies an end, whereas at this point you want to open and build a relationship. Getting commitment to what happens next is therefore a successful outcome from a cold call. The outcome is unlikely to result in an immediate sale, but could lead to an appointment at which the sale is able to take place. In many respects, this is earning the 'permission' of the recipient to contemplate a commercial relationship with you.

It's important that you record notes as to this interaction in case it's a colleague rather than you who attends the prospect or has to make a follow-up call that could ultimately result in a sale.

How to turn a warm call into a sale

In many respects, prospects who started as a cold call have graduated into being a warm call, as they have agreed to a follow-up call or a meeting at which you're able to make a presentation or to get a deeper appreciation of their needs and requirements.

The rules of turning a warm call into a sale are exactly the same as those outlined above.

In other cases, the warm call could be as a result of a recommendation or referral from an existing customer or client – which again emphasizes the consultative nature of the interaction. Again, you should resist going for the 'close' without understanding, listening and asking the prospect about his or her needs and requirements – and suggesting a number of alternative solutions in helping to solve those challenges. In this way warm calling can bring about far better and faster results than a traditional cold call.

Based on the law of averages, you're likely to have more cold calls to make than warm calls – and of course it's preferable that every call is a qualified success whether you have had dealings with that person or not.

As you've read in this chapter, up-selling is one of the most effective and profitable ways to achieve incremental sales, but it's not guaranteed that simply because a customer or client has bought goods or services from you in the past they will automatically do so again.

The process of up-selling needs to be very carefully managed – whether this is face to face, by mail or via the telephone or internet. At the core of up-selling sits effective communication, and this necessitates the ability to listen very carefully.

A golden rule is 'Don't ask, don't sell.' In other words, without asking customers or clients what's important to them, don't expect to gather any meaningful information. And if you don't gather any meaningful information you can't expect to expand that relationship.

To be successful in up-selling, cross-selling, cold calling and warm calling, keep the following points in mind:

- Convey enthusiasm in what you do, tempering sales zeal with pragmatism.
- Remember, listening can be more powerful than talking.
- Keep it simple.
- Remove preconceptions.
- Have a plan and anticipate what can be said but don't provide a stock answer to objections.
- Know when there's little point attempting to up-sell.
- Have a realistic view of what customers or clients want to do with you, and their timescale for making such a decision.

- Keep control of the up-selling process, but don't dictate what customers, clients or prospects should do. Instead influence their thinking and their behaviour.

References

Books

Etherington, B (2012) *Cold Calling for Chickens*, Marshall Cavendish
Fisk, P (2009) *Customer Genius*, Capstone
Harding, F (2002) *Cross-Selling Success*, Adams Media
Kolah, A (2013) *Essential Law for Marketers*, 2nd edn, Guru in a Bottle®, Kogan Page
Maslow, A (1962) *Toward a Psychology of Being*, Wilder Publications
Sales and Marketing Procedures for Sales Pipeline Management (2008) Bizmanualz
Schiffman, S (2005) *Upselling Techniques That Really Work*, Adams Media
Sobczak, A (2010) *Smart Calling*, John Wiley & Sons

"Look into my eyes...look into my eyes"

4

Effective approaches to prospective customers and clients

Introduction

Imagine you are standing in front of a dartboard and are holding 10 darts in each hand. What are your chances of hitting treble 20 at 12 o'clock or the bull's eye if you were to throw the darts all at the same time? I'll leave you to think about that for a moment.

This chapter explores effective approaches to prospective customers and clients. The earlier chapters in this book dealt with the psychology of selling and building a realistic sales pipeline and some of the key skills you need to be effective in sales. Now it's useful to explore effective approaches that will open the way for you to use those skills.

Let's get back to the dartboard. Successful salespeople tend to hit their sales targets because they are precise in their sales efforts. They didn't become successful by chucking everything they had at a dartboard in the vain hope they'd hit the target.

Ever heard of the 80:20 Rule? And, no, it hasn't got anything to do with darts! Back in the 19th century, the Italian economist and philosopher Vilfredo Pareto noticed that with an amazing regularity things weren't evenly distributed. Then, as now, it was just a handful of people in Italian high society who controlled most of the wealth. His theory was that 80 per cent of the land in Italy was owned by 20 per cent of the population. And of course he was proved correct. What he didn't know at the time was that this truism had a much wider application than he envisaged.

What Vilfredo Pareto hadn't appreciated was that the 80:20 Rule also applies to prospective customers and clients. Irrespective of the market or customer segment you're in, it's highly likely that 80 per cent of your profits come from just 20 per cent of your customers. That may sound incredibly inefficient, and you may ask yourself the question: why bother serving the needs of the remaining 80 per cent of unprofitable customers? It's probably also the case that 80 per cent of sales come from just 20 per cent of the sales force. And, conversely, it's more than likely that just 20 per cent of your sales generate around 80 per cent of the profits. This is why pipeline management and customer relationship management are so important in business.

For a discussion on qualifying leads and relationship management, see Chapter 2.

This chapter explores effective approaches to 20 per cent of profitable customers and clients.

We deliberately talk about approaches rather than 'winning' customers or clients, which some sales books are obsessed about. The reason we prefer not to use the word 'winning' is because it presupposes someone else is 'losing' – and that kind of thinking gets sales and marketing a bad name.

This chapter also discusses how to negotiate successfully with prospective customers and clients in order to achieve desired shared outcomes – a sale of the product or service that's delivering value for all parties on either side of the transaction.

Six ways to make a lasting impression

An effective approach starts with making an effective impression. There's a saying that is worth remembering: 'There's only one chance to make a good first impression.' However, the good news is that there are several ways to make a lasting impression.

In today's connected world, a lot of thought and investment is given to engaging with desired customers and clients in an online environment. In many respects, this is driven by expediency rather than a genuine desire to engage in a personal or human way. Let's face it: computers haven't been around that long relative to the way we've chosen to conduct communication and business over the centuries.

In this brave new world, we've become obsessed with having 'friends' and 'followers'. The reality is that such people may not be known to you personally and you may never have met them. You may simply have agreed to allow them to be added to a growing database of 'friends' and 'followers' because it somehow conferred some form of social status in the eyes of your peers.

Leaving cynicism to one side, clearly those who are 'friends' or 'followers' are engaged in what you have to say and at a basic level they may have something of value to offer in exchange. 'This is the price of great, sustainable impact, whether two or 2 million people are involved. Yet it's only when generosity and trust are communicated artfully and authentically that the benefits are mutual', explains Brent Cole of Dale Carnegie & Associates in the United States.

Many people are under the illusion that to succeed in negotiations with customers and clients they've got to be tough or highly competitive. Adopting such a stance can make many salespeople extremely uncomfortable, because they want to succeed in negotiation but don't like acting tough. So many opt to be cooperative because they want the other party to like and trust them and, frankly, it's just more comfortable being this way rather than pushy. The reality is that you don't have to adopt either stance, because an effective approach to a customer or client is built on cooperation as well as competition.

According to US sales legend and management guru Dale Carnegie, there are six tried and trusted ways that are guaranteed to make a lasting impression with a customer or client:

1 Take an interest in others' interests.

2 Smile.

3 Reign with names.

4 Listen longer to customers and clients.

5 Discuss what matters to customers and clients.

6 Add value that leaves customers and clients better for the experience.

Take an interest in the customer or client's curiosity

This may sound like an obvious thing to do, but most salespeople are far too interested in themselves or their products and services to notice the customers or clients standing in front of them. The bottom line is that you must become genuinely interested in others before you can ever expect anyone to be interested in you and what you have to say or sell.

One curse of social media is that it's spawned the idea that we must become obsessed by what we want to think, act and communicate to others via Facebook, Twitter, LinkedIn, MySpace, YouTube and the rest. And yet there are now so many more opportunities to stay connected, learn from others and show appreciation of another person's point of view (POV).

Changing how your customer or client engagement strategy works will dramatically change how the market and customer segments perceive you and your enterprise.

So, instead of each day refining your digital media, spend time relating to your friends, colleagues, customers and clients. Post brief, admiring notes. Interact and engage with these audiences by listening. Find out what problems you might help them solve or what pursuits you might help promote.

'We are all driven by pain and pleasure, so such prospects exist in every person. When you are sincere in your endeavours to connect with others, chances are always higher that meaningful connection will occur. Progressive, mutually beneficial collaboration is then possible. And today genuine connection and collaboration can quickly become infectious', observes Brent Cole.

Smile!

Part of the huge success of the Guru in a Bottle® Series is in its ability to entertain, inform and engage. The intention is to use a pinch of humour. A smile – provided it's not artificial, unnatural or false – is a key social asset. Researchers in the United States used statistical analysis of social networks to show that people who smile tend to have more friends and are also at the centre of a social network rather than on the periphery of the online world.

A smile, someone once said:

Costs nothing but gives much.

It enriches those who receive without making poorer those who give.

It takes but a moment, but the memory of it sometimes lasts forever.

None is so rich or mighty that he can't get along without it and none is so poor that he can't be made rich by it.

Yet a smile can't be bought, begged, borrowed or stolen, for it's something that's of no value to anyone until it's given away.

Some people are too tired to give you a smile.

Give them one of yours, as none needs a smile so much as he who has no more to give.

So show us your pearly whites!

Reign with names

Today, we are surrounded by brands of every description, shape and size. There are company brands, organization brands, product brands, services brands and – perhaps the most powerful of all in a sales situation – the personal brand. Increasingly, the name game is becoming much more important.

For example, on Twitter your commercial worth is commensurate with the number of names who follow you – assuming that these people are worth holding a candle to. The opportunities to be known by others and to know others are two sides of the same coin. Remembering people's names and referring to them by their names, and even spelling their names right – particularly an unusual name – may seem trivial details but they have a massive impact. We must never forget the magic in a person's name and that this word is wholly and completely owned by the person with whom we are dealing and nobody else.

Listen longer

This book is entitled *The Art of Influencing and Selling* but the alternative title could have been 'The Art of Listening'. This is one of the most under-rated skills of salespeople: the ability to use their ears rather than their mouth in that ratio.

It's often said that women rather than men make better listeners.

Undoubtedly, the power of listening is the power to influence hearts and minds – and wallets will follow. In a sales context, it's the power of giving people what they desire most.

Throughout this book we talk about two modes of communication – 'transmit' and 'receive' mode. It's the latter that in fact is much more power-ful, and yet as sales and marketing professionals we spend all our time trying to perfect our abilities in using the transmit mode without placing an equal weight or importance on perfecting our abilities in using the receive mode.

Few people possess the listening qualities that were endowed to the man who is described below:

It struck me so forcibly that I shall never forget him. He had qualities which I'd never seen in any other person. Never had I seen such concentrated attention. There was none of that 'piercing soul penetrating gaze' business. His eyes were mild and genial. His voice was low and kind. His gestures were few. But the attention he gave me, his appreciation of what I said, even when I said it badly, was extraordinary. You've no idea what it meant to be listened to like that.

Dale Carnegie was describing the experience that a correspondent had with none other than the brilliant psychoanalyst Sigmund Freud.

In today's networked world of Twitter, Facebook and LinkedIn, our circle of influence has expanded beyond the boundaries of family, friends, acquaintances and colleagues and now includes those who want to be our 'friends' on LinkedIn and other networks. As a consequence, individual networks can spawn not just hundreds but potentially thousands of such friends or 'followers'. However, while the number of people to whom we might listen has exploded, the number of people to whom we actually listen is in fact diminishing.

Listening is a powerful weapon in the armoury of the salesperson. Listening imparts a great deal of respect – more so than a planned sales pitch ever could. This is why asking questions of prospective customers or clients can evince a stronger sales signal than bombarding them with sales messages. 'It's often said that you live and learn, but perhaps an equally important lesson for us all is that, if you listen and learn, you live more harmoniously', reflects Brent Cole.

Discuss what matters to them

In Chapter 1, we discussed starting with the customer's or client's POV in order to be successful at selling and influencing. Yet how many of us give this but a momentary thought before launching into a sales pitch in the misplaced belief that we'll convince the hapless prospect of the power of our offer and achieve the sales outcome we're hoping for?

Successful selling is what Dale Carnegie described over 80 years ago as a bridge-building exercise. This begins when you flip conventional sales and marketing on its head and begin all interactions from the POV of the other person.

For a detailed discussion on making an effective sales pitch, see Chapter 6. US social network blogger Valeria Maltoni offers this advice:

Everyone is wrong about influence except your customers. Think about that before you get into trouble for not delivering meaningful results. True influence flows from drawing together people with shared interests. It's a process of identifying areas of relevancy among your customers and prospects, community building and allowing others to amplify your influence as you meet their needs. You'll be chasing the popular kids (even those who demur) until the cows come home if you keep thinking that influence is about you. It's not. And you don't need the following of celebrity to build something of significance.

You're ultimately building a network when you initiate interactions with what matters to others. And a community is what really matters to you in a sales context – whether it's building and launching a new brand, product or service.

If the foundation of all long-term sales success is trust-based relationships, then the goal of such interactions must be to convey value as soon and as often as possible. Such communities don't need to be large in order to have influence over purchasing behaviour – they just need to be real.

Some research suggests that the human brain can only cope with 150 contacts who are deemed to be within your 'inner circle', so having thousands of followers or 'friends' within the context of social media doesn't necessarily translate into a healthy sales pipeline.

According to US social network blogger Mitch Joel, influence shouldn't be confused with the sheer volume of friends or followers you're able to attract on Facebook or Twitter:

True influence comes from connecting to individuals, nurturing those relationships, adding real value to the other people's lives and doing anything and everything to serve them, so that, when the time comes for you to make an ask, there's someone there to lend a hand. Worry less about how many people you are connected to and worry a whole lot more about who you are connected to, who they are and what you are doing to value and honour them.

Add value that leaves customers and clients better for the experience

Have you ever had the sinking feeling of having left a wallet or a mobile phone in the back of a taxi? We're sure that's happened to many people reading this book. But then, when you're able to call the cab company or you ring your own mobile phone and the cab driver answers and voluntarily makes arrangements to return your wallet or phone to you, such an act of kindness is guaranteed to make a lasting impression.

Applied to a sales context, being attentive and focusing on small things can make a big difference.

In the heart of London's fashionable Oxford Street a small revolution in retailing is taking place. Acclaimed British retail expert Mary Portas has opened a concept store concession. Customers are blown away by the welcome that each of the handpicked sales staff gives as they wander around the rails. Instead of the sales team focusing on what they are selling and pushing this as hard as they can, they have been personally trained by Mary Portas to focus on making their customers' days a little better for the experience. And of course the concession is one of the most profitable sales floors in the whole of Oxford Street as a result.

Understanding the short cuts to getting what we want

Given that most of us exist in a highly complicated environment, we need short cuts to deal with it. Researchers have shown that stereotyped behaviour is prevalent in much human interaction because it's an efficient way to behave and in other cases it's simply a necessity.

For example, a typical salesperson can't be expected to recognize and analyse all the aspects of a prospective customer or client, event or situation every day. Let's face it: even with the best will in the world, all of us lack time, energy and capacity at some point! So it's human nature to fall back on relying on stereotypes, 'rules of thumb' and classifying things according to a few key features and then to respond without thinking when one or other of these trigger features are present.

For example, a favourite short cut for salespeople is the 'contrast principle' whereby customers' behaviour is influenced when they are presented with a contrast.

Salespeople in a clothing store are often instructed to sell the most costly item first. Common sense may suggest the reverse: if a man has just spent a lot of money on a suit he may be reluctant to spend much more on the purchase of a sweater – but this isn't always the case. The shop assistant behaves in a way consistent with the contrast principle: sell the suit first because, when it comes time to look at a sweater, even expensive ones, the price won't seem that high in comparison with the suit! The same effect is achieved when the sales assistant nonchalantly enquires whether the customer needs a new belt, tie and shirt to complement the suit that's just been bought. These secondary purchases feel relatively painless on the wallet!

'Presenting an inexpensive product first and following it with an expensive one will make the expensive item seem even more costly as a result – hardly a desirable consequence for most sales organizations', observes US psychologist Robert Cialdini.

New car dealers are experts in the art of the contrast principle (they may not know it yet!). They'll focus on selling the vehicle first and then provide a series of options that will upgrade the vehicle, such as offer alloys, a slicker CD and in-car entertainment system, a superior air-con system and metallic paint. All these 'extras' are designed to make you feel that you have bought a customized product for your taste and requirements where the incremental costs are almost academic to the main purchase and therefore the customer feels powerless to resist.

Robert Cialdini concludes:

> More and more we are forced to resort to the shortcut approach in which the decision to comply (or agree or believe or buy) is made on the basis of a single, usually reliable piece of information. The most reliable and therefore popular single triggers for compliance are commitments, opportunities for reciprocation, the compliant behaviour of similar others, feelings of liking or friendship, authority directives, and scarcity of information. And because of the increasing tendency for cognitive overload in our society, the prevalence of shortcut decision making is likely to increase proportionately.

The art of sales negotiation

A major weakness in the armoury of salespeople is often nothing to do with the product or service or even their own personality. Rather, it's their ability to be able to negotiate a sale.

According to British sales negotiator and trainer Peter Thomson, there are seven mistakes most often made by salespeople when it comes to negotiating with a customer or client, which can often end up in no sale being made or, worse still, a sale that's uneconomic as it doesn't generate a profitable return.

The seven deadly sins in trying to negotiate a sale

1 Not giving a reason why it's important for the customer to act now

It's important that there's an imperative for the customer to want to buy – this could be as a result of a limited offer, for example, or that there's a scarcity of the type of products available to be purchased.

Another way of grabbing attention in the negotiation with the customer is to use a small but very powerful word that is guaranteed to get a response – F-R-E-E.

For example, many business consultants will provide a free download to a document in exchange for your name and e-mail. In other words, you opt in to receive it. They know that if they can touch a raw nerve you'll respond in a way that could lead to a monetary purchase at another time. Getting you to take the 'free of charge' step gets them closer to you taking a paid-for next step in the sales process.

2 Assuming that the purchaser holds all the cards in the buying process

'There's a complete misunderstanding as to who has the real power in any conversations that involve buying and selling. The vast majority of salespeople believe erroneously that the buyer is the final arbiter in any selling/buying conversation. And that's totally and utterly wrong', observes Peter Thomson.

One of the deadly sins for salespeople is trying to get a sale before they've asked sufficient questions to expose the needs and wants of the buyer and then selling the product or service at a price point that's not capable of generating a profitable return.

'Far too many businesses are dealing with clients where the price negotiated in the past now simply doesn't make them enough profit to make the business sustainable and rather than stop dealing with those customers they keep on taking orders – and as a consequence continue to lose money', warns Peter Thomson.

For a further discussion on buyer types, see Chapter 10.

3 Focusing on selling, rather than allowing customers to buy

You multiply your chances of success if you can identify those challenges, issues or problems faced by the customer and only then start to talk about features, benefits and advantages in the context of how the product or service provides a workable solution.

4 Being arrogant rather than having a ring of confidence

Many salespeople can come across as pushy or belligerent. Conversely, a professional salesperson should walk away from a deal where there's no genuine effort made to create a win–win outcome, that is, a negotiated outcome in which the parties have reached an agreement that can't be mutually improved upon.

5 Failing to learn from the mistakes of others

The collective wisdom of experienced salespeople is available in virtually every format imaginable. Model your thinking around a salesperson or organization that you admire and the guru will be out of the bottle!

6 Not adding a premium to the price for the knowledge applied to solving a problem or providing a service

In the services sector, solving issues, challenges and problems is about delivering a service that makes a difference. But failing to price this service by taking account of the experience invested in the person delivering this is a deadly sin. For example, a news release can be written by a PR executive with two years' experience or a PR professional with over 20 years' experience. But the client wouldn't expect to pay the same fee to both if the PR professional could deliver this in half the time and create more interest as a result of their experience. The client, more importantly, is also paying for 20 years' as opposed to two years' experience.

7 Forgetting to ask for a referral that can help to generate the next sale

Asking for a referral is one of the best retention sales strategies known to professional salespeople. 'How on earth could a customer stop buying from you when they've just given you the name or names of colleagues and friends and by implication recommended that those contacts buy from you?' asks Peter Thomson.

Knowing when you're in the zone of possible agreement

Assuming that there's a genuine will to want to buy and that the customer or client has a clear view about acquiring the product or service and the benefits that will flow from its acquisition, then the salesperson will have reached the zone of possible agreement (ZOPA). The ZOPA represents the overlap between the most the buyer is willing to pay and the least the salesperson is willing to accept for the product or service. Professor Leigh Thompson of the Kellogg School of Management at Northwestern University in the United States, who's conducted academic research in the area of negotiation, explains:

I always think of ZOPA like a dance floor. I envision two negotiators dancing, each trying to lead the other to his reservation point. It's possible that there's no space on the dance floor, meaning that the maximum a buyer is willing to pay is less than the minimum a seller will accept. It's also possible that the dance floor is the size of a football field. The most common mistake people make is to assume the bargaining zone is much smaller than it actually is. I call this ZOPA myopia. ZOPA myopia often occurs because people are anchored by their own reservation prices.

Two basic types of negotiations

According to Leigh Thompson there are two types of negotiations: fixed-sum negotiations and variable-sum negotiations.

Fixed-sum negotiations

In such instances, the parties' interests are diametrically opposed and, however much one party gains, the other loses and vice versa.

For example, if there's a negotiation over price, Party A's (buyer) secret reservation price is $80, whereas Party B (seller) has a reservation price of $60. In such an example, the ZOPA is always going to be $20.

However, if the parties can identify another negotiable issue that at least one of the parties cares about, then there's the potential for a win–win deal.

Variable-sum negotiations

In such instances, the ZOPA can be expanded. For example, if Party A's reservation point for a cash deal is $80 but Party A is prepared to go to $100 for a credit deal, and Party B's reservation point was $60 for cash but $70 for credit, then in terms of the ZOPA for the cash deal only it's $20, but the ZOPA is $10 greater when considering a credit deal. In such a situation, the purchase price has been separated from the method of payment (cash or credit).

Many negotiations are disguised as single-issue, but sales negotiators can prevent them from becoming fixed-sum negotiations by adding an issue, such as an additional product or service, or splitting the issue into multiple issues, such as offering credit terms. 'By unbundling single-issue negotiations into multi-issue negotiations, sales negotiators can create more opportunities for win–win trade-offs', says Leigh Thompson.

The future is about collaborating for profit

The future of the sales process is going to be radically different – and it's already starting to happen. Instead of the dance that the majority of sales situations appear to resemble, the professional salesperson will soon be dancing to a different tune – collaboration.

This isn't some conceptual pipe dream – a utopian state where producers and consumers join forces for the sake of capitalism. Collaboration is rapidly becoming the de facto way in which products and services are developed, road-tested and marketed.

For example, Threadless is a phenomenally successful US business that gets its customers to design a new range of T-shirts every week, which are sold through its website as well as retail stores. The best designs submitted win a US$2,000 cash prize, which the online community vote for. T-shirts cost US$3 to produce and retail for US$15, which shows that customers are prepared to pay a premium for collaboration. What's really cool is that they keep coming back for more – as the community customers want the latest designs. This is a great example of doing things differently. It's about collaborating for profit.

In summary, key points to remember are:

- Remember that 80 per cent of profitable sales are generated by just 20 per cent of customers and clients.
- Take an interest in others' interests.
- Smile!
- Reign with names.
- Listen longer to customers and clients.
- Discuss what matters to customers and clients.
- Add value that leaves customers and clients better for the experience.
- Remember to deploy the contrast principle in order to negotiate a successful sale.
- Provide customers with a reason why they need to act now.
- Remember, you're the expert and can walk away from the sale if it's unprofitable.
- Focus on allowing customers to buy rather than focusing on selling to them – you may be ready to sell, but are they ready to buy?
- Be confident, not arrogant.
- Be prepared to learn from others' mistakes as well as your own.
- Be brave and consider knowledge and experience as part of the product and service value.
- Don't forget to ask for a referral.
- Avoid ZOPA myopia.
- Avoid fixed-sum negotiations wherever possible.
- Negotiate by collaborating with the customer or client.

References

Books

Carnegie, D (1936) *How to Win Friends and Influence People*, Cedar
Cialdini, R (2009) *Influence: Science and practice*, 5th edn, Pearson
Thompson, L (2008) *The Truth about Negotiations*, Pearson Education

Websites

Ardi Kolah's view of the death of the average customer published by the Institute
    of Customer Service: http://www.instituteofcustomerservice.com/5976-6009/
    Death-of-the-average-customer.html (accessed 18 June 2011)
Chris Gourlay's article about Facebook Friends can be found on the website:
    http://technology.times.online.co.uk (accessed 9 December 2010)
Mitch Joel's view on the value of building networks can be read on his blog:
    http://www.twistimage.com/blog (accessed 9 December 2011)
Peter Thomson's view on how to approach prospective customers and clients can
    be seen on his website: http://www.ultimateleadgensystem.com (accessed 10
    January 2012)
Valeria Maltoni's view about influence can be read on her blog:
    http://www.conversationagent.com/2010/07/everyone-is-wrong-
    about-influence.html (accessed 7 July 2010)
Wisdom Commons: http://www.wisdomcommons.org (accessed 9 November 2011)

"Thinking outside the box isn't easy –
keep trying"

How to interrogate a database of contacts to get more sales

In this chapter:

- Developing a customer, client and supporter database
- Basic principles of data mining
- Customer, client and supporter acquisition strategies
- Using survival analysis to understand customers, clients and supporters

Introduction

Customers, clients and prospects are 'leads' and as such are the lifeblood of all commercial organizations. Within the voluntary and not-for-profit sectors, such 'leads' are frequently supporters, donors and volunteers.

As discussed in Chapter 2, it's important to have a realistic sales pipeline where 'leads' are qualified and also where there's a clear lead conversion process. Such an approach applies to any size of organization in any sector – public or private.

Typically, such data will need to reside in a centrally organized database system. This repository will be a key foundation for any outbound or inbound telemarketing or direct marketing campaign like those described in Chapter 3.

Inbound sales leads are often generated as a result of marketing activities that have influenced customer, client or supporter behaviour, such as competitions, prizes, special offers and other activities that require some form of participation and registration. Typically, the respondent will need to input some demographic and/or psychographic information in order to participate in the promotion.

For all organizations, acquiring and then retaining customers, clients and supporters is a critical success factor given the current challenging economic conditions. At the same time, the nature of sales has increasingly become a more sophisticated exercise and can often involve multifaceted workflows and internal procedures that are often difficult to synchronize, track and manage.

For example, sales representatives may be required to follow up on hundreds of new sales 'leads' while juggling existing sales cycles at the same time.

Marketing professionals must often plan and develop an increasing number of sophisticated campaigns that are capable of being delivered across a variety of offline and online channels. Customer service teams may be required to resolve rapidly a growing volume of customer and client problems and issues as they arise. Managers need to oversee customer, client and supporter-facing operations across all areas to ensure that interactions are handled in an appropriate, legal, responsive and helpful manner. Taken together, none of these tasks can be effectively managed in the absence of a database, and it's likely that such a database of contacts will have been built up over several months or even years.

Such a database is only useful if the information it contains can be easily accessed and applied. That's why customer relationship management (CRM) systems were devised as a way to automate the process of interrogating these data sets.

Over the last couple of years, CRM systems have had to go much further as a result of the rapidly changing nature of communication with customers, clients and supporters, which is now much more collaborative, and the tightening of privacy and data protection laws in jurisdictions around the world that affect the use of personal data and the constant need to cleanse and maintain accurate data sets that can so rapidly become obsolete.

In this chapter we explore what best practice looks like in the interrogation of a database of existing customers, clients, supporters and prospects in order to drive more sales. Although 'database' is referred to in the singular in this chapter, it's often the case that there'll be more than one database involved, so 'database' should also be interpreted in its plural context.

Developing a customer, client and supporter database

Data sits at the heart of many core business processes. It's generated by transactions in operational systems irrespective of the market segment – retail, telecommunications, insurance, banking, healthcare, transport, utilities and other market segments. Adding to the deluge of internal data are external sources of demographic and psychographic data, which often includes lifestyle information, credit information and financial and marketing information. In order to get the most out of a database, it should include details of prospective as well as existing customers, clients and supporters. People who enquire about your company or organization should be included and 'flagged' for approach in the future.

'The promise of data mining is to find the interesting patterns lurking in all these billions and trillions of bits lying in a computer disk or in computer memory. Merely finding patterns isn't enough. You must respond to the patterns and act on them, ultimately turning data into information, information into action, and action into value', observes US data mining guru Gordon Linoff.

For example, only a small percentage of the total population is likely to want to purchase your products or services or become volunteers and supporters. If you segment your sales and marketing effort by focusing on the most valuable segments, then it's more likely to be successful. Conversely, if you aim to appeal to very wide customer, client or supporter segments, you'll run the risk of failing to engage with those with whom you can genuinely have a dialogue as well as spread your resources too thinly without achieving the sales outcomes you've planned for.

Refer to Guru in a Bottle®'s *High Impact Marketing That Gets Results* for a detailed discussion on best practice in customer and client segmentation.

Not all customers, clients and supporters have the same needs. It makes sense to build up a profile of your customers and group them according to their different requirements. This will give you a good idea of how likely they are to purchase or support what you are offering. Having established a customer profile, you should then consider looking for additional prospects by buying in a tailored database or list from a list broker. Bear in mind that it's only usually possible to buy and sell personal information held in a database if the people concerned have agreed that their information can be passed on ('opted in').

Refer to Guru in a Bottle®'s *Essential Law for Marketers* (2nd edition) for more information on data protection principles.

When dealing with list brokers, you can specify exactly what type of person or organization you want to target in terms of size and type of organization, if you're involved in business-to-business (B2B) activities, or age, gender, income or lifestyle, if you're involved in business-to-consumer (B2C) activities.

Such lists are usually offered for rent, ie one-off use only, or for sale, ie unlimited usage of such data.

If the list is rented, then most conditions of use exclude the right to add names on the list to your own database, except when you've received a response to your approach. In order to achieve this, there should be a compelling reason or attractive incentive, such as a generous promotional offer, to encourage a prospective customer, client or supporter to respond.

Basic principles of data mining

Data mining is a business process for exploring large amounts of data in order to discover meaningful patterns and trends within data sets that can predict sales outcomes. Typically, sophisticated modelling techniques are used in order to make such predictions.

Data mining is also an ongoing process and starts with the identification of sales opportunities, which is followed by the conversion of raw data into useful information, which through analysis informs and inspires action on the part of the brand owner; this in turn creates sales leads, which then generate more data, and the whole cycle begins again (Figure 5.1).

Figure 5.1 Virtuous cycle of data mining

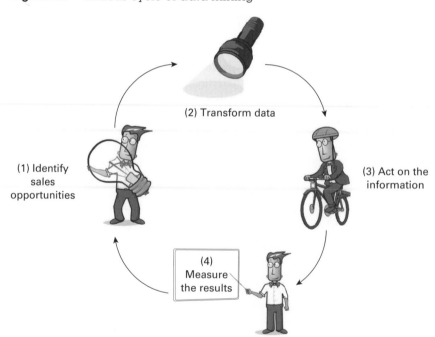

Identifying sales opportunities

In the retail sector, this is particularly important, as purchasers don't tend to be brand loyal and will often shop around for the best price, making it challenging to build a database of potential customers. Quality products and competitive pricing may not be enough to create brand loyalty.

As discussed in Chapter 1, in such a dynamic economic and trading environment the retailer needs to focus on the attitudes, values, beliefs and behaviours of valuable customer and client segments. This is best done by grouping subsets of customers, clients and supporters with different characteristics and developing differentiated strategies that most accurately address their specific needs and requirements.

Market research in the retail sector is typically used to gain insights into customer attitudes, requirements, views, preferences, and opinions about the brand owner and its competitors. In addition to external and market research data, transactional data can also be added to the data sets used in order to develop effective segmentation solutions that will help to drive sales (this is often referred to as 'market basket analysis').

A value-based segmentation scheme allocates customers, clients and supporters to groups according to their spending or donation amount. In this way, it can be used to identify high-value customers, clients and supporters and prioritize their importance to the brand owner according to their economic value.

Successful organizations that want to use data to drive sales embed data mining deep within their sales and marketing efforts.

Transforming data into information

This sits at the heart of any data mining exercise, particularly in the retail sector (Figure 5.2).

Sales success will be a consequence of turning data into useful information such as:

- recency, frequency and monetary value of purchases (often referred to as 'RFM analysis');
- relative spending amount per product group and subgroup;
- size of basket;
- individual spending amount on a per-item basis;
- preferred payment method;
- preferred period and time of day for making purchases; and
- preferred retail outlets and offline channels.

The ability to have this level of insight into behaviour will allow for a differentiated and targeted approach to sales prospecting amongst these segments based on their recognized consumer and spending habits.

Figure 5.2   Transforming data into useful information

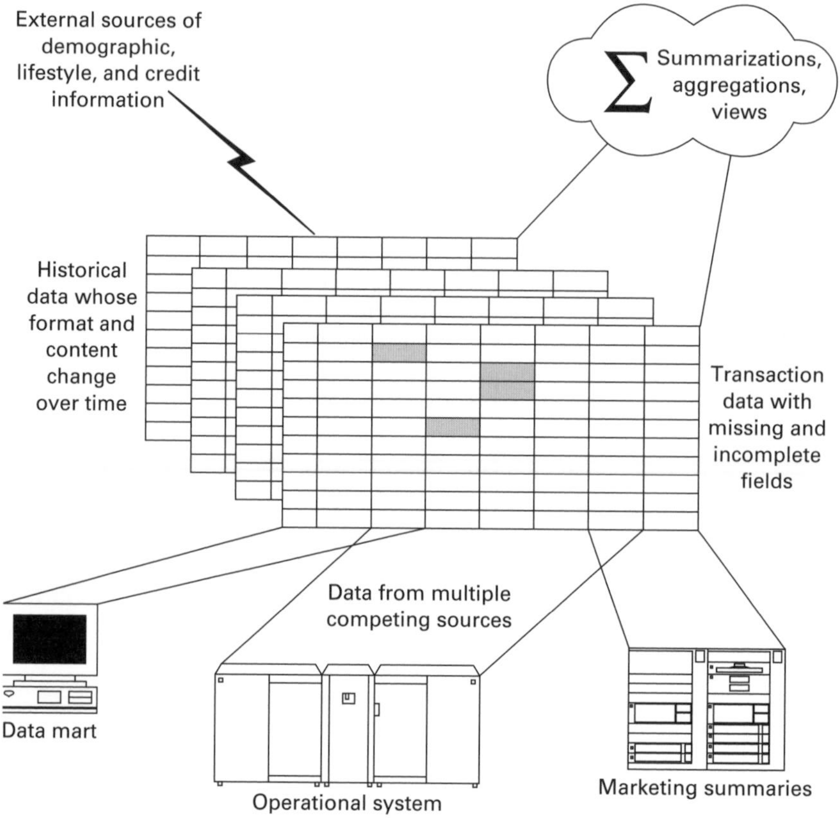

Source: Data Miners, 2012

Another important data set is transactional details that are logged at the point of sale by an electronic point of sale (EPOS) system and typically record detailed information of every transaction. Where the universal product code (UPC) of each item purchased has been logged, this allows the brand owner to carry out more sophisticated monitoring of the groups and subgroups of products that each customer tends to buy.

A prerequisite of behavioural segmentation is that every transaction is identified with a customer. Within the retail sector, this is usually achieved by introducing a customer loyalty programme that assigns an identification field to each transaction and permits tracking of the purchase history of each customer and aggregation of the transactional information at a customer level. This data set can be extremely valuable.

That said, there are many potential pitfalls for sales professionals when attempting to turn raw data into information, and these include:

- bad data formats such as not including the postal or zip code in the customer, client or supporter address field;
- confusion between different databases, where 'planned delivery' and 'actual delivery date' can mean one and the same thing;
- lack of functionality within the database, for example not allowing annotations on a per-customer basis by the outbound or inbound telemarketing team; and
- a lack of timeliness in updating the database rendering it unreliable.

Acting on the information

For example, outputs may include sending messages to prospective customers, clients and supporters via e-mail, direct mail and telemarketing, with different messages being sent to different people.

Measuring the results

This part of the cycle can so easily be overlooked in the heat of wanting to drive sales leads, but it's vital to understand how the plan is performing against actual sales in order to appreciate what can be done to improve sales in the future. Measurement should be inbuilt at the commencement of thinking about how to drive sales through data mining rather than as a 'nice to have' afterthought.

For example, a brand owner that distributes money-off coupons for a brand of coffee can measure the redemption rate of such a promotion relatively easily through a unique promotion code. However, coupon redeemers might have purchased the jar of coffee anyway irrespective of the money-off incentive, so other metrics will need to be added to the data sets being mined.

Another appropriate measure is examining incremental sales in a particular store or region, and these can also be tied to a particular sales and marketing campaign. Such measurements can be difficult to make because they require more detailed sales information, but assuming the objective is to drive incremental sales then there'll need to be a way to measure this directly and indirectly.

Customer, client and supporter acquisition strategies

As discussed in Chapter 4, the Pareto principle applies where typically 80 per cent of the profit is likely to come from just 20 per cent of your customers, so accuracy in targeting and engaging with the most valuable and profitable customer, client and supporter segments is critical.

Turning prospects into customers, clients and supporters is dependent on a number of factors, including advertising, marketing and word of mouth, as well as collaborating with them.

Value-based segments can provide useful information for the development of effective acquisition models. Acquisition campaigns aimed at increasing market share through expansion of the customer, client or supporter base tend to be focused on growing existing segments as well as acquiring customers, clients and supporters from competitors. For example, in mature or more established market segments, such as telecommunications, there's often fierce competition for acquiring new customers.

In such instances, predictive models can be used to guide customer acquisition efforts.

A common issue with acquisition models is the availability of input data. The amount of information available on people who don't as yet have a relationship with your company or organization is generally limited compared with information on existing customers, clients or supporters. In such cases, acquisition of data through third parties such as list brokers may be required and, depending on the value of the data, will dictate the cost-per-name rate. The usual approach in such cases is to run a test campaign on a random sample of prospects, record their responses and analyse these with predictive modelling techniques (see Figure 5.3) in order to identify the profiles associated with the increased profitability of accepting an offer. The derived predictability models can then be used to score all prospects in terms of acquisition probability.

At the top of the decision tree in Figure 5.3 is the root node that contains the demographic data used to grow the tree. In this simple example, it's the age of the customer, client or prospect. The point of the tree is to split these segments into four categories (the under 18, 18–35, 36–55 and over 55 age groups) in order to determine which age groups are the most profitable. These are further segmented by income and marital status. The nodes that ultimately get used are at the ends of their branches. These are the 'leaves' of the tree. The path from the root node to a leaf describes a rule for the records in that leaf. For example, an under-18-year-old prospect on a low income has a higher propensity to buy than someone with a higher income in the same age group. Conversely, prospects within the 36- to 55-year-old segment who are single are also likely to have a higher propensity to buy compared with those who are married within this segment. The least valuable customer, client and supporter segment is the 18- to 35-year-olds, so the sales and marketing effort shouldn't be targeted at this segment, as it's unlikely to generate incremental sales.

Although there are many variations on the core decision tree algorithm, all of them share the same basic method for creating the tree. You need to click on the decision tree icon in your tool of choice or call up the appropriate decision tree procedure. Within each section, the data divides into more detail, helping you use the decision tree more effectively and making the results easier to understand. The decision tree algorithm repeatedly splits the data into smaller and smaller groups in such a way that each new set of nodes has greater purity than its ancestors with respect to the target variable.

Figure 5.3 Example of a decision tree

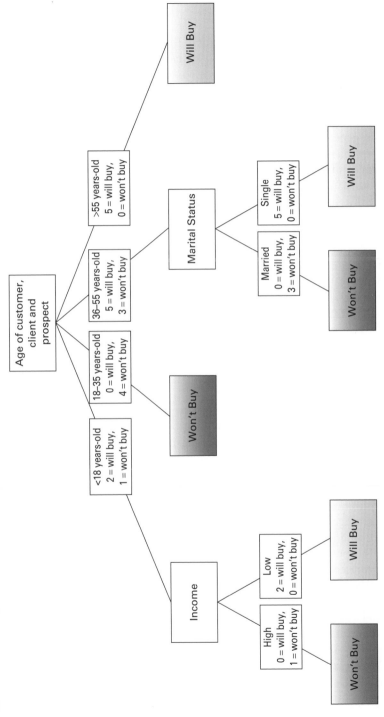

Segmenting customers and clients according to their value

One of the key tasks of data mining is segmenting customers and clients according to value. Undertaking such an exercise differentiates customers and clients according to their profit contribution and can be used to prioritize customer and client handling. As a result, this is one of the most important segmentation types, since it can be used to identify the most valuable customers and clients and track value and value changes over time.

In general, high-value customers and clients should receive a higher level of service in every interaction with the brand owner. Since high-value customers, clients and supporters account for a significant share of a company or organization's income, the brand owner has to build loyalty by offering incentives and benefits that 'reward' and recognize this status. At the same time, this works as a defensive strategy by placing an emotional and rational barrier in the way to prevent customers, clients and supporters falling into the arms of other competitor companies and organizations.

These customer and client segments should be thoroughly monitored, and any 'at risk' warning signs should immediately trigger retention sales strategies.

For example, an insurance company could decide to segment its customer base according to marginal revenue, a value index calculated previously and readily available on its database. In this example, the insurance company can segment customers by rank in respect of their marginal revenue and subsequently segment them into groups of equal size – known as 'quantiles' or 'tiles'.

Customers with a zero and negative revenue contribution can be distinguished and assigned to two distinct groups. Customers who are loss making for the insurance company can form tile 10, and customers with no profit contribution can form tile 9. The remainder of the company's customers can be grouped into eight value segments of about 10 per cent each (Table 5.1).

As can be seen from Table 5.1, the relative revenue contribution of each derived segment doesn't correspond to its size. On the contrary, respective value steeply decreases from the top to the bottom segments, despite the fact that each segment has approximately the same number of customers. The top 10 per cent of the most valuable customers (tile 1) account for about 60 per cent of the total insurance company's revenue. Similarly, the second most valuable segment (tile 2) also accounts for a disproportionately large part of the revenue. The Pareto principle holds true in this example, as tiles 1 and 2 provide about 80 per cent of the insurance company's overall marginal revenue. In essence, these are the vital few customers on which the insurance company should focus its sales and marketing efforts.

One way is to try to develop a dialogue with customers by listening to what their needs and requirements will be in the future. This will go some way to preventing churn, since possible customer attrition will drastically affect the company's profits.

Table 5.1 Derived value-based segments for an insurance company

Tiles	No. of customers (%)	Marginal revenue sum (%)	Cumulative no. of customers (%)	Cumulative marginal revenue sum (%)
1	10.0	60.4	10.0	60.4
2	10.0	20.5	20.0	80.9
3	10.0	10.8	30.0	91.7
4	10.0	5.8	40.0	97.5
5	10.0	3.1	50.0	100.6
6	10.0	1.4	60.0	102.0
7	10.0	0.5	70.0	102.5
8	10.0	0.1	80.0	102.6
9	15.7	0.0	95.7	102.6
10	4.3	(2.7)	100	99.9

The characteristics of the top-value customers also indicate the profile of the potentially profitable prospects that should be the acquisition target of the insurance company in this example.

Segmenting customers and clients according to their behaviour

This is sometimes referred to as 'cluster modelling', and the attributes that can be used for this type of segmentation of customers and clients include: product ownership and utilization; volume, type and frequency of transactions; and the payment and revenue history that resides on the brand owner's database.

For example, in retail banking, the following behavioural segmentation will be useful in helping to drive incremental sales:

- depositors (savings products);
- future investors (insurance and investment products);
- consuming borrowers (credit cards and loan products);
- frequent travellers (a mix of products and international transactions);
- shoppers (credit cards and hire purchase products); and
- needs borrowers (mortgage and consumer loans).

Propensity-based segmentation

This is particularly useful in industry sectors where there's a high level of churn amongst customers, such as mobile phones, and financial services such as credit and loans.

Customers are first sorted into groups according to their propensity to churn (low, high or medium propensity), and a churn model then assigns churn propensity scores to all customers. These scores denote the likelihood of defection and enable brand owners to rank their customers according to their churn risk.

Data mining can go one step further by combining propensity models and scores in order to produce compound segmentation schemes, which can also be achieved through cluster modelling.

Cluster analysis can be applied to the retrospective propensity scores in order to reveal the segments of customers with similar future needs for specific product groupings. This approach can be useful in support of cross-selling activities.

Further insight can be gained by combining propensity scores with other segmentation schemes such as value-based segments.

For example, when value-based segments are cross-examined with churn probability segments, it produces 'value-at-risk' segmentation – a compound segmentation that can help in prioritizing the churn prevention campaign according to each customer's value and risk of defection.

Loyalty segmentation

This is used to identify different groupings of customers according to their loyalty and to separate brand advocates from migrators or switchers. The segments are created by the application of simple business rules and/or cluster models to survey or database information.

By analysing loyalty segments, a brand owner can gain a valuable insight into its own strengths and weaknesses. As can be seen in Figure 5.4, brand advocates and brand switchers can be further segmented according to the main reason for loyalty or migration.

Brand advocates can be associated with specific usage behaviours and customer database attributes. In order to achieve this, the brand owner can use a market survey to reveal the loyalty segments and then build a classification model with the loyalty segments' field as a target. In doing so it will be able to identify the behaviours associated with each loyalty segment and use the relevant classification rules to extrapolate the loyalty segmentation results to the entire customer, client or supporter base.

Socio-demographic and life stage segmentation

With demographic segmentation, customers, clients and supporters are grouped according to basic information, including:

- age;
- sex;
- ethnicity;

Figure 5.4 Loyalty segmentation in data mining

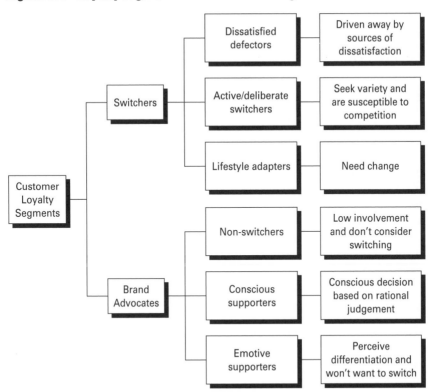

- marital status;
- children;
- educational level;
- address;
- home ownership;
- occupation;
- financial income bracket; and
- employment status.

Typical family lifestyle segmentation is mainly determined by customers' age, marital status and number of children in the household.

For FMCG brand owners, family life cycle segmentation could include:

- retired;
- empty nesters;
- young families without children;

- young families with children under five years old;
- growing families with children over five years old; and
- young singles.

This type of data goes out of date extremely quickly, as it's time-bound, and it's important to ensure that any data mining exercise is conducted with the most recent available data sets, which can be supplemented through list acquisition and market research (where appropriate). In a data mining framework, demographic segmentation is mainly used to enhance insight into the revealed behavioural, value and propensity-based segments.

Life stages are the various milestones that individuals will pass on their journey through life, which could include puberty, relationships, first job, promotion, change of career, rental of accommodation, home or apartment purchase, marriage, children, looking after an elderly parent, grandchildren, retirement and death. A brand owner should try to identify the important life stages and link them to purchase behaviour (Figure 5.5). In this example, the brand owner will have opportunities to sell financial services and savings products to the customer that link to the life stages as shown.

Needs and attitudinal-based segmentation

This segmentation goes further than a basic demographic segmentation as described above and explores attitudes, values, beliefs and behaviours as well as the preferences and perceptions of desired customer, client and supporter segments.

Figure 5.5   Life stages in financial services

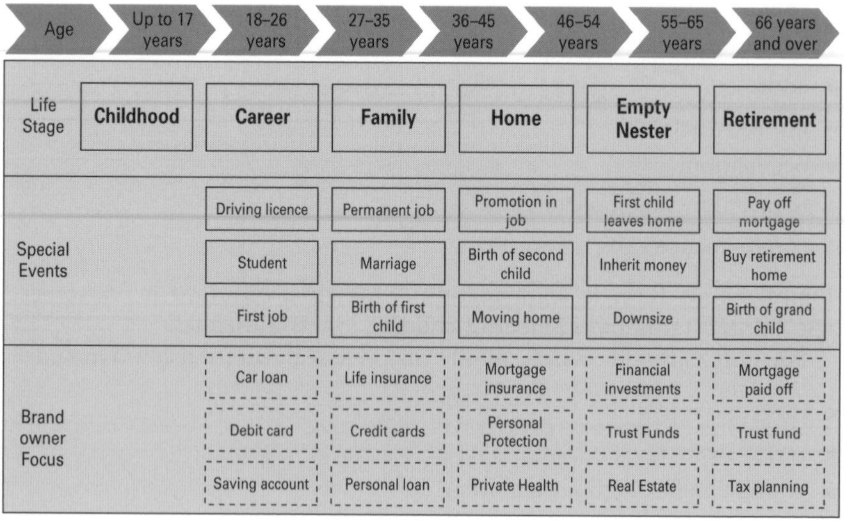

Age	Up to 17 years	18–26 years	27–35 years	36–45 years	46–54 years	55–65 years	66 years and over
Life Stage	Childhood	Career	Family	Home		Empty Nester	Retirement
Special Events		Driving licence	Permanent job	Promotion in job	First child leaves home	Pay off mortgage	
		Student	Marriage	Birth of second child	Inherit money	Buy retirement home	
		First job	Birth of first child	Moving home	Downsize	Birth of grand child	
Brand owner Focus		Car loan	Life insurance	Mortgage insurance	Financial investments	Mortgage paid off	
		Debit card	Credit cards	Personal Protection	Trust Funds	Trust fund	
		Saving account	Personal loan	Private Health	Real Estate	Tax planning	

Relevant information is gathered through market surveys, and customer, client and support segments are typically identified by the application of a cluster model on gathered questionnaire responses.

In the data mining framework, needs and attitudinal-based segmentation is mainly used in combination with behavioural and value-based segments to enrich the profile of the revealed segments as well as provide insight into their qualitative characteristics. This is particularly useful in respect of:

- projection of the brand;
- new product development;
- communication of the product features; and
- public relations and promotions.

Up-selling and cross-selling

A major focus for CRM with existing customers and clients is up-selling and cross-selling, and data mining can be used for figuring out what to offer and to whom as well as when to offer it.

For example, US investment company Charles Schwab noticed that customers generally opened an account with a few thousand dollars even if they had considerably more stashed away elsewhere. Naturally, the company wanted to see if it could attract the rest of this money as well. By analysing historical data, it discovered that customers who transferred large balances into investment accounts usually did so during the first few months after they opened their first account. After a few months, there was little return on trying to get customers to move in large balances. This window was closed. As a result, the company shifted its strategy from sending a constant stream of sales and marketing throughout the customer life cycle to a more focused and concentrated effort in the first few months of the relationship.

Affinity modelling

This is becoming more widely used, particularly by companies and organizations on the web that store a large volume of data and want to drive incremental sales to existing customers.

One of the best exponents of this technique is Amazon. You may have noticed when browsing for this book on the Amazon website that there were other recommendations that popped up and suggested other titles that you might be interested in. 'Customers who bought this book have also bought the following books' can sometimes be highly persuasive and effective in helping to drive incremental sales. Most of the time, these recommendations are useful since they take into account the recorded preferences of past customers and are usually based on association or affinity data mining models.

These models work by analysing past co-occurrences of purchases and attributes and detecting associations. They associate a particular product category, for example business books, with a set of conditions, for example a set of other products such as sales and marketing planning software. They are typically used to identify purchase patterns and groups of products purchased together.

Association modelling techniques generate rules of the following general format:

IF (antecedents) THEN (consequent)

So, for example:

IF (product A, B, C and D) THEN ⟶ product X

The antecedent is a condition or a situation where, when it is true, the rule applies and the consequent shows increased occurrence rates. In other words, the antecedent part of the rule contains the product combinations that usually lead to some other product.

Association modelling techniques are particularly useful in helping to understand which products are commonly purchased together, which can help inform the sales and marketing effort. In the case of Amazon, it's developed a sophisticated association model where it can analyse shopping carts and help direct sales and marketing (through e-mail communication) by producing personalized product suggestions according to the customer's previous recorded behaviour.

Using survival analysis to understand customers, clients and supporters

On first appearance, survival analysis sounds like some desperate strategy to save the life of a company or organization in the absence of sales revenue and income. Yet survival analysis or, as it's sometimes referred to, time-to-event analysis is nothing to worry about, even though its roots are in the statistical analysis of critically ill patients in medical studies.

Gordon Linoff explains:

In the medical world, doctors often want to understand which treatments help patients survive longer – and which have no effect at all (or worse). In the business world, the equivalent concern is when customers stop being customers. This is particularly true of businesses that have a well-defined beginning and end to the customer relationship. A good example is a subscription-based relationship, which may be found in a wide range of industries including insurance, communication, cable television, newspaper and magazine publishing, banking and utilities.

The basis of survival data mining is 'hazard probability', which statisticians define as the chance that someone who's survived for a certain length of time ('customer tenure') is going to stop, cancel or expire before the next unit of time. This definition assumes that time is discrete and such discrete time intervals – days, weeks or months – fit business needs.

By contrast, traditional survival analysis in statistics usually assumes that time is continuous, and this is the major distinction when looking at survival analysis in order to interrogate a database of contacts to get more sales.

This type of statistical analysis was pioneered by British statistician Sir David Cox and has been adopted by brand owners around the world with very large data sets on customers, clients and supporters that could run into thousands, hundreds of thousands or even millions of records.

Gordon Linoff observes:

> *When I try to understand a company's customers by using data collected in its databases, my first inclination is to apply survival data mining. Over the years, I've found that this approach provides rapid feedback about the customers and their behaviours, while at the same time providing a solid basis for quantifying customer value and measuring customer loyalty. This is customer insight in practice.*

Survival analysis is like an early warning system, as it tells the brand owner:

- when a customer is likely to switch brands;
- when a customer is likely to migrate to a new customer segment;
- when a customer is likely to broaden or narrow the customer relationship; and
- how to identify the factors that can increase or decrease the long-term value of the customer.

This aspect of data mining is extremely useful, as it's not always easy to predict how long someone will remain a customer, but past customer behaviour can be a useful indicator for determining whether the customer will continue to purchase goods and services in the future.

Hazard probability

'Given the right data, calculating the hazard probability for a given tenure *t* is simple', explains Gordon Linoff.

> *The probability is the number of customers, clients or supporters who succumbed to the risk (hazard) divided by the population at risk during that tenure. That is, the numerator is the number of customers who stopped with exactly tenure* t *and the denominator is everyone who had tenures greater than or equal to* t. *Customers with shorter tenures aren't part of the risk group.*

Figure 5.6 illustrates hazard probabilities for customers in a typical subscription business. The horizontal axis is the tenure of customers measured in days; the vertical axis is the probability that customers stop at a particular tenure point.

Figure 5.6
Hazard probability of customers of a typical subscription service

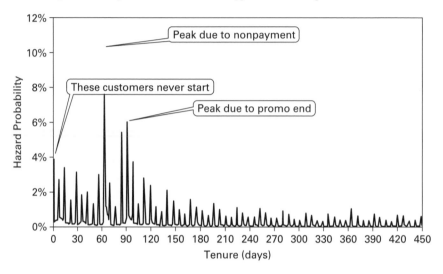

Source: Gordon Linoff, 2012

According to Gordon Linoff, the hazard chart is an 'X-ray into the customer life cycle' because it highlights different important events. The very first hazard probability at time 0 is about 4 per cent, as this is due to customers not starting and is often caused by poor customer information being gathered at the point of sale. This is to be compared with the change in hazard at 60 days, which corresponds with those customers who start with the subscription service but then don't pay. At around 90 days, there's another significant hazard spike, but this time it's due to the end of the initial subscription promotion when there's significant customer churn of customers who initially signed up but lapse once that promotional period ends. After these two initial hazard peaks, the hazard probability gradually declines between 0.5 and 1 per cent as a result of the fall-off of customers as they come to the end of each monthly billing cycle.

'The gradual decline is also interesting and in fact it says something quite important about customer loyalty; the longer customers stay with the company, the less likely they'll leave. In this respect, long-term decline in hazards is a very useful measure of customer loyalty and predictor of future sales', Gordon Linoff says.

Survival analysis has many applications beyond measuring the probability of customers, clients or supporters leaving. For example, it's often a fundamental component of customer value calculations, and it's also used for forecasting customer sales levels as well as providing insights into customer, client and supporter behaviour. These insights can directly feed into marketing and make it possible to understand how long different groups of customers, clients and supporters are likely to be around and as a result the likely profitability of these segments. It also makes it possible to forecast numbers of customers, taking into account both new customer acquisition and customer churn.

For a further discussion on market and customer segmentation, refer to Guru in a Bottle®'s *High Impact Marketing That Gets Results*.

Survival analysis also makes it possible to determine which factors, both at the start of a customer's relationship with the brand owner and in later experiences, will have the biggest impact on customer loyalty.

'The more data you collect from customers, the more value you can deliver to them. And the more value you can deliver to them, the more sales you can generate', concludes Gordon Linoff.

References

Books and papers

Kolah, A (2013) *Essential Law for Marketers*, 2nd edn, Guru in a Bottle®, Kogan Page
Linoff, G (2004) *Survival Data Mining for Customer Insight*, Data Miners
Linoff, G and Berry, M (2011) *Data Mining Techniques*, Wiley
Tsiptsis, K and Chorianopoulos, A (2009) *Data Mining Techniques in CRM*, Wiley

"And it's on special offer for today only –
batteries included..."

Making an effective sales presentation

Introduction

One of the most successful sales trainers in the UK, who has worked with Santander, Swiss Post Document Solutions, GSK, the Orbis Group, npower, RBS, Certus Sales, KPMG and many others, is Andy Bounds. He was born with a hereditary condition known as Stickler syndrome. His mother lost her sight when she was just eight years old, and Andy Bounds was about the same age when he lost all sight in his left eye. This gave him something that few sales professionals possess. As a child, Andy Bounds learnt to explain things to his mother in a way that others would struggle to cope with:

> As long as I can remember, I've known something very few people truly know: that the natural way you speak isn't the natural way for somebody else to understand. That's because audiences are blind to a speaker's agenda. And unless you can see – and say – things from their point of view, your communication is unlikely to work. But learn and apply a few simple techniques and everything is easier. Your communication becomes more effective, more pleasant, shorter and more successful.

And of course he's so right.

Businesspeople say too much irrelevant stuff – all the time, every day and to every type of person. And, hand on heart, we probably all do.

Andy Bounds observes:

> When you speak like this, it's very much like filling a bucket with jelly and flinging it at the other person, hoping some of it will stick. Some will, sure. But most won't. And it's doubly inefficient. It wastes your effort, money, resources and that priceless commodity, time – and that of the people you talk to. But there's an even bigger problem with 'jellying' someone. When you're on the receiving end, you feel like you're on the receiving end of a big, wet, useless barrage. A needless barrage. You feel like a target, not a person. It puts you off doing what they want... from buying into them and their ideas. And, flipping it round, when it's you 'jellying' someone else, they don't always do what you want either, or buy into you or your ideas. But imagine how much more you could achieve if you could overcome all this. Imagine if you knew how to say only the stuff that was 100 per cent relevant to your audience.

In modern times, there's one person that stands head and shoulders above all others as the ultimate 'salesman showman'. In the wake of a boardroom coup staged by a small but powerful group of disgruntled shareholders, he returned to rescue the company from near bankruptcy and was the mastermind behind a series of phenomenal product launches that turned the world of computing, mobile telephony and downloadable music on its head. In doing so, he confounded his critics, his enemies and the cynics on Wall Street who'd written off the company he founded in his lock-up garage with Steve Wozniak back in 1975. And – as if you need reminding – today Apple is the world's most valuable company.

For more than three decades, Steve Jobs worked tirelessly to transform his sales pitch technique into something close to an art form, and his rise to the top as the world's most celebrated 'visionary digital entrepreneur' is the stuff of legend. But then Steve Jobs was no ordinary salesperson, and his legacy will live on well after his untimely death in 2011.

What made him so successful was that he did three things absolutely brilliantly: he entertained, he informed and he engaged. His sales presentations at Apple's annual Worldwide Developers Conference in San Francisco attracted the kind of hysteria normally reserved for a Hollywood 'A list' star. And creating this level of interest wasn't part of some self-indulgent ego trip. In fact, Steve Jobs was an extraordinarily humble person and eschewed material wealth. His attention to detail was so fanatical that even the wrong Pantone colour on a press ad for one of his beloved iMac or iPad products could send him into a high-velocity tail-spin. Steve Jobs lived and breathed what he believed in. Apple products were his life and the stars of his show. Nothing else mattered, and he cared deeply that we bought them, which we did – in our millions.

If we flash back to a time when the sun was always shining, many sales executives didn't spare a nano-second's thought to the quality of their sales pitch. Why should they? The old adage that 'nobody ever got fired for buying IBM' had more than a whiff of truth about it. You simply had to turn up and get the deal in the briefcase. That was about the extent of the sales training IBM-ers were getting in those days.

However, it wasn't just IBM but many other big blue-chip companies that succumbed to becoming complacent about selling and as a result took their foot off the gas. By the time they looked in the rear-view mirror, their competitors had not only caught up with them but were poised waiting for the right opportunity to overtake, a bit like the Olympian marathon runner with eyes set on winning gold.

Of course, the world today is a different place to what it was back in the heady days of the early 1970s. A previously unheard-of Chinese company, Lenovo, bought IBM's personal PC business to become the world's second-largest PC vendor after Hewlett-Packard, and in an instant it had transformed itself into a global brand. Another brand owner from Asia – Tata – bought Land Rover and Jaguar and turned these prestigious car marques into profit, something the previous owner, Ford, had never been able to do. Tata is now one of the most successful companies in the world, having started as a Parsee-owned family business in India in the late 19th century and become a highly respected global conglomerate with interests from industrial mining, construction and car production through to consultancy services, consumer goods manufacturing and tea.

In contrast, the fortunes of Western brands aren't faring as well, as the economic recession in the West looks like being the 'mother of all hangovers' with little prospect of an immediate end in sight.

The party really is over. And it's time to focus on selling.

For many, the thought of having to stand up in front of a group of strangers and get them to buy a product or service is akin to a visit to the dentist – or worse. But it doesn't have to be this way. This chapter unlocks the secrets of what can make a good sales presentation great. Everyone's capable of achieving this level of performance, whatever their previous experience or inexperience may have been. All you need to do is read on and, like Andy Bounds and Steve Jobs before you, keep an open mind, free of innocent preconceptions and expectations, judgements and prejudices. That's a great place from which to start your journey to becoming an accomplished sales presenter. Finding your positive energy won't just make you a more successful sales presenter. As with Andy Bounds and Steve Jobs, it could change your life.

It's about them, not about you

The most important consideration in terms of the content of your sales pitch isn't your product or service. It's the audience you're selling to. It's also not the length of your PowerPoint presentation, the number of slides you've decided to include or whether there's a video in it or not. Everything starts and finishes with the audience, so getting a deep understanding of the prospective customers or clients you're presenting to, as well as their attitudes, values, beliefs, perceptions and behaviours, is absolutely vital if you're to stand any chance of closing the sale.

Let's suspend making a sales pitch for a moment and say you found yourself wanting to make a proposal of marriage or civil partnership to someone you wanted to spend the rest of your life with. Ask yourself – would you use the hard sell in order to get the 'yes' answer you so want to hear? Of course not! So why then use the hard sell in a sales presentation?

'The sales pitch is the hinge on which the door opens. Everything else in life is about process – the pitch is about decisions. If you get the pitch right, everything else follows. And, if you don't, nothing follows', observes Roger Mavity, chief executive of the Conran Group in the UK.

It may sound like we're stretching the point a bit to compare a sales pitch to a proposal of marriage or civil partnership, but the best relationships are those that endure, rather like a marriage or civil partnership.

The best customers and clients are those we collaborate with. These are our brand ambassadors – where there's alignment of what both parties want to get out of the relationship, a 'shared destiny' and a genuine investment in each other's outcome.

Getting inside the head of the person you're trying to pitch to

According to Daniel Kahneman, the recipient of the Nobel Prize in Economic Sciences for his seminal work in psychology, we tend to use information that comes quickly to mind in order to form judgements, which tends to produce predictable biases. Understanding this element of human psychology could hold the key to becoming a successful sales presenter. The list of biases all of us carry within ourselves is a long one, which is all the more reason why the sales pitch must be about the buyer rather than the seller.

Daniel Kahneman's research shows that there are two types of thought processes at work in the mind of the decision maker that we need to be aware of. System One is quick, intuitive and automatic, but prone to being forced by its own mental short cuts. System Two is more contemplative, deeper and harder to deploy. It can correct for error, but more often acts like a lawyer and lobbyist for our emotions.

From a sales perspective, understanding how to 'read' the personality styles of those we are presenting to will dramatically improve the chances of closing the sale, as we'll get an insight into how to handle them without changing our own natural personality in the process.

Personality styles

There are four well-established personality styles depending on whether the decision makers are active or passive, as well as whether they tend to be extroverts or introverts (Figure 6.1).

In the majority of cases, your gut intuition about the dominant personality style of the key decision maker you're making the sales pitch to will be spot on in the first 30 seconds of meeting the person.

If there's an opportunity to sit in on a real-life sales pitch being conducted by one of your colleagues or an experienced sales manager, why not suggest you'd like to go along to observe. When you're in the room, quietly try to assess each of the personality styles of the prospects, and when you return to the office have a chat about this with your colleague to get your colleague's input and explore whether he or she agrees with your analysis or not.

Figure 6.1   Four personality styles (DISC)

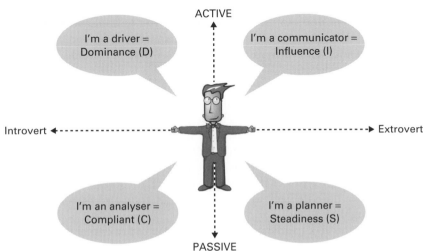

Table 6.1 Presenting to someone with a dominant personality
style (D)

Body language	Keep your distance.
	Have a firm handshake.
	Lean forward when listening.
	Keep direct eye contact without staring.
Tone of voice	Strong, clear, confident.
	Direct, fast paced.
Energizers	Challenges.
	Opportunities.
Sales buzz words	Win.
	Leads the field.
	Results.
	Now, immediate.
	Bottom line.
	Challenge.
Dos and don'ts	Be clear, specific and to the point.
	Stick to business.
	Be well prepared.
	Provide alternatives and options.
	Take issue with the facts, not the person.
	Let it be the other person's idea.
	Don't waste time.
	Seek a win–win opportunity.

When the stakes are high and it's an important sales pitch, then next time around your preparation should include creating a sketch of each of the decision makers prior to the sales pitch that you're about to make. This should include trying to break down their personality styles and how you're going to interact with them as a result. Tables 6.1 to 6.4 should help guide you in the right direction.

Dealing with multiple personality styles is a challenge even for the most seasoned sales presenter. It may help to determine quickly who in the room has the most influence and also the person with the power and authority to make it happen – it could be the same individual or two different people. It's important that you connect with them.

In the absence of having a strong sense of which direction to take based on the personality styles of those you're meeting, the guidance in Table 6.5 is offered as a fail-safe back-up plan in terms of your own personality style that you ought to adopt.

Whether you've a handle on the audience you're presenting to or rely on the back-up plan, the sales pitch will only work when it's about them and

Table 6.2 Presenting to someone with an influence personality style (I)

Body language	Get close. Sit next to. Smile, relax, have fun. Friendly eye contact. Expressive gestures.
Tone of voice	Enthusiastic. Persuasive, colourful.
Energizers	People interactions. Social recognition. Inspiration.
Sales buzz words	Fun. I feel. Socialize, recognition. Exciting. Picture this. People.
Dos and don'ts	Support the person's dreams. Talk about the person's people and goals. Ask for opinions. Provide ideas for implementing actions. Don't talk down. Allow time for socializing. Don't drive for facts and figures. Provide case studies and testimonials from important customers and clients. Make the person feel special. Offer incentives.

not about you. Andy Bounds provides these five tried and tested 'golden rules' to ensure success:

- *Golden rule 1: Always start with context first.* Always explain the big picture first so that any subsequent detail is related to something.
- *Golden rule 2: Always have the frame of the other person.* Always think from the perspective of the other person, which means you need to get under that person's skin.
- *Golden rule 3: Thoroughness is key.* Expand on the relevant and important subjects to give more detailed information.
- *Golden rule 4: Double-check on whether the person needs extra information.* Always ask if anything else would be helpful, so you know the person has all the information needed.

Table 6.3 Presenting to someone with a steady personality style (S)

Body language	Relaxed, calm.
	Methodical.
	Lean back; don't rush.
	Friendly eye contact.
	Small gestures.
Tone of voice	Warm, soft, calm.
	Low tone, low volume.
	Slow paced.
Energizers	Defined territory, security.
	Closure.
	Team harmony.
Sales buzz words	Step by step.
	Guarantee, promise.
	Think about it; take your time.
Dos and don'ts	Start with a personal connection.
	Listen!
	Present your sales pitch logically.
	Look for hurt feelings.
	Don't mistake willingness for agreement.
	Provide information.
	Show interest in the person as an individual.
	Don't force a quick response.
	Don't interrupt.
	Provide personal assurances.

- *Golden rule 5: Present on required information only.* Ask the audience what information they want rather than flinging jelly at them and hoping some sticks. This could be done as part of the pre-presentation planning and will ensure that what you present is exactly what they want to hear.

Overcoming your fears

Let's get one thing out of the way first of all. All excellent presenters are nervous before giving a presentation. It's irrelevant that they've done it countless times before. Every presentation is a new experience, and presenters are only as good as their last presentation.

That should provide those with limited experience of sales presentations with a lot of comfort. If you're not nervous, then that's a cause for concern!

Table 6.4 Presenting to someone with a compliant personality style (C)

Body language	Keep your distance. Sit across from. Firm posture. Direct eye contact. Few or no hand gestures.
Tone of voice	Controlled, direct. Thoughtful, precise. Little modulation. Slow pace.
Energizers	Information. Quality standards, analysis, research. Compliance with rules.
Sales buzz words	Here are the facts. Data. Results.
Dos and don'ts	Prepare the sales pitch thoroughly. Approach in a straightforward way. Provide policies and rules to follow. Give time for decisions. Don't over-promise. Prove with facts. Demonstrate customer and client loyalty. Don't be disorganized. Build credibility. Present specifics. Take time, but be persistent. Help the person to do things 'right'. Be fair and consistent.

But this shouldn't be confused with being frightened. There is a world of difference between the two. You need to be full of expectation. You need to be totally in control over what and how you want to present. In short, you need to be 'in the room'.

British sales coach Nigel Risner adds:

You'd think so, wouldn't you? It makes sense. After all, where else could you be but in the same place as the one you're standing in? If only it were that simple. In all aspects of your life, if you're not 'in the room', you're not in the game. Period. By that I don't mean physically; I mean mentally in the room, right where you're supposed to be. In short, you have to be exactly where you need to be – you need to focus on that moment or opportunity to make it count and block out everything else.

Table 6.5   Back-up or fail-safe personality style to adopt in a sales presentation

Don't be arrogant or assume you know more about their business than they do	Maintain a confident and positive attitude humbled by facts and skill. Never try to tell them how to run their business. Never assume you know how to run their business.
Be diplomatic	Communicate with rather than to. Listen. Try to understand their perspective and determine if they understand you. Check that they do understand what you're saying. Take responsibility if the message isn't clear. Tweak the sales message if necessary in order to ensure understanding.
Show your passion	Be passionate about your ideas and the ideas of others that you can champion for them. Passion is a quality customers and clients look for and are attracted to. Project positive energy in the room and make them feel good about themselves. Make them gravitate towards you.
Keep an open mind	Be curious. Be open to the ideas of others. Be open to the opinions of others. Be motivated always to find the best solution, even if it's not your own.
Know when to follow	Sometimes leading means following someone else's lead and having others follow you down a path by supporting their efforts.
Know when to shut up	Be aware that the sales pitch is also an opportunity to listen rather than fill the silence. In cultivating a relationship, you need to build trust by actively listening.
Demonstrate emotional intelligence	Use your judgement to ask questions to broaden your understanding – the difference between what someone is saying and what that person really means to say. Understand the underlying motivation for the customer or client's behaviour. Keep an open mind. Figure out how you can help the customers or clients without forcing your opinion on them – spotting the opportunity for collaboration, sharing views and ideas and focusing on the challenge or issue at hand.

And he's got a point.

It's a fact that the state you're in will affect everything else going on in and around you. Professional sales presenters know how to do two very important things: 1) how to be in the right state for what they want to do; and 2) how to be able to change their state at will.

The state we're in before a sales pitch refers to our emotional state – the way we feel at any moment. We may feel happy, sad or depressed. Alternatively, we may feel highly energized and confident.

When we're feeling good in ourselves, we are going to behave differently from when we're feeling bad about ourselves. Most of us know this from our own personal experience. We can all remember our behaviour when times were good compared with when times were much harder. As illustrated in Figure 6.2, a good state of mind enables us to get far better results.

Figure 6.2 Why keeping a positive state of mind is important when presenting

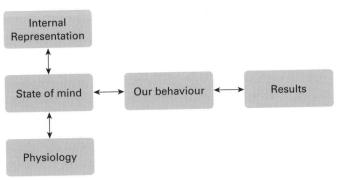

Try this exercise. Take a few moments to remember any event in your past where you did something and it didn't work out the way you expected. For example, it could be sitting a particularly difficult exam paper, taking your driving test for the first time, being at the starting line for the 100-metre sprint – anything. And, as you think about that event, how do you feel? Notice how you're feeling in your body as you recall that event. You probably don't feel as good.

All right. Come back 'in the room'. Take a breath and, as you breathe out, let the memory go.

Now think of a time when you did something in the past that worked out brilliantly and you did an even better job than you thought you had, for example fixing the meeting with a prospect and closing the sale, supporting your sales manager in landing a major contract, passing an exam with excellent marks, or preparing a new dish following a recipe you've never used before. Now how do you feel? Notice anything different? Great.

You would've observed, like everyone else doing this, that what you hold in your mind determines the way you feel.

Just before a big sales presentation, many professional presenters take a few moments to 'get in the room' and prepare themselves ahead of that presentation. When no one is there, they'll stand up tall and focus on a point on the wall, say the clock or another object. They'll keep their arms by their sides. They'll keep looking at the clock or the object on the wall ahead of them but start to listen to their own breathing. Then they'll listen to all the external noises that are in the room and outside of the room, and they'll stand very still. They'll hear what's going on in the street outside, on the floor above, and outside the door to the room they're standing in. They'll then tell their brain to slow down their heartbeat. After a few moments, they'll take their left hand and with the forefinger and thumb pinch the right hand between the thumb and forefinger as they tell themselves out loud in a single sentence the core reason that they'll be successful in what they're about to do. They'll then smile and as they smile they will project a massive amount of energy from their body as if they had a hosepipe and were spraying a beautiful garden on a hot summer's day. The energy will come from the centre of their body and is aimed to reach the wall ahead of them.

Try it for yourself. You'll notice you feel remarkably different. You feel incredibly energized and confident.

The pinch coupled with the positive thought is known as 'anchoring' in neurolinguistic programming (NLP). Your body and mind are tuned into the space that you're about to occupy before you do your sales pitch. You'll have calmed yourself and are ready to share your positive energy with those you're about to present to. You're now 'in the room'.

There's another technique to the one described above that deals directly with your subconscious mind (System Two), which is remembering the fear you felt after you'd delivered a sales pitch in the past and is trying to transmit this fear to the other part of your brain (System One) so that you feel fear again. Don't panic! Help is at hand. You can reprogramme your System Two so this doesn't continue to happen to you every time you're asked to give a sales pitch, or any presentation for that matter.

Time Line Therapy

The core of this theory is that the emotion of fear is a response that you felt after you'd done something in the past and after it had occurred. Before it happened, you couldn't have predicted how you would respond. Fear is one possible reaction to what happened but not the only reaction that can affect how you feel about that event when you recall it in the future. When you anticipate a similar event happening again, you project the fear out into the future – in other words, you anticipate fear based on past experience. But you can change this.

Try this exercise. Do you remember a situation when you had to get home in the face of extremely bad weather, for example having to drive through a snow blizzard or flooding in your area? The situation was fraught with danger but you made it. Recall how you felt – relief, and gratitude that everything turned out all right. It's only later when you are recalling what you've been through that you actually feel fear.

This is the way fear is supposed to work. System Two of our mind controls a System One response that kicks in only after the event has already happened, so that you know to get afraid. What System Two is trying to tell you is to avoid that situation in the future. However, by going back to the very first event, the one that made you afraid afterwards, you can do something about it (Figure 6.3).

Figure 6.3 Time Line Therapy technique

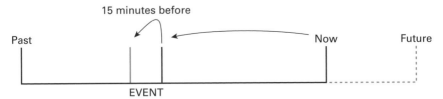

Source: Tad James, 2012

The Time Line Therapy technique was developed by US NLP guru Dr Tad James, and in essence it's extremely simple and effective.

According to Tad James, when it comes to 'stage fright', 'performance anxiety' or 'fear of making a sales pitch' or appearing at any public speaking event, there has to be a first event at some point in your own time line that you have in your mind after which you learnt to be afraid of presenting in front of an audience. Otherwise, you wouldn't know to do that. Generally, people aren't born with stage fright. For example, children have the incredible ability to express themselves in front of an audience without feeling inhibited, and it's only at a later point in their lives that some of these children develop a fear of public speaking that in fact they never had in the first place!

Look at the Time Line in Figure 6.3 and ask yourself two questions: 1) What was the first significant event after which you became afraid of making a sales pitch or presentation? 2) Fifteen minutes before that event started, where was your fear?

Interestingly, 15 minutes before the event that you're recalling there was no fear, because it couldn't be there.

Now look again at the Time Line and the two arrows. Think back along the time line to that first significant event in your past, and then go back just a little further to a time before it all happened. And, from that perspective, your memory will be different. By altering your perspective on any such event stored in your System Two memory you'll be able to change your System One response to it.

The reason you were afraid after that very first event is because there were certain things you didn't know then but you know now. If you'd known them at the time, you wouldn't have been afraid. It's only when you look back at those past events that you realize that your fears were groundless, as there was nothing to be afraid of.

Before you let go of that event and everything that it triggered in you afterwards, you need to get the rest of the learning from it, advises Tad James.

> *Once you've done that, your unconscious mind will be willing to let the fear go. So looking back from the safety of now, to that time 15 minutes before the event, with the resources and the understanding you now have, knowing that you survived, then you can simply go through that event again, consciously or unconsciously learning from it, and continue to grow as a person, as you come forward in time... until you are again in the present. Your memory of that situation will now be different.*

Each time we revisit a memory, we alter it in some way. The Time Line Therapy technique allows us to benefit from how our unconscious mind works. Once we have all the learning from the event, the fear disappears.

Our unconscious mind will recode the memory, allowing it to become a positive memory that we can use to build a new version of the future from that point on.

Tad James recommends:

> *When you use hindsight to illuminate some aspect of your past, there's no need to hang on to any unnecessary emotional baggage. You can let all that go. It's often said that we have 20:20 vision when it comes to hindsight. You can make useful changes by recoding those memories as learning opportunities, and then your unconscious mind will revise your experience in the light of what you know now.*

Be yourself

Most people need to let out more of who they really are. The more of you that's available to the audience sitting in your sales pitch, the more they'll be able to connect and bond with you, and the more comfortable you'll feel with them and vice versa.

Provided that time allows, some relevant self-disclosure lets the audience get to know you as a person rather than as some disembodied source of product information! This doesn't mean you have to tell them your life story. It does mean that you need to remove barriers so that your true self can emerge – the lively, spontaneous, inquisitive, playful, energetic self that you really are.

For a discussion on how to build rapport, see Chapter 3.

When you have rapport with the audience, they'll be in the same state as you. You and the audience will be 'in the room'. If you're feeling agitated or stressed out, then it's likely your audience will too, and neither you nor they will be 'in the room'. If you feel balanced and calm and all right about being yourself, they will too. The sales pitch will then be much easier for you.

Prior preparation prevents poor performance

There's no substitute or short cut to doing your homework on the customer or client prospects you'll be presenting to.

Lynn McBain, head of sales at the Chartered Institute of Marketing in the UK, says:

> *The work starts before you get to the pitch. You've really got to know your customer, what their business is like and how they stand with their competitors. Personal background helps, too: have a look at LinkedIn or Facebook or one of the other networking sites. There's a lot of information out there about the individuals you may be pitching to – even about things such as their hobbies. It's all useful. You need to start building a relationship with them if you're going to sell to them.*

You may also be able to discern some of this information from customers' or clients' websites, from speeches they've made, from talking to people who know them personally, from speaking with journalists who may have interviewed them or simply from asking around where you work.

It's always worth double-checking who's going to be there at the sales presentation, as this can often change at the last minute. If the finance director is there, you'll need to concentrate on cost a bit more. For operational people you may need to look at logistical issues.

'You may come away from a pitch without closing the sale, but then make sure you walk away from that meeting with a clear idea of what happens next. You need to do what you've said you'll do and when you have said you'll do it', adds Lynn McBain.

Peter Coughter, former advertising agency guru and now at Virginia Commonwealth University in the United States, agrees: 'The power of making an emotional connection with the audience, convincing that audience that you want the business, and the willingness to do anything necessary to win the business is sometimes all it takes. Simply having the best work or the best ideas isn't always enough.'

It's often said that the sale is done in the first two minutes not the last two minutes of the sales pitch and that people buy from people before they buy products and services. So rather than trying to work to a sales cycle, turn it on its head and work to customers or clients' purchasing cycles. That way you'll be more in tune with their needs and requirements rather than trying to drag them slavishly on to yours.

Preparing your sales pitch the Steve Jobs way

Thousands of articles on the web about Steve Jobs talk about his genius, but before we try to peel back what made his approach to making a sales pitch so effective it's worth bearing in mind that Steve Jobs didn't simply turn up at an auditorium having just left his swimming pool, put on his flip-flops and taken to the stage to deliver a knock-out sales presentation to shift Apple products like handing out candies to kids.

The secret is he spent hours rehearsing, rehearsing and rehearsing.

Every slide he used had its purpose in telling the story. Every presentation he made was like a theatrical experience. He made it look easy, but that's the hallmark of a great sales professional.

Don't give up before you've begun. It takes many years of dedicated practice – in Steve Jobs's case, 20 years of practice – to perfect your sales pitch technique.

Don't think you need to be word perfect. You don't. Mistakes and slip-ups show the audience that you're human and also, if you handle them well, they can remove an emotional barrier and make the audience warm to you. It's about being authentic.

Another observation to make here is never to assume that you know more than the audience – in fact many of those sitting in front of you have a lot of knowledge and experience that you can also learn from.

Acknowledging their expertise and experience and putting your own in that context helps to rebalance what could be a one-way conversation that won't help you close the sale. You genuinely need two-way communication: asking questions, seeking their input, involving them in the conversation and getting them to talk about themselves – now that's selling!

1 Pen and paper

Steve Jobs was all about the future, and his products defined the way the current generation prefers to communicate. But he planned his sales pitches with pen and paper, and he would use a whiteboard to sketch out what he wanted to say without turning on his iMac.

'His presentations had all the elements of a great movie – heroes and villains, stunning visuals, and a strong supporting cast. And, like a movie director, he "storyboarded" the plot. Brainstorming, sketching, and white-boarding came before building slides. The narrative always came first for him; the slides were there to complement the story', explains leading US communication skills coach and Steve Jobs fan Carmine Gallo.

Steve Jobs never gave his audience time to lose touch with what he wanted to say. He wanted them to be 'in the room' the whole time he was on stage. His presentations involved demonstrations, video clips and even other speakers – all expertly crafted to form a sales narrative from start to finish that took the audience on a journey, maintaining the pace and momentum of the sales message. All of these elements were planned well before he opened his iMac.

2 Making it Twitter-friendly

This was distinctive of Steve Jobs, but it could work for you too. He created a single-sentence description for every Apple product. These headlines helped the audience categorize the new product and were always concise enough to fit into a 140-character Twitter post.

When the MacBook Air was launched in 2008, Steve Jobs described it as 'the world's thinnest notebook'.

'That one sentence spoke volumes', observes Carmine Gallo. 'The audience needs to see the big picture before they can digest the details. A product or idea that can't be described in 140 characters or less needs to go back to the drawing board.'

Steve Jobs filled in the details during his presentation and on the Apple website, but he loved one sentence or phrase and wrote this in white on a black background as a way to position every product, adding drama as well as keeping it simple and memorable for the audience.

3 Adding a villain to the story

Every classic story can be reduced to its basic elements – cops and robbers, good versus evil, cowboys versus Indians. You get the idea.

In 1984, Steve Jobs was in a commercial battle with IBM and created a dramatic story around the little guy taking on 'Big Blue'. Branding guru Martin Lindstrom says that great brands and religions have one thing in common: the idea of vanquishing an enemy. Steve Jobs created a villain that allowed the audience to become sympathetic to the underdog – Apple and its products.

An alternative to slugging it out with a competitor is to focus on an issue, problem or challenge of the customer or client that needs to be resolved as the 'villain' of the story. For example, when Steve Jobs introduced the iPhone in 2007, his sales pitch at Macworld focused on the problems that mobile phone users were having with other models. The iPhone was the antidote to those problems, and the product was the hero of the story.

4 Answering the question 'What's in it for me?'

Steve Jobs understood that, in order to influence purchase behaviour, he had to answer that question in a highly compelling way. It was the question that was in the minds of every potential customer exposed to the sales pitch he was about to deliver. No matter how brilliant the Apple product, he had to connect on this level in order to unlock the wallets of his customers. It's the reason why Steve Jobs created a sales proposition from the point of view of Apple's customers: 'Twice as fast at half the price' (iPhone 3G) and 'All your irreplaceable photos, videos and documents are automatically protected and easy to retrieve if they're ever lost' (Time Capsule).

Steve Jobs knew how to connect the rational and emotional side of the proposition and make this relevant for his customers.

5 Three's company

Nearly all of Steve Jobs's presentations were divided into three parts. When he made a sales pitch he would often talk about the iPhone, iTunes and iPod.

Along the journey, he would give verbal signposts such as 'iPhone. The first thing I wanted to talk about today. Now, let's move on to the second, iTunes.'

The number three is a powerful artistic device. For example, there's more tension and drama with three rather than two people. Ask anyone who has three children and they'll tell you how sometimes two of the children gang up on the third child. Stand-up comedians know that three is funnier than four, and Steve Jobs knew that three was more memorable than six or eight.

The point here is that the audience can only hold a limited amount of information in their heads so they remember three rather than forget everything they've heard.

6 Selling attitudes, values, beliefs and dreams, not products

In much the same way that the airline industry awoke to the fact that it wasn't just transporting people from one location to another but creating the opportunity for dreams to come true, so it was that Steve Jobs was driven by an almost messianic desire to create new experiences. He wasn't there to sell more computers or phones; his mission was to sell us the promise of a better world tomorrow. In many respects, this is a much more powerful platform that can stand the test of time as new products that now roll off the Apple production line testify to his legacy.

In 2001, when Steve Jobs made a sales pitch for the iPod, he said 'In our own small way, we're going to make the world a better place.' Where some customers may have seen the iPod as yet another MP3 player, Steve Jobs saw it as a tool to enrich people's lives.

'Of course, it was important to have great products. But passion, enthusiasm and a sense of purpose beyond the actual product are what set Jobs and Apple apart', reflects Carmine Gallo.

Steve Jobs was passionate about his customers. He famously said at the conclusion of a sales presentation in 1997 that 'Some people say you have to be a little crazy to buy a Mac. Well, in that craziness we see genius – and that's who we make tools for.'

Steve Jobs was all about vision and purpose. Passion, emotion and enthusiasm are often greatly undervalued in business communications, and yet this was the magic dust that was sprinkled into his sales presentations that made them so effective. He prophetically once said: 'My goal isn't to die the richest man in the cemetery but to go to bed at night thinking that we'd done something wonderful today.'

7 Keeping it simple

Steve Jobs never used a bullet point. He simply used photographs and images. Where the average PowerPoint slide has 40 words, it was difficult to find seven words on many of Steve Jobs's slides. This technique is often referred to as 'picture superiority' – information is more effectively stored and recalled when in visual form and when text and images are combined.

When Steve Jobs did a sales pitch for the MacBook Air, he showed an image of the ultra-thin computer inside a manila inter-office envelope. That image was worth a thousand words. 'Simplicity is the ultimate sophistication', said Steve Jobs. And he was bang on.

8 Making numbers count

Big numbers can impress, but they always have to be put into context. For example, in 2009, 220 million iPods had been sold, which represented 73 per cent of the market for MP3 players, with Microsoft pulling up the rear with 1 per cent market share. For Steve Jobs, this was as much about playing to the audience as it was having a dig at his much bigger rival.

9 Using colloquial language instead of jargon

It's surprising but true that most companies tend to speak in their own formal language rather than stop to think what would be preferred by the audience they're speaking to. A conversation between two people after all is conducted in colloquial language. In fact we spend most of our lives speaking colloquially, and this fact wasn't lost on Steve Jobs, whose preferred style of communication was simple, clear, direct, colloquial English.

10 The reveal

Every presentation Steve Jobs ever made had built into it an emotionally charged event that was meant to be an anchor point for the audience to remember when the sales pitch was consigned to their short-term memory.

At Macworld in 2007, Steve Jobs could've started his sales pitch by telling the audience that Apple was unveiling a new mobile phone that played music, games and a video. Instead he decided to have some fun with the audience. 'Today, we are introducing three revolutionary products. The first one is a widescreen iPod with touch controls. The second is a revolutionary mobile phone. And the third is a breakthrough internet communications device... an iPod, a phone, an internet communicator... an iPod, a phone, are you getting it? These are not three devices. This is one device!'

The audience knew they were in the presence of the master and erupted in cheers because it was vintage Steve Jobs – he had entertained, informed and engaged as no one else could.

Body talk

Research by Professor Albert Mehrabian, professor emeritus of psychology at UCLA, is often cited as evidence that the visual impact of a presentation has the greatest influence on an audience (55 per cent), followed by the tone of voice of the presenter (38 per cent) and the text and content of that presentation (7 per cent).

'It's not that the content isn't important; of course it is. But if you fail to get the visual side of it, such as body language and pictures right, and then compound that failure by not sounding right, then the content doesn't matter at all', warns veteran US sales trainer Bob Etherington.

Some experienced presentation coaches downplay the usefulness of body language in a presentation context and instead focus on the voice and how you should speak. They argue that the words that you say and how they come out of your mouth are far more important than anything the rest of your body is doing. Treat that point of view with extreme caution!

It's a fact that the human brain is constantly processing vast amounts of information from a variety of sources simultaneously, not just what's heard but also from the other four senses – sight, touch, smell and taste. In many instances, actions will definitely speak louder than words.

When actors are performing in front of an audience, they're trained to use every fibre in their body to convey emotion – the slightest sideways look of the eyes may convey as much meaning in a few seconds as would be expressed by 10 pages of dialogue.

In many respects, the human body acts like a billboard. Non-verbal communication transmits information just as the spoken word does, except it's achieved through facial expressions, gestures, touching (haptics), physical movements (kinesics), posture, body adornment (such as clothes) and even tone, timbre and volume of voice.

Experienced presenters use their energy to get their points across to the audience in the most effective way possible. They have stage presence as a result. It's body talk.

Three Circles of Energy

This theory describes how energy moves around the body, and has been used as the basis of coaching actors at the world-famous Royal Shakespeare Company (RSC) in the UK. This energy is tangible and can be felt by others. It's what gives actors presence.

You can move through the Three Circles of Energy very rapidly, within seconds (Figure 6.4).

You can experience any thought or emotion in any of these Three Circles of Energy with different degrees of intensity, according to Patsy Rodenburg, the former voice coach at the RSC. 'Each one of us have a favourite Circle of Energy, one that's habitual to us. And it's this favourite energy that's blocking our presence', she explains. According to Patsy Rodenburg, we mostly live in the Second Circle, and the First and Third Circles take us out of our natural presence in the Second Circle.

First Circle – the Circle of Self and Withdrawal
The whole focus is inward, and the energy you generate tends to fall back into you.

Figure 6.4 Three Circles of Energy

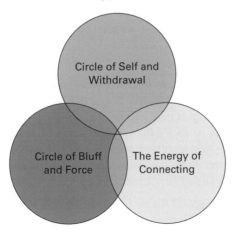

Source: Patsy Rodenburg, 2007

The First Circle absorbs other people's energy and draws all outward stimuli inwards; in other words, a person in the First Circle is an 'energy taker' rather than an 'energy giver'. This isn't the state you need to be in when making a sales presentation, as you're unlikely to be that observant or perceptive about people or objects outside of yourself.

The First Circle is about introspection and reflection. 'This is very useful at times but to live predominately in First Circle is very limiting, if not disabling. You can come across to others as self-centred, uncaring and withdrawn, and you tend to drain rather than enliven others. Your personal power and impact on the world is compromised and you are vulnerable to being victimized', warns Patsy Rodenburg.

The body language of people in the First Circle includes the following:

- They are withdrawn physically from people, feelings or ideas.
- They tend to hold their breath or breathe rapidly and shallowly.
- They are asked to repeat themselves when they speak.
- People have to lean forward to hear them or to notice them.
- They are frequently ignored.
- They often feel left out.
- They tend to be self-conscious.
- They tend to wear clothes that help them disappear.

The point of a sales pitch is to get noticed, so people who exhibit the traits listed above won't make it as successful salespeople unless they can move themselves into the Second Circle.

Second Circle – the Energy of Connecting

This is the most appropriate place for the sales presenter to occupy, as the energy is focused and moves outwardly toward the audience, as well as being received back.

Patsy Rodenburg explains:

You react and communicate freely and spontaneously within the energy you are giving and receiving. You are in the moment – the zone – and moment to moment you give and take. Both giving and taking, in that moment, are equal to each other. In the Second Circle, you touch and influence another person rather than impress or impose your will on them. You influence them by allowing them to influence you. You hear others and take in what they're really saying.

The downside of the Second Circle is that it touches people who don't want to be fully engaged as well as those who have no clear path of escape from you and who don't want to be 'in the room'. That said, positive presence through the Second Circle is the most powerful, creative and intimate way of making a connection with the audience that you're trying to sell to.

The body language of people in the Second Circle includes the following:

- They feel centred and alert.
- They are in control of their body.
- They feel the earth through their feet.
- They feel that breathing is easy and complete.
- They can reach an audience, and the audience will listen to what's being said.
- They can read the details of the audience: their eyes, their moods and their anxieties.
- They are curious about new ideas and keep an open mind, free of innocent preconceptions and expectations, judgements and prejudices.
- They listen clearly.
- They acknowledge the feelings of others.
- They can use all five senses when presenting.

This is a powerful presence and one that all salespeople should habitually gravitate towards – they are noticed, heard and remembered.

Third Circle – the Circle of Bluff and Force

This is undirected energy, rather like a hosepipe that's out of control and spraying anything in its vicinity indiscriminately. Your attention is outside of yourself but unfocused and lacking in precision and detail.

'The world is a dimly lit audience to whom you are performing', observes Patsy Rodenburg.

In the Third Circle, you attract attention and you may even make a good first impression. This is deceptively useful in some selling situations where you need to engage superficially with people in groups and gain their immediate compliance and cooperation.

The downside is that you're not engaging specifically with anything and as a result can't take energy back in as you can when in the Second Circle. This energy lacks intimacy and makes others feel that they don't really matter to you and therefore the energy is impersonal to them. You may speak eloquently and sound enthusiastic and charming, but you don't listen well. You look through people rather than at them and skim the surface of every interaction, appearing shallow. In many respects, the Third Circle is a force field that shields you from the intrusions of others and puts you into a kind of 'bubble'.

If this energy is the norm, then you're not going to be open to receiving energy from others, and as a result it's unlikely to be effective in a sales pitch situation; you could come across as overbearing, arrogant and aloof even if your intention isn't to.

The body language of people in the Third Circle includes the following:

- They notice people withdrawing from them or making space for them.
- They find themselves taking up more space than they need.
- They breathe with noise, pulling the air into their body and taking oxygen from others.
- They are told often that they are too loud, in either speech or laughter.
- They don't really notice people they are speaking to or in the room.
- They don't notice if people aren't enjoying or engaging with them.
- They take command of a discussion even though they've only heard a fragment of what's being discussed.
- They wear clothes that get them noticed.

People working in service industries such as hospitality are normally highly skilled in the Third Circle. They have to feign charm and concern for hundreds of people on a daily basis. This is impossible to do and still be fully present with all those strangers, so the solution is the Third Circle.

Many celebrities, Olympic athletes and members of the royal family keep their distance from the public with Third Circle energy pushing strangers away. In such cases they pretend intimacy but stay defended.

'If you know you fall into a Third Circle habit, it's probably because your back was pushed up against the wall at some time in your life and you came out fighting! You were desperate to be felt and seen, not reduced and ignored. Maybe now you'll realize you don't have to fight all of the time', says Patsy Rodenburg.

Delivering an effective sales pitch

The primary difference between a poor sales pitch and a good sales pitch is in its delivery. Effective delivery techniques have always been recognized as being critical to the success of communicating a message to an expectant audience.

In 1912, the Irish playwright George Bernard Shaw remarked: 'It's impossible for an Englishman to open his mouth without making another Englishman hate or despise him.' Although that may now appear to be an extreme point of view, what Shaw was referring to primarily was the differences in regional accents.

Over the last century, the importance of an accent has become almost obsolete as a barrier to communication unless the accent is very pronounced and hard to decipher. It's been replaced by the importance of non-verbal communication, which accounts for approximately 83 per cent of all the face-to-face communication process.

What this means in practice is that how the sales pitch is delivered can be more important than what's being said.

In order to make an effective sales pitch, a number of skills can be developed over time.

1 Overcoming your nerves

This is important in delivering an effective sales pitch but, as we said at the beginning of this chapter, being a little nervous is a good thing. It encourages you to practise and focus on the presentation and means you're 'in the room'. On the other hand, being overly nervous will have a negative impact on the delivery of the sales pitch, and so coping strategies as outlined above will definitely help.

Other practical steps that can help reduce nerves are planning the presentation well in advance, arriving at the venue nice and early to allow plenty of time to set up the sales pitch, and getting plenty of rest the night before the presentation.

For novice sales presenters, it's often helpful to hold a paper or a note card with key or transitional points on it in one hand. However, the best way to overcome fear of public speaking is to gain as much practice and experience as possible.

2 Making the sales pitch flow naturally

A sales presentation needs to flow smoothly if it's to be successful. If you lose your train of thought or jump from one idea to the next and back again, the audience will struggle to follow what you're trying to say and the sales message will be lost in the confusion.

The key is crafting a well-prepared sales pitch. In order to achieve this you should be focused on the outcome – what you want the audience to do in behavioural terms as a result of having the sales pitch. That may sound obvious to you, but don't assume it's obvious to them. You need to think carefully what happens next and explain this to them clearly, in words that resonate with them and from their point of view.

3 Creating your own unique stage presence

As we've already discussed, stage presence refers to the ability of the speaker to acquire and keep the audience's attention by sharing their energy. When in front of an audience, your poise, posture, gestures and movements can all significantly add to or detract from the presentation, so it's important to be self-aware and conscious that such behaviour can have an effect on others. The goal is to control these aspects of delivery so they reinforce the sales message you want to deliver.

When delivering a sales pitch, it's important to convey the sales message clearly and powerfully. Stage presence and voice qualities will contribute to the expression of the message, but you should also consider the flow, filler words, enthusiasm and facial expressions as part of the presentation mix.

4 Poise and posture

The poise and posture you adopt are among the first indicators to the audience of how confident and comfortable you are in their presence.

Before you've said a single word, the audience you're presenting to will have made a number of judgements on you – about the colour of your hair, what you are wearing, whether your tie clashes with your shirt or even the length of your skirt! Maintaining a calm approach and presenting a comfortable appearance will normally be reciprocated by those to whom you are presenting. Facial expressions can also help enormously – so don't forget to smile!

Your posture is an important element of non-verbal communication, so stand tall and straight, and avoid slouching. Feet should be planted about shoulder-width apart and weight distributed evenly on both feet. Proper posture will not only illustrate confidence to the audience, but also discourage undesirable nervous movements such as pacing and fidgeting. It opens the diaphragm so that when you speak your voice is loud and clear.

If you're working with a radio mic, then there's no need to over-modulate the normal volume of your voice and, in any event, never shout at the audience!

5 Gestures and movements

Gestures and movements, like many other non-verbal communications, can either reinforce and clarify the sales message or distract the audience from the sales message you want to deliver (Table 6.6).

Typically, when people get nervous, they tend to use a variety of movements to release their nervous energy. These nervous mannerisms include,

Table 6.6 Typical physical gestures and interpretation

Gesture or posture	Message it sends to the audience
Stroking fingers across the palm or rubbing hands together	Indicates serious concerns or anxiety
Chewing on an object	Nervousness
Leaning forward or facing the audience	Intensity of interest in them
Hands pushing forward	Seriousness and importance
Hands open at chest level, palms facing upwards	Helplessness, pleas to be understood
Head nodding	Affirmation, agreement
Hands or fingers in front of mouth	Reluctance to talk
Deep sighing	Impatience, boredom
Pointing at the audience	Aggressiveness and always negative
Crossing arms	Rejection, disagreement, discomfort
Open arms	Open to thoughts and ideas
Covering the neck dimple or playing with a necklace	Indicates insecurity, emotional discomfort, fear or concerns
Rubbing the forehead	Indicates struggling with something
Touching the neck	Indicates doubt, insecurity, emotional discomfort
Touching the face	Indicates irritation and nervousness – it's a pacifying behaviour
Exhaling with puffed-out cheeks	Indicates releasing stress; often happens after a mishap
Adjusting a neck tie	Indicates insecurities and discomfort
Massaging or stroking the neck	Pacifying behaviour to alleviate stress
Yawning	Rather than lack of sleep it can indicate stress
Ventilating the neck area under the short collar	Pacifying behaviour to alleviate stress
Toes pointing upward towards the audience in the standing position	Shows you're in a good mood or are thinking or hearing something positive
Crossing of legs in a standing position	Shows you're comfortable
Body turned to the audience but feet pointing away	Indicates you want to be somewhere else and will be interpreted as distancing
Crossing arms and smiling	Waiting for an answer from the audience
Crossing arms with hands tightly gripping the arms	Indicates discomfort

Table 6.6 *continued*

Gesture or posture	Message it sends to the audience
Partial shoulder shrug	Indicates lack of commitment or insecurity
Shoulder shrug	Lack of knowledge or doubt
Arms behind back ('the regal stance')	Indicates 'Don't draw near', and keeps people at a distance
Both hands on hips and legs apart	Territorial display and can be used to establish dominance or to communicate there are issues
Frowning of the forehead and squinting	Facial distortions are indicative of stress and discomfort
Head tilt	Demonstrates in a powerful way that you're comfortable, receptive, friendly
Pupil dilation	Indicates emotional attachment
Constriction or squinting of the eyes	Indicates anger or that we hear sounds and voices we don't like. It can be very brief, such as an eighth of a second, but in real time may reflect a negative thought or emotion
Eye blocking with the hands	Indicates that you don't like what's being said, seen or heard
Brief touch of the eyes during a conversation	Indicates a negative perception of what's being discussed
Delay in opening of the eyelids on hearing information, or a lengthy closure	Indicates negative emotions or displeasure
Tightly squeezing the eyes shut	Indicates trying to block out information, news or an event
Eyes relaxed	Contentment, no tension
Eyebrows arched slightly, defying gravity	Positive feelings
Flashbulb eyes	Excited to see someone or full of positive emotions we can't hold back
Looking askance at people	Indicates distrust or being unconvinced
A natural smile forcing the corner of the mouth up toward the eyes	Sincerity, genuinely happy, comfortable
A polite smile where the corners of the mouth point towards the ears and there's little emotion in the eyes	Insincere
When lips disappear, mouth is tight shut, pursed lips, corners of the mouth turn down	Indicates stress or anxiety, emotions at a low point and concerns running high

Table 6.6 *continued*

Gesture or posture	Message it sends to the audience
Pucker of the lips	Indicates disagreement
Sneering	Shows disrespect or disdain and being uncaring
Licking of lips	Indicates anxiety, as it's a pacifying behaviour
Tongue jutting through the teeth very briefly	Indicates being caught doing something that you shouldn't or making a mess of something or getting away with something
Face blushing	Embarrassment or being caught doing something that's wrong
Crinkling nose very briefly	Indicates dislike or disgust
Tucking the chin in, forcing the nose down	Indicates low confidence or concern for yourself
Chin out and nose high	Feeling positive; indicates comfort and confidence
Palms up or 'rogatory' position	Indicates you want to be believed or accepted; not a dominant display
Palms down and fingers down resting on a table whilst standing up	Making a confident and emphatic statement
Steepling of hands, fingertip to fingertip	One of the most powerful displays of confidence
Hand wringing or clasping both hands tightly together	Shows stress or concern
Hand in pocket but thumb sticking out	Indicates high confidence and associated with a high-status individual
Interlocking hands with thumbs up	Positive thoughts
Interlocking hands and thumbs suddenly disappear	When there is less emphasis on the point being made or where emotions are turning negative
Thumbs in pocket with hands outside the pocket	Indicates low status, low confidence and insecurity

but aren't limited to, pacing, shifting weight, swaying, leaning, crossing legs or moving arms unnaturally. However, these tendencies can be eliminated with a little effort.

In order to control such involuntary responses, you must first identify any tendencies you may have to do this. One of the best ways to do this is by videotaping a practice delivery to camera and analysing the recording. It often helps to have someone else assist with the recording analysis, since we all tend to hate how we sound rather than focus on our mannerisms, of which we may be blissfully unaware!

You should review the recording to affirm those nervous habits and to see how they distract from the presentation – that's the first step on the way to eliminating them. For example, if you find yourself unconsciously playing with a ring or a bracelet, then simply remove the item before the sales pitch. In that way, the distraction has gone!

Another way to eliminate nervous movements is to plan to expel some of the nervous energy in a way that will energize and reinforce the sales pitch. For example, moving across the stage or even coming off the stage and into the audience provides an opportunity to give energy and also to receive energy, as discussed earlier in this chapter.

Movement can also assist in making a transition in the presentation. Consider moving from centre stage to stage right as a transition between the introduction to the first main point; then move again when transitioning to the next point, and so on. This physical movement creates energy and provides non-verbal communication with the audience to help them follow you through the presentation or sales pitch. The other benefit is that it provides an easy way for you to remember when to move next, keeping your energy levels high.

A further benefit of movement is that it helps to engage the audience in a way that speech on its own can't achieve. Audiences tend to pay more attention, especially if you move towards them. As you learn to read the audience's feedback, you can use movement to respond. For example, if you notice someone is daydreaming, or someone is answering a text message, you can move towards that person in order to recapture his or her attention and eliminate the distraction.

Humour is an excellent way of getting people 'back in the room', but ensure that you laugh with them, not at them.

Care should be taken to not go overboard with using these movement techniques. Pacing and overuse of gestures and movements distract from the presentation. However, when moving, move with purpose; otherwise it's simply a distraction and can be irritating for the audience as they struggle to focus on you. And, when making an important point, stay rooted and maintain eye-level contact with the audience before moving again.

6 Maintaining the appropriate pace of delivery

The pace of delivery of the sales pitch can also affect your flow. If you speak too slowly, research shows the audience will lose interest quickly and turn off. On the other hand, if you speak too fast, the audience won't be able to follow the thought process clearly and will be trying to play catch-up as you keep the foot on the accelerator in order to get to the end of the presentation.

Humans are capable of listening to and absorbing words five times faster than we are capable of speaking, so slow speakers don't engage the speaking capacity of an audience. This lack of engagement means that those in the audience have plenty of capacity to think of things other than your sales pitch. Before the end of every sentence they may lose the will to live let alone stay 'in the room'.

Excessive use of change of pace should be avoided. Some US sales presenters can deliver remarkable clarity at 400 words per minute, and non-stop talking can be very effective. However, to keep your audience 'in the room' you may want to vary the pace of delivery throughout the sales presentation. For example, in order to emphasize a point you may consider putting in a slightly longer pause at the end of that point, allowing the audience to digest it fully before you move on to your next point.

7 Using your voice as a foundation for your performance rather than relying on your slides

Your voice can communicate in ways that a static PowerPoint slide will have difficulty in matching. The appropriate use of volume, enunciation and tone can ensure that the audience can hear, understand and internalize what's being said and also respond to what's being presented. In addition, these aspects of delivery can contribute to the enjoyment of the audience. Remember that Steve Jobs entertained first. He then informed and engaged.

Try to introduce vocal variety when delivering a sales pitch. The volume and tone should be fluctuated to reinforce what's being said as well as to emphasize important points and information.

What will help you achieve this is to listen. Research shows that the accuracy with which we listen relates directly to how we respond vocally. It's something we take for granted because it's such a basic thing.

We tend to listen much less accurately in daily life than we'd care to admit. As we listen we are preparing for what we are going to say or do after we've finished listening. System One in our mind is coming to a conclusion before we've fully listened to the audience in front of us.

Engaging with the audience may well involve asking a question or a series of questions. Listening accurately to their response is one of the most important factors in using the voice fully.

Cicely Berry CBE, the voice director of the RSC, warns:

When rehearsing a piece of text, either by themselves or in rehearsals, actors often form conclusions of what the text should sound like or what they should be presenting before they've discovered what they're actually saying and what the text can say. This of course is part of the actor's situation: the pressure that comes from being judged and the anxiety to present a finished product. But unless they allow themselves time to listen for the possibilities to affect them, the vocal result will always be predictable.

8 Moderating the volume at which you deliver the presentation

The first consideration is that the voice quality is audible. When on a stage, a radio mic will fix this and you should be able to speak at a normal conversational volume.

Where the gathering is much smaller, say in a room, then judge how far the person is who is furthest away from where you are and ensure that you project your voice to reach that person – this isn't shouting, but using posture and breathing to increase the energy behind your voice so that it's audible.

If you're speaking too loudly then the audience can become uncomfortable and won't be receptive to what you have to say.

9 Enunciating your words clearly, particularly where the language you use is a second language for some of those in the audience

Those who are fortunate enough to have been trained as broadcasters will recognize immediately the importance of clearly enunciating the words that are being spoken. Mispronouncing words affects the quality of what's being said to a disproportionate level because it creates a negative perception very quickly with the audience. This is particularly relevant when referring to people by name within the context of the presentation and those who are in the audience. Get this right and people will feel good about you and the presentation, even those for whom it's in a second language. Get a name wrong or mispronounce it and you won't be forgiven, as it's assumed you should get it right.

10 Tone of voice

The tone of voice conveys so much more than simply the words being spoken. It adds a quality to what's being said that can capture precision, emotion, energy, enthusiasm, fun, empathy and seriousness in a way that can touch the soul of those to whom you are presenting.

Get it wrong, and it's curtains. They may never want to buy anything from you, no matter how good the product or service you're trying to sell.

Using inflection in tone makes the speech more interesting. It's also helpful in sharing emotions to reinforce ideas. As we've said earlier in this chapter, using colloquial language can be extremely effective in helping to engage with the audience you're presenting to. Remember it's a conversation rather than a monologue that you're trying to create.

11 Facial expressions

Facial expressions can help set the mood of the sales pitch and also relax you and the audience. Remember that the audience want to know you're a real person, not a robot, so when you make a mistake then roll with it;

have a bit of fun with the audience and smile with them. It's a great way to get them on your side and removes any barrier that there may be between you and them. Let them in on the joke. They'll appreciate it.

12 Eye contact

Eye contact is an important aspect of communication, as without it you're not communicating. However, it's also one of the aspects that novice sales presenters struggle with the most.

Where possible, try to organize the room so that it fits with the way you prefer to present.

There are no right or wrong ways of doing this, and to a large extent it does depend on the number of people you're making the sales pitch to.

Figure 6.5 illustrates the cabaret-style format that's favoured by many presenters where the audience is up to 25 people dispersed across five tables. This makes for a much more relaxed atmosphere compared with the usual serried ranks for the theatre-style presentation (see below).

Figure 6.5 Cabaret-style room layout for a sales presentation

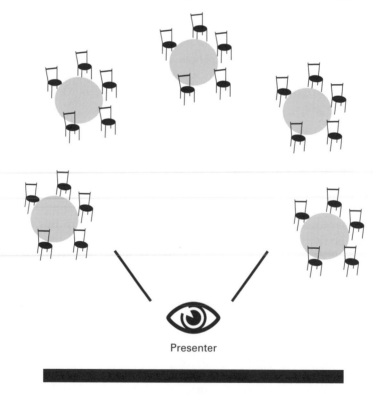

Presenter

Stage

In such a situation, it's important that you're not reading from a prepared script but have committed it to memory. It's much more important to look at the audience and not at the script, the screen with your PowerPoint presentation in the background, or indeed the floor, ceiling or clock at the back of the room.

A common technique is to find one person in the room and maintain eye contact with that individual for three to five seconds. Then find another person in another part of the room and do the same thing again.

It may be easier to start with people you have met previously and then move to those with whom you must also build a dialogue.

Feel free to walk off the stage and into the audience – this makes it more entertaining and more personal, and also allows for more natural interaction with the audience, inviting two-way conversation rather than having the audience staring at you throughout the presentation.

Maintaining eye contact is more of a challenge with a larger group, but you should strive to reach as many people in as many areas of the room as possible.

Where the audience is over 25 people, then the horseshoe-style layout is useful for presentations up to 50 people (Figure 6.6).

Figure 6.6 Horseshoe-style room layout for a sales presentation

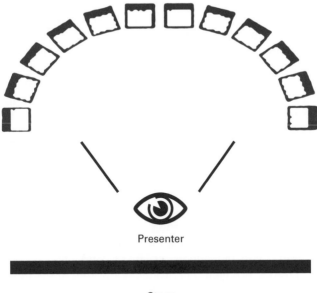

However, even with a substantially larger audience you can increase the feeling of intimacy by grouping the audience in theatre-style format, which can be two or three rows deep (Figure 6.7).

Figure 6.7 Theatre-style room layout for a sales presentation

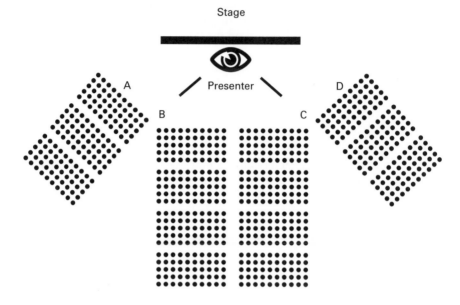

An audience between 50 and 500 people will also expect some level of intimacy, but don't even try to make eye contact with every single person in the room. Instead, you should be aiming for the illusion of eye contact.

This type of set-up is very common for a major sales conference to a large number of distributors, for example. In front of the presenter could be as many as 200 people. Think of the audience as being divided into four blocks, A to D. This is where the illusion starts. If you look at someone in block A for say three or four seconds, then approximately 10 people in that vicinity will believe that you've addressed them personally too. But the illusion goes further and, despite knowing that they've not had eye contact with you, everyone else in block A will also start to feel that you've at least made an effort to include them. The energy you share with the one person who's in your line of sight and whom you look at for three or four seconds is then contagiously spread to everyone else in that block, even though you haven't made direct eye contact with any of them. This illusion needs to be repeated through to those sitting in blocks B, C and D, although the sequence should be random to give the effect that you're establishing eye contact naturally with individuals within the audience. To complete the eye contact illusion, also glance occasionally to those in the front row who have a clear view of you as well as those sitting in the middle and back rows.

How to avoid 'death by bullet points'

Standing in front of an audience you have the chance to inspire, inform, influence, motivate and impress, which could make all the difference in closing the sale or losing the sale.

To present well, we need to understand when and why to use visual aids, what audiences are looking for and how to make our sales messages stick.

Presentations work well when slides and presenter work together – seamlessly delivering the right information, at the right time, to captivate the audience as well as influence its behaviour so that they want to make a purchase (Table 6.7).

Table 6.7 Benefits of using presentation aids

For the sales presenter	For the audience
Provides visual cues in the journey of telling the story	Illustrates a sequence of events or procedures
Helps gain and maintain the attention of the audience	Helps the audience to organize their thoughts
Enhances the memory of all key points	Enhances memory, understanding and relevancy
Reinforces the key sales messages	Simplifies complex ideas and information in a digestible and memorable way
Entertains, informs and engages with the audience if done well and not as a distraction	Helps to maintain concentration and interest in what the presenter has to say

Research shows that on average bullet-point slides yield a 15–20 per cent recall of information after just an hour, and yet most sales presentations are a stream of never-ending bullet points and poor click art interspersed with graphs and charts that are hardly legible on the screen.

Death by bullet point really is an issue for many sales professionals. However, it's possible to use PowerPoint to communicate effectively by using it as a tool in a more considered way as part of the sales pitch.

Think in terms of pictures, not bullet points

As children, we learnt to read by understanding stories and pictures. In fact, this way of learning has never left us. As adults, we forget about this method that's been around for thousands of years and don't think of getting our sales messages across by using pictures and telling a story. That's a missed opportunity.

If we want to capture attention with a fact or particular message, then make it a few words and one number and make sure that this dominates the slide in terms of its font size. As you speak, those few words and that number will burn into the memory of the audience along with their 'internal video clip' of you explaining the significance of that. Their brain will store this so that, when it comes to recall, what you said and that packet of information stored in their memory will be much more powerful than the presentation of five slides of closely typed information and a snowstorm of bullet points to accompany it.

Use a quote to make a point that'll have resonance with the audience

There's a lot of collective wisdom in the world of business and it doesn't all come from one place but can be found across a gigantic landscape – the web. The selection of an appropriate quote can be extremely powerful. For example: 'Wherever you see a successful business, someone has made a courageous decision.' This is a quote by management guru Peter Drucker and is very motivational depending on the context of the presentation being made.

Graphical alternatives to bullet points

It really doesn't take a lot of imagination to avoid using bullet points.

Graphs and charts can be useful, such as cluster charts and perceptual maps. Less complex but equally powerful are words in tables, where there's a tick or a cross against certain strategies or options.

Other alternatives include a decision tree or mind map diagram, which can present complicated information very simply and effectively all on one slide.

Using a photograph or image as a background to a chart or a table adds graphical interest but also requires you to present to the audience, so again the slide shouldn't be overloaded.

These are some of the most common pitfalls to avoid when using a PowerPoint presentation to create a sales pitch:

1 *Cut down on the company overview.* Most sales presentations talk in great detail about the company's history, locations, values, mission and even diversity policy. Most of the time, for most of this content, nobody cares and it's irrelevant in the way that Andy Bounds described earlier in this chapter. Say enough to build credibility and establish empathy, but no more.

2 *Decide which benefits are most powerful and relegate the others.* A common mistake made is to list all the benefits you offer, which leads to information overload for the audience, and your sales message is either completely buried or forgotten.

3 *Move the 'Summary of Benefits' slide from the end to near the start of the presentation.* Another common pitfall is talking in terms of benefits only at the end of a presentation when the audience are already bored. Maximum attention levels are often after about three or four minutes – so start talking about benefits then. Remember to talk about what you deliver as opposed to what you offer, as this is much more powerful from a selling perspective.

4 *Sixty slides of text is too much detail.* If your sales pitch usually lasts more than an hour, your prospects might wish they'd never met you. Often, information can be cut without being missed. When presenting a particularly complex product or if you're expected to present for a long time, consider using multiple presentations and presenters or hyperlinks to present in a non-linear way. This keeps the audience focused and allows your prospects to set some of the agenda. Remember, you're trying to create a dialogue with the audience, not bore them into submission.

5 *Let the audience know where you are in the presentation.* Have you ever been reading a book and flicked to the back to see how many pages you have left? How would you feel if, once you started reading, you'd no way of finding out how much was left? Without an agenda slide and reference to the agenda during the presentation, your audience can feel lost in space and will start to read their e-mails on their smartphones.

6 *Reconsider the slides full of technical specifications.* Technical details are often important when selling, but don't fall into the trap of including every technical detail. Eliminate the details that are commoditized, and don't illustrate any competitive advantage of your product or service over and above what the competition offers. Think about presenting the Steve Jobs way.

7 *Listing all your products is not the same as selling solutions.* Don't just present a few slides on each product you offer. If you want to sell solutions, understand the problem that you can solve, and then present one integrated view of the solution you offer. Finding slides from five different product presentations and putting them into one jumble of a sales presentation isn't the same as presenting a solution.

8 *Eliminate bullet points wherever possible.* The audience read the text and ignore the presenter – they can't listen and read at the same time, so don't encourage them to blank you in favour of reading a slide. It's the same reason why we stop and look up when somebody disturbs us reading a good book. Instead of a bullet point, find visuals that help you explain the same points in a more dynamic way.

9 *Think about when to open the laptop.* Some salespeople 'show up and throw up'. That's to say they get face to face with a prospect, open the laptop, and present everything that they have to say without stopping to find out anything about the specific needs or interests of the audience. Psychologically this may be easy to do – but it isn't effective. Instead, think of your sales presentation as just one part of a broader conversation.

10 *Be prepared not to slavishly follow your carefully constructed PowerPoint presentation.* In a small sales situation, there may be points that the prospects are much more interested in and want more detail on – this could be a surprise, and in the time you have allotted you may not be able to get through the rest of the deck. Don't panic. Deal with their enquiries and use the time to qualify their interest in the product or service further. If necessary, suggest a follow-up meeting, but always agree next steps before leaving the room. After all, the sales pitch was a step on the way to achieving an outcome. Never lose sight of that.

How to make a great close

The fact that your sales presentation to 50 people went incredibly well – in fact, much better than you thought possible – is fine, but the only outcome you're interested in is what happens after and whether these outcomes are enough for you.

'Audiences don't care what you say. They only care what they are left with after you've said it. Since audiences are only interested in their "afters" (outcomes). The sequence in which you present your ideas is critical in ensuring audiences engage, buy in and ultimately act on what you say', observes Andy Bounds.

It's important that the sales pitch leaves the audience with a message about the outcome they want to achieve rather than continuing to push a product or service you're trying to sell (Table 6.8).

It's important to state categorically what outcomes prospective customers or clients will be left with if they decide to go with you. Andy Bounds concludes:

> If not, leaving them to draw their own conclusions about the [outcomes] you can deliver will never be as powerful as you stating them and proving you can deliver them. Understanding the real reasons why people should buy from you is the beginning of sales wisdom. It's the strong foundation of your sales argument, the firm platform on which you build all else.

The following checklist is a summary of the key points covered:

- Understand your audience – spend as much time as necessary to know their attitudes, values, beliefs, perceptions and behaviours. Remember that people buy people, not things, so this is an essential part of your preparation for the sales pitch.

- Be in the room – focus on what you are there to do.

- Keep it simple – follow Steve Jobs's approach and use powerful pictures and a few words. Simplicity is clearly expressing your message. Make sure your visuals convey only the most important information, and wherever possible avoid the dreaded bullet-point approach to PowerPoint.

Table 6.8 Focusing on the outcome when closing a sales pitch

Seller	The outcome being sold
IT trainer	Freeing up employees' time
Corporate financier	Access to capital in order to expand the business to take advantage of stronger demand in emerging markets
Graphic designer	Improved profile and identity of your organization amongst its key audiences in order to help drive sales
Public relations agency	Protecting, enhancing and strengthening the reputation of the business so that it is trusted
IT installation	Time saved, less inconvenience, increased profits through greater efficiency
Architect	A building you are proud of, which meets your needs
Nutritionist	More energy, thinner or healthier weight
Life coach	Being the best you can be and proud of your achievements
Recruitment consultant	The right people in place to take your business forward
Financial planner	Your money working for you, not you working for your money
Health insurer	Your children and loved ones protected and safe
Accountant or accountancy firm	A larger, healthier business, or a smaller tax bill
Marketing agency	Increased sales
Telesales	More sales appointments
Printer	Contacts who are impressed (by your brochures, stationery, letterheads)
Business coach	Increased company value, more time with your children
Commercial lawyer	Protecting intellectual property rights and seeking compensation for infringement

- Don't assume your audience can listen to you and read your slides at the same time – they can't! Avoid the temptation to bombard them with so much information that it becomes information overload – they won't remember what it was you said. You want them to spend less time staring at the slide and more time listening to what you have to say.
- Use your slides as the backdrop to the points you want to make – the sales message is on the slide and they see you talking about it. Think of

the sales pitch as entertainment; don't make it boring. Visuals are important, but so too is your energy.

- The font you use for the sales pitch is nearly as important as the message it's delivering. Using a non-default font (in other words not standard to PowerPoint or Keynote) is one way to individualize your sales pitch. Given that computers differ greatly, some may not be able to read a non-standard font. In order to use the font you want, save the words you want to use as an image file.

- The size of the font is a major consideration, and it's not good practice to go below 30 points for the simple reason that it gets difficult to read if smaller. Remember, less is more. Using a sans serif font is usually preferred.

- Use imagery to convey themes and ideas. Two sites worth checking out are iStockPhoto.com and Flickr.com – both having original user-generated content (UGC) images. In some cases, permission may be needed and/or a royalty may be payable. Avoid posed, businesslike images of corporate people smiling or shaking hands. Not only are these forced but they have no impact for the audience and convey a poor image.

- A sales presentation is the sum of its parts – it's not only PowerPoint or Keynote but also your ability to convey a story with passion. Remember to entertain, inform and engage.

- Creating an effective sales pitch isn't easy – there's a lot of information and a limited amount of time to deliver it. It's best to give yourself more than one day to prepare it, revise, create, practise, get feedback, refine and practise some more. Creating a presentation in haste is a recipe for disaster.

- It's essential to establish what the prospective customers or clients want as outcomes as a result of buying your product or service. Remember, you're selling solutions for them, not your business capabilities and leaving it to them to work out whether they should buy from you or not.

- In creating your presentation don't feel tied immediately to working in PowerPoint or Keynote. Mind mapping software or even a flip chart is just as good a place to start to prepare your presentation.

- The saying that 'practice makes perfect' is very apt when considering that the majority of sales presentations today are rushed and ill thought through and never actually achieve close of a sale. Steve Jobs used to begin to prepare his sales pitches months in advance, and there was a lot of fine-tuning before he was satisfied with the final sales pitch. This level of preparation and practice creates a sales pitch that flows so well and naturally that it won't seem as though it was practised at all.

- You can run through the presentation on-screen or alternatively try setting up a video camera and using this as the proxy audience. Use the playback on a monitor and see how the presentation comes across. It's a great way to get another perspective on the presentation as well as observe little things like the use of your hands and general body language.

- A common mistake is actually to read your own slides to the audience! Remember that the slide deck is simply a visual backdrop to your presentation, so don't treat it like a script. The danger about reading your slides is that you give the perception you don't have a clue what you're talking about or that you didn't care enough about the audience to prepare properly for the sales pitch.

- A sales pitch is a conversation, even though you're doing most of the speaking. As we said in this chapter, the sales pitch at its best is the art of influencing. You need to connect, both rationally and emotionally. It starts with your body language and importantly eye contact. Avoid looking at your own slides when talking, or staring at the floor or ceiling, or at a laptop and your notes. It's the surest way to lose the audience and make them feel you are detaching yourself from them. You need to acknowledge their presence as well as feel their energy, and that means getting them involved. They'll thank you for it, and you'll close the sale.

- Don't talk yourself out of a sale. Once they've agreed to buy from you there's no need to keep talking, even if you haven't got to your main selling point. When the prospective customer or client says 'yes', then shut up!

For more guidance on closing a sale, see Chapter 10.

References

Books

Berry, C (2000) *Voice and the Actor*, Virgin Books
Bounds, A (2010) *The Jelly Effect*, Capstone
Buzan, T (2010) *Mind Maps for Business*, Pearson
Coughter, P (2012) *The Art of the Pitch*, Palgrave Macmillan
Davies, G (2011) *The Presentation Coach*, Capstone
Etherington, B (2012) *Presentation Skills for Quivering Wrecks*, Marshall Cavendish Business
Honey, J (1989) *Does Accent Matter?*, Faber and Faber
Isaacson, W (2011) *Steve Jobs*, Little, Brown
James, T (2008) *Presenting Magically*, Crown House Publishing
Moon, J (2008) *How to Make an Impact*, FT Prentice Hall
Navarro, J (2008) *What Everybody Is Saying*, HarperCollins
O'Leary, C (2008) *Elevator Pitch Essentials*, Limb Press
Risner, N (2006) *The Impact Code*, Capstone
Rodenburg, P (2009) *Presence*, Penguin Books

Articles

Gallo, C (2012) The presentation genius of Steve Jobs, http://ebookbrowse.com
Thomas, J (2012) 10 tips and techniques for more effective presentations, http://www.presentationadvisors.com

Websites

An excellent source of free non-standard fonts that can be downloaded to your PC or laptop: http://www.dafont.com (accessed 8 August 2012)
An excellent website on the way to create PowerPoint presentations for sales pitches and other uses: http://www.m62.net (accessed 13 August 2012)
Dr Tad James is the creator of the NLP Time Line Therapy system: http://www.nlpcoaching.com (accessed 5 August 2012)
Two of the best places for finding original photography for helping to tell your story as part of the sales pitch: http://www.iStockPhoto.com (accessed 8 August 2012) and http://www.Flickr.com (accessed 8 August 2012)

"It's a good start. Needs more gibberish."

How to write effective sales materials

Introduction

In the 1976 epic *Taxi Driver*, directed by Martin Scorsese, actor Robert De Niro plays Travis Bickle, a mentally unstable Vietnam war veteran who works nights as a taxi driver in New York. Back in his rented apartment, he is shown staring at himself in the bathroom mirror, brandishing a high-calibre handgun.

'You talkin' to me? You talkin' to me? You talkin' to *me*? Then who the hell else are you talkin' to? You talkin' to me? Well, I'm the only one here. Who the f*** do you think you're talking to?'

Yes, it's the rhetorical question of a madman staring at himself in the mirror. But we have more in common with Travis Bickle than you may care to realize. How insane is it that we don't stop to think who we're writing for before we invest time and resources in producing a small mountain of sales collateral that could be destined for the recycle bin?

'The problem with a lot of copy is that it isn't talkin' to me. If anything, it's talkin' at me. That's a big difference, because the centre of the universe for that kind of copy is the writer. But who cares about the writer? Certainly not the reader', says British copywriter guru Andy Maslen.

Of course, he's absolutely right. It's highly unlikely that taking such an approach will open a dialogue with the desired customer, client or prospect or indeed lead to closing a sale.

In the world of sponsorship, it's the biggest strategic error made by the vast majority of rights holders seeking financial support for their properties from well-endowed brand owners. Typically, a glossy sponsorship brochure will talk about how great the property is and how successful it's been in engaging with fans and generating media coverage. It will contain a never-ending list of 'benefits' that reads more like a shopping list than a focused piece of copy. The fundamental flaw is that the sales collateral has been produced entirely through the lens of the rights holder, not the intended sponsor who could use those intellectual property rights. And typically no effort whatsoever is made even to attempt to explain how making such an investment would help achieve the brand-building and commercial objectives of the potential sponsor. Doh! It's no surprise that this ends up in the bin in at least 95 per cent of all mailings.

As we've said in other places in this book, the starting point in the journey of making a sale must be the desired customers, clients or prospects. This holds true whether it's up-selling, cold calling, warm calling, making a sales pitch, networking, closing the sale or writing a piece of sales collateral. It's their point of view that counts.

This may sound like a challenge. How could we possibly know everything that intended recipients will be interested in? After all, how do they know they'll want something when they don't know it exists?

In this chapter, we'll explore how such a barrier in our own thinking can be removed if we're prepared to learn to write with our eyes and our ears – something that we weren't taught at school but could be one of the most valuable lessons of our sales career.

Outside in, not inside out

In *The End of Marketing as We Know It,* former Coca-Cola chief marketing officer Sergio Zyman gave a textbook definition of 'seller-centric' communication. He said: 'Convincing consumers to buy your products is the only reason why any company should spend its money on sales and marketing. Buy my product. Period. If what you are doing now doesn't get consumers to do that, try something else.'

His book is more like a polemic on the virtues of getting back to sales and marketing basics. It was written over a decade ago and was a reaction to a time in the 1980s when the global economy was in better shape than it is today and when marketing tended to be about the 'sizzle' rather than the 'sausage'. He was tired of spending millions of dollars on commercials for Coke that made us feel good about ourselves but didn't actually translate into incremental sales of its products.

To be fair to Sergio Zyman, the world of buying and selling is now a very different place, where the accent is on buyer-centric approaches and collaboration rather than the 'buy my product' school of sales and marketing. We're sure his opinion about seller-centric communication would be very different today.

Without doubt, the point of view (POV) of the prospective customer or client is now a highly valuable commodity. As a result, the practice of 'selling' is much more 'outside in' rather than 'inside out'.

Set aside any thoughts about selling stuff for the moment and put yourself in the shoes of today's consumer venturing out on a shopping trip in the space of a couple of mouse clicks. Chances are you wouldn't say no to the following:

- impartial advice on the best baby buggy to buy that can be folded with one hand and stored in the boot of a small car;
- the views of others who've stayed at a resort you're thinking of booking for a fortnight's holiday in the sun with your family;
- visiting a price comparison site in order to find the cheapest household insurance; and
- finding out how to save at least 40 per cent on textbooks you must buy for your course.

Today's sales materials must be created from the POV of the buyer, not the seller. Consumers are looking for sellers that are on their side, helping them to fulfil their hopes, desires, needs and requirements, with the minimum of fuss and at the best possible price.

It goes back to writing with your ears and eyes.

'The thing that really astounds me is that most copywriters really haven't bothered to listen deeply enough', remarked the legendary US copywriter Eugene Schwartz. He used to get into a taxi and start interrogating the cab driver, because that's one way to tap into what the market's saying. He also used to go and watch all the top 10 box-office movies. Even if he didn't like them, he'd watch them anyway because that's what the market was thinking and feeling. This allowed him to write copy that directly appealed to this mindset.

Before rushing to the keyboard or briefing an agency for sales literature it's worth building a psychological profile of the readers to whom the sales collateral is attempting to talk:

- Are they male or female?
- How old are they?
- What do they want more of and less of in their lives?
- Where would they rather be right now?
- What do they want more than anything else out of life?
- What are their values?
- How do they see themselves?
- How do others see them?
- Are they head or heart people?

'Whether you're selling to consumers or people at work, ignore the baser human emotions at your peril. Yes, people will want to rationalize their decisions, so make sure you provide plenty of objective reasons why buying your product or service is a sensible thing to do. But remember that people buy on emotional grounds first', observes Andy Maslen.

Content is king

So said Microsoft co-founder Bill Gates, way back in 1996. At that time, he prophesied:

> Content is where I expect much of the real money will be made on the internet, just as it was in broadcasting. One of the exciting things about the internet is that anyone with a PC and a modem can publish whatever content they can create. In a sense, the internet is the multimedia equivalent of the photocopier. It allows material to be duplicated at low cost, no matter the size of the audience.

Reading this a decade and a half later (which in internet years is a lifetime!) you're struck by the limitations in Bill Gates's vision. The comparison of the internet with a photocopier rather gives this away. It wasn't long after this that brands effectively turned themselves into broadcasters and selling moved from being all about 'push' to being all about 'pull'. At the heart of this movement was content.

Case study approach

From a sales material perspective, the case study is one of the most powerful forms of content you can create. There can be no better way of getting your sales messages across to desired customer and client segments than by having these delivered by your customers and clients (Table 7.1).

Table 7.1 Case study template

1	Identify the problem, issue, challenge or opportunity	Describe this clearly and succinctly in business terms.
2	What did the customers, clients or intermediaries do about this?	For example, did they research the market and draw up a shortlist of potential solution providers? Need to explain. Why did they choose your company or organization compared with others? Need to explain this in rational and unemotional language.
3	What did your company or organization do?	What was your company or organization's response? Did your company or organization map out a strategic plan? Did your company or organization scope the problem or issue? Did your company or organization do some initial analysis? What were the findings of this? Did your company or organization undertake a short research study or programme? At this part of the case study you need to create quotes from the customers, clients or intermediaries and quotes from your own company or organization that provide some 'colour' to the story. This is where emotional language can be used.
4	What did your company or organization deliver?	Here you need quotes from the customers, clients or intermediaries. 'The influencer' quote could be from a chairman or someone very senior within the customer, client or intermediary organization, but someone who didn't authorize the contract. 'The specifier' quote could be from a boss within the customer, client or intermediary who sets the framework or direction for the work to be done but who may not personally sign off the invoice. 'The authorizer' quote within the customer, client or intermediary is from someone responsible for the scope of work to be done and who also signs off the invoice.

Table 7.1 *continued*

	It's also important to have numbers or statistics (measurable stuff) that back up and validate what is said that your company or organization has delivered. This is the evidential basis part of the case study and in many respects one of the most important ingredients.
5 Did this work?	This is also evidential in nature. Where possible, it's useful to find an external third party who can give an external and objective perspective or endorsement on the work your company or organization has done. Input from an institute, professional body, recognized university or academic can be extremely powerful and add a level of credibility and authority to the case study.
6 What are the measurable benefits for the customer, client or intermediary?	Need to describe the benefits delivered. Benefits should be from the perspective of the customer, client or intermediary (B2C or B2B or B2B2C). For example, the expression of benefits can be in terms of cost savings, income generation, new product development, security, added value for the end user or opening a new revenue stream. It's also important to have numbers or statistics (measurable stuff) that back up and validate what is said to have been delivered.
7 Within a B2B context, how did this affect the customer or client's own customers?	Here your company or organization needs to get some insight from the customer, client or intermediary that validates the decision to use your company or organization rather than a competitor. This part of the case study is with quotes from the customer or client's own customers or clients and other stakeholder groups. This is often ignored or forgotten in case studies and yet could be the most interesting bit. Using these stakeholders' own quotes will be powerful (and permission from the customer or client will be required).

Table 7.1 *continued*

8	(Where relevant) what can the customer, client or intermediary now do in terms of its own market segment that it couldn't do before?	Where relevant, your company or organization may have empowered customers, clients or intermediaries to be able to do something that is important for them. Explain what this is. This part of the case study is about delivering a competitive advantage to customers, clients or intermediaries or some other advantage that has value for them.
9	(Where relevant) what are the future opportunities for the customer, client or intermediary?	This is a forward-looking bit of the case study. This can be described in terms of competencies, capabilities, market position, market share, new product development, increase in productivity, decrease in risk or other such measurable benefits that link back to the other parts of the case study.
10	(Where relevant) what experience and capability does your company or organization now have as a result of this work?	This is a more 'sales'-orientated type of case study. This bit could be a useful round-up of your own competencies, capabilities, market position, market share, new product development and other meaningful 'sales'-type messaging. This part of the case study ends on your company or organization, so it's much more selling focused. Try to make this bit more future orientated. Include contact details at the bottom.
11	How can all of the above be encapsulated by a photograph, video or film?	There is a need to break away from linear thinking and consider expressing the case study through the medium of photography, video and film and not just through the printed word. This helps to add emotional intelligence in the way the story is told. It is the most powerful way to assist in getting the audience to engage with the case study.

The likelihood of getting every single element of the case study template in place will be a tall order, but even getting 50–70 per cent of it would be a fantastic step forward in creating some really compelling content that can be used as a media asset in both offline and online environments.

Sales copy tips

Failure to plan is a plan to fail

The reality is you can't get going unless you have a plan that you want to follow and execute. Spending time thinking and planning will ensure that the sales copy will work. Remember, you need to shift your point of view to that of the recipient, and that takes some thinking and planning to do.

Look beyond your own 'field of view'

Some of the best sales copy ideas may in fact not be in our own market segment. They may be found in other markets, professions and sectors.

A good example is the impact that salespeople from a retail background have had on the selling of professional business-to-business (B2B) services. Good practice exists in a variety of places – go seek it out, give it a twist and apply it in your field. You could be surprised as to the results you can achieve simply by looking outside your own field of view.

Be authentic, above everything else

There's a lot of wisdom out there about writing great sales copy – often written by those who've been doing it for years both offline and online. On the other hand, you've got to develop your own style. You have to find the voice of your company or organization. Your copy should reflect your company's or organization's personality, to be the best it can be.

Remember, more than ever, it's about being 100 per cent authentic. This is what this chapter is all about. Don't try to be something you're not. Apart from the fact that it won't work, you can damage your credibility and destroy your reputation, perhaps irreversibly.

The oil company BP learnt this lesson the hard way – a huge amount of time, effort and resources was spent globally giving it the 'green makeover'. It even changed its logo in 2000 to one that looked like a sunflower in an attempt to win over environmentally conscious consumers, at a reported cost in excess of US$25 million. Mind-blowing. Then a decade later, in 2010, the company was held responsible for creating the worst oil spill in US history, which turned stretches of the Gulf of Mexico into a lifeless ocean. Heart-breaking.

And it wasn't just a matter of human error, although that did play a part. It was a corporate culture where the interests of shareholder return were more important than saving the environment, no matter what the company was saying publicly about its environmental record. No amount of copy on 'protecting the environment' could reverse the environmental disaster that had its fingerprints all over it. BP had tarnished its reputation, some say to such a degree that it would take a lifetime to put the record straight. Actions will always speak louder than words.

Talk to an audience of one

Forget target audiences, stakeholder groups, target customers or typical buyers, visitors, viewers or listeners. You're not writing for the masses. You're writing for a human being: the reader, the recipient of your communication, a real person.

Remember, it's a conversation, in the first person, so use colloquial language to express ideas, thoughts and information. By paying importance to the tonality of the language you use, you'll be much more effective in getting your sales messages across. And, provided you can write simple sentences in plain language, grammar shouldn't be an issue for your copywriting.

Andy Maslen says:

You can write copy that's hard-hitting, persuasive, even entertaining and also avoid thrashing the English language. But maybe there's something that matters even more than correct English, something to do with the fundamental truths about your product or service. Like is it any good? Do enough people want to pay for it? And, ultimately, will your revenues from selling it outweigh your costs in producing and promoting it?

Mirror and match

This is a technique most commonly associated with body language but can apply equally to creating sales collateral, as pictures of the type of people you're aiming to connect with need to be present visually amongst the words of the copy. The connection has to work on both a rational and an emotional level. Visual images, such as photography, can be immensely powerful if used appropriately.

Call to action (CTA)

In the past, copywriters tended to put the CTA at the end of the sales brochure, sales letter or press advertisement. They'd taken the reader on a journey and at the end of this was 'payback time' – to get something in return. This may have been getting the reader to complete a tear-off strip and stick it in the postbox.

As we said in other places in this book, the art of closing a sale is orchestrating a series of small closes, so there's no reason why a CTA must always come at the end of the sales copy. It could come at the beginning, in the middle or even in the headline. You could pepper your copy with CTAs.

Andy Maslen says:

Just as the CTA seems to go last, it often gets written last. But maybe that's not such a good idea. After all, you're tired... and elated... the copy is almost finished. You can go home – just as soon as that pesky CTA is done. So you dash off an 'order now', save and close and you're clear. But this is the whole point of the sales letter, flyer or web page.

This is where it all comes down to a 'yes' or 'no' from your reader.
So it needs the most effort, creativity and precision to get it right.

In an online environment, a call to action isn't as simple as including your phone number in the body of the e-mail or giving the recipients lots of links to click. They need directions and compelling reasons for taking specific actions, particularly if these incur time and money.

It's important that any CTA looks like 'action'. For example, simply stating 'Click here' in the body of e-mail copy isn't likely to get a higher response rate than if you'd said 'Contact us today!'

Words are the building blocks to an effective CTA, and the quantity and type of words you use have a significant impact on the response rate. The most effective way to write a CTA is to start with one or more action words: verbs that propose a specific task that you want the recipient to do (Table 7.2).

Table 7.2 Verbs that influence the recipient to accept a call to action (CTA)

Call to action	Words that can influence this behaviour
Make an appointment	Sign up, register now.
Contact your company or organization	Call us now! Call toll free now! We are waiting for your call! Call now!
Attend a webinar	Sign up, register now.
Attend event	Register – few places left. Sold out. More dates coming.
Meet you at an exhibition or event	Download a free meeting app. Click here to make an appointment to meet us at our stand.
Open e-mail newsletter	New! Read, look in here. Scroll down.
Complete form	Takes just 60 seconds. We want to hear from you.
Save your e-mail	Do not delete.
Visit web page	Click here. Visit. Give us your feedback.
Make a purchase	Shopping cart. Buy now. Add to shopping cart. Order now! Order now and save money!
Request information	Download, request, learn, e-mail.

Avoid clichés 'like the plague'!

It's a bit like seeing someone with a poorly matching shirt and tie – you know it doesn't work but you haven't the heart to tell him. You just avoid sitting next to him.

If your copy is to be the best dressed in town, then avoid the most commonly used clichés in sales copy (Table 7.3) and rewrite the cliché in plain language.

Table 7.3 Clichés to avoid in sales copy

Let me be honest	Just between us	Step change
Honestly speaking	Let me be sincere	What do I have to do to get you to say yes?
If I were you…	I know	We need to look at this holistically
To tell you the truth	You may have heard this before	This is a game changer
Let me be frank	It's never too late	It's a win–win
Trust me	Paradigm shift	Exclusively for everyone

Avoid emotional adjectives

Poor copywriters leave all the hard work of bringing their product or service to life to the reader by using emotional adjectives like 'super', 'outstanding', 'fabulous', 'important', 'exciting' and 'great'. If you want to tighten up sales copy, it's best to expunge emotional adjectives altogether. Instead focus on choosing the precise noun rather than qualifying vague or abstract ones with adjectives.

A supreme example of the use of language in a precise way is the telegram British prime minister Sir Winston Churchill sent to General Alexander, commander-in-chief in the Middle East, on 10 August 1942: 'Your prime and main duty will be to take or destroy at the earliest opportunity the German–Italian army commanded by Field Marshal Rommel together with all its supplies and establishments in Egypt and Libya.' In the space of just 35 words, he'd packed in an entire campaign, from target to objectives and timescale. As they say, less is more.

Whatever you're selling online, make sure you write copy that engages readers' attention instantly. You don't have time to warm them up. But that doesn't mean all sales copy must be short. Rather, it's about losing a sentence when one word will do.

Length matters

The perceived wisdom is that everything on the web needs to be short, including sales copy, and that long sales copy doesn't work. In fact, any length of sales copy won't work if it's boring and dull and fails to capture and hold the attention and interest of the reader. Flip this on its head, and long copy does work where it's interesting and can sustain interest.

Long copy in a sales letter can be broken down into:

- short paragraphs;
- opening with a direct CTA appealing to the reader's self-interest;
- bullet points and cross-headings that break up the page;
- press cuttings;
- using the first person;
- using lots of specifics; and
- citing lots of benefits.

Like a fine wine, let your copy breathe

Resist the temptation to say absolutely everything possible about your product or service. Leave something for the salesperson to explain!

Overloading sales copy and cramming it into the space of the media you're working in doesn't make any sense. It could look like a mess.

Let the words and images work together in harmony. Give them space and as a rule of thumb allow around 30 per cent of the available space to be blank and design the sales collateral accordingly.

If you're in the luxury product sector, copy tends to be in a classical serif typeface such as Palatino or Perpetua. Use lots of white space and the best-quality paper you can afford.

Use the power of the narrative

A story that brings to life the reasons why someone may want to buy your product or service is one of the most powerful ways of getting your sales messages across to a prospective customer or client. As discussed in Chapter 6, storytelling in the way that Steve Jobs did is incredibly powerful and memorable. All you need is a problem, a hero, a narrative of the journey taken and a happy ending!

E-mail

One of the most significant challenges in using e-mail as sales collateral is targeting recipients with highly relevant content. Get this right and the return on investment is considerable.

Sending print newsletters and direct e-mails has long been a proven method to stay in touch with customers, clients and prospects. According to the US Direct Marketing Corporation, every US$1 spent on e-mail marketing generates US$45.06 return on investment – the highest response rate for all direct response methods.

With the right tool, not only can you create a newsletter within 30 minutes or less, but you can also track:

- who opened your message to find out who cares enough to read what's inside it instead of deleting it;
- who clicked on any of the links that are inside your message to read more or to place an order; and
- which addresses are no longer valid so you can maintain a clean list.

Sue Coakley, senior director, customer contact strategy at Yahoo!, explains:

> *At the end of the day, we all need to drive revenue, but it may not be the sole focus of every e-mail and I would argue it shouldn't be the sole focus of every e-mail that we send. We want to develop that relationship because we know that when we build a relationship people are more likely to respond when we want them to take action and they're less likely to simply tolerate or, worse yet, unsubscribe from our messages.*

Yahoo! (2012)

In order to engage with recipients of e-mail sales and marketing outbound activities, Yahoo! pursues a three-pronged contact strategy (Table 7.4):

Table 7.4 Yahoo! Three-step contact strategy for e-mail campaigns

Step 1: Build on the relationship	Step 2: Keep it relevant	Step 3: Respect recipients' preferences
Why did they start the relationship?	What do you know about them?	Obviously honour their preferences
Why do they use your products or services?	Demographics?	Do all you can to retain them
What's their end goal?	Interests?	Think about frequency
Continue to fulfil on that value	Response behaviour	Avoid permission creep
Surprise and delight	Never assume what you don't know	Consider your message in the larger context
Give your e-mail social legs	Listen – both positive and negative	
	What standard metrics don't tell you	
	Beyond the campaign	

- *Step 1: Build on the relationship.* This involves thinking back to why people started the relationship with you to begin with. It's probably because they had a very specific need. Did they provide the e-mail address and are you building off that? For Yahoo!, it's because somebody signed up for a Yahoo! Mail account. 'We should really start and build that relationship first and foremost before we look at expanding it further', says Sue Coakley.

- *Step 2: Keep it relevant.* This is probably one of the biggest buzz words for e-mail marketers. The starting point for Yahoo! is finding out what it knows about the consumers. Knowing your audience helps you to understand your purpose. In the case of Yahoo! this is done through data that's been provided as well as through behavioural tracking on its site. Another key strategy is listening as well as thinking beyond the campaign.

- *Step 3: Respect recipients' preferences.* According to Yahoo!, you have to do all you can to retain that permission. 'It's really permission to go into someone's inbox and doing that by thinking about things like frequency. At Yahoo, that currently stands at no more than one e-mail per user, week. That seems to be intuitively right, but also in terms of both positive and negative metrics', explains Sue Coakley.

The frequency that you send these messages will depend on your audience's ability to read each message and your ability to keep up with the ongoing workload. As a rule of thumb, if you think you've got a busy audience, don't send too many messages. And if you don't think you can maintain consistency on a twice-monthly basis, then opt to send only one message each month.

Typical uses for e-mail copy

You can use e-mail copy for exactly the same range of goals as you can for a sales letter:

- to generate sales enquiries;
- to generate downloads for a free white paper or research document;
- to generate a free trial of software products over a time period;
- to make incremental sales to existing customers and clients;
- to entice prospects to visit your website;
- to get discounts and special offers;
- to provide a voting mechanic;
- to drive participation for promotions, prizes and competitions; and
- to invite to a conference, seminar, exhibition or symposium.

Response rates

It won't come as any surprise that response rates are much higher when using opted-in lists. E-mail copy is particularly suitable for campaigns where you want to integrate the sales message with a website, for example for sign-ups or registrations for an event, or you want to provide a free demo or download of your software.

Subject line or headline

E-mail copy will live and die on the strength of the subject line or headline. The reason is that the recipients will be looking at your e-mail message in the preview pane and will be making an instantaneous decision to decide whether to read the whole message by clicking it open. Alternatively, they may have selected the reading pane and so will read the top of your message without having to open the whole e-mail.

According to Andy Maslen, it's clear why subject lines work in e-mails: 'They need to appeal directly to the reader's self-interest and promise a benefit of some kind. They should be personal, urgent, practical, irresistible, specific and related to the promise (not the picture if you have one).'

A headline in an e-mail can also be used as a hyperlink to a landing page. It's worth testing different sample subject lines in order to go with the one that achieves the optimum result for you.

The following are known subject lines that could throw your carefully crafted e-mail copy straight into the junk e-mail box:

- vague headlines that look like spam e-mails, such 'Hey you' or 'Check this out';
- a blank subject line (yes, really!);
- symbols in the subject line;
- words with all capital letters (offends 'netiquette' as it's synonymous with shouting at someone); and
- the recipient's first name in the subject line.

For a discussion on the legal restrictions on e-mail copy, refer to Guru in a Bottle®'s *Essential Law for Marketers* (2nd edition).

Addressee of the e-mail

One sure way of getting the e-mail deleted is to address it to 'Dear Sir or Madam' or 'Dear Subscriber' or 'Dear Customer'. It must be personal and have the person's full name. A first-name reference when you don't know that person can come across as disrespectful and over-familiar.

First paragraph

Get straight to the point. Don't waffle. Think of it as your 'elevator pitch'.

Subsequent paragraphs

Again, these need to be succinct.

If the main purpose of the e-mail copy is to promote your products or services then you should consider including descriptions and images that support the promotion and ensure that this is seen through the lens of the customer or client.

Text links

Consider using clickable words and phrases that result in certain actions when clicked, for example connecting to another piece of content or linking to an e-mail address.

Text-only e-mails are preferred by customers and prospects who check their e-mails on portable devices such as a smartphone. To avoid running into technical difficulties, it may be possible to offer users the choice of HTML or text-only versions, so that the integrity of the way the e-mail looks and reads can be maintained.

Most commonly used fonts

The protocol is to use fonts that are easy to read (10 or 12 point) and will ensure that the text displays properly when received (Table 7.5).

Table 7.5 Most commonly used fonts for e-mail copy

Arial	Arial Narrow	Calibri	Comic Sans MS
Courier New	Garamond	Georgia	**Impact**
Lucida Console	Tahoma	Times New Roman	Verdana

Sign-off

Again, keep it friendly, open and personal by using a name rather than signing off as an organization.

Web page

Good copywriting existed well before the web was conceived or direct mail had ever made its way through a single letterbox! In the opinion of Andy

Maslen it all comes down to one thing: 'Good online copywriting must sell, first and foremost. The paradigm may have changed from promotion to education, but the underlying purpose remains unchanged. And that means holding people's attention and stopping them clicking off your site.'

Ideally, copy that will produce results will need to grab the attention of visitors, hold their interest, create desire for the products or services that you deliver, make them comfortable that they can do business with you in confidence and finally lead them to take some action, such as landing on the checkout page in order to complete a transaction.

Headlines

Whether writing copy for a website or a news release, the headline is probably one of the most important – and perhaps one of the hardest – things to get right. A headline is basically the hook for what follows next. You'll quickly lose the interest of readers if the headline doesn't grab them by the throat.

Headlines do a number of really important jobs:

- They encapsulate succinctly the main benefit of your product or service.
- They give the visitor a compelling reason to read on.
- They summarize the story they introduce.
- They stop the visitor from clicking away.
- They serve as a taster for your web page when Google or other search engines deliver search results.

The most effective headlines share a number of characteristics:

- They are short – 15 words or fewer is ideal.
- They focus on benefits.
- They speak directly to the reader.
- They tell a story.

Online headlines are sometimes the only chance to hook your readers before they click off somewhere more interesting. It helps to be really specific. For example, if you have a service that could save home owners money on their utility bills, you could just say 'Save money on your utility bills', but that looks a bit lame. It's much more powerful to add specifics into the headline, such as 'You could be saving $350 a year on your electricity bill.'

You don't need to be a professional copywriter in order to write great copy:

- Write a list of all the ways your product or service makes your customer or client's life easier.
- Rank these benefits in order of importance.

- Pick your strongest, most compelling benefit, which you'd choose if you had only 10 seconds in which to tell the prospective customer or client. This forms the basis of the headline.
- Leaving aside the length or style of the headline, write a sentence that explains how the benefit makes a difference for the customer.
- Now remove as many words from the sentence as possible (called tightening up).
- Check that it addresses the reader directly.

Tone of voice

Tone of voice is incredibly important, as it can dramatically change the emphasis of the words being used. Think of it as the decor of your writing. It's not just about what you say, but also the way you say it.

On the web, it's important to make visitors to your website feel welcomed and reassured and make it easy for them to do business with you. The tone of the language used has a major role to play in achieving this. On the whole, the web is a more informal place in which to communicate. Bear in mind people Skype, IM, chat, blog, twitter and re-tweet – all in a very informal tone of voice.

You need to find your own distinctive tone of voice that's real and reflects your brand personality. The best way to achieve a realistic tone of voice is to write copy the way you would have a conversation with a friend or an acquaintance. It's the style adopted by the Guru in a Bottle® Series, which has gone down extremely well in Europe, Asia and the United States.

Online style

As a general rule, keep it simple! Use shorter words instead of long ones when writing for the web. Keeping sentences shorter – aim for 10 words on average – also improves the readability of your copy. 'Get into the habit of replacing long words with short ones and you'll be writing crisper, punchy online copy that engages your visitors and costs them less time and effort to read', says Andy Maslen.

One area where writing for the web and e-mail is distinctly different to writing for print is in the length of paragraphs that appear on a website. The difficulties of reading online mean avoiding overlong paragraphs that could be overlooked or at worst prompt visitors to leave the page they're on in search of something more manageable.

Relevancy

More important than length of copy is the relevancy of the copy, as once the purple prose starts to take visitors to a place they have absolutely no interest in going they'll soon click off.

It's usually best to avoid hyperbole and keep your writing as factually based as possible – what's known as evidence-based marketing. That way, you can easily avoid making wild, unsubstantiated claims and in turn vastly improve your reputation because you become a trusted source of information rather than trying to push a product or service irrespective of the context that the prospect will be facing.

Doing business with confidence

This is particularly important if the website is expected to take orders – before customers click through to check out, they need to be reassured they can do so with confidence.

Given the numerous web scams, many brand owners treat security as a major part of the customer experience and have clear, express security policies that are prominently displayed, which help to engender confidence for customers to do business with them. There are also data protection requirements that must be observed. Brand owners such as eBay handle this extremely well, and it's worth visiting eBay's website to take a look at how they manage this part of the communication process.

For more information about legal requirements that websites need to comply with, refer to Guru in a Bottle®'s *Essential Law for Marketers* (2nd edition).

Testimonials and case studies

One of the most powerful ways to demonstrate what you deliver – as opposed to what you offer – is through the lens of your customers and clients, and one of the most efficient ways to do this is through a testimonial or case study.

A common mistake is to ask for an endorsement or testimonial from customers or clients and find that (should they agree) it doesn't actually say very much as a piece of communication. Simply saying that the company was 'great to do business with' doesn't tell the website user why. Nor does it deliver some of the key messages that you may wish to communicate to your desired market and customer segments – about quality, service and cost or indeed the way you dealt with problems when they occurred and how these were resolved with the minimum of fuss. All of these elements can help strengthen reputation, confidence and trust, and it's a unique selling opportunity too.

The best way to achieve this is to pre-draft testimonials or case studies – keeping them factual – and get customers or clients to approve them. That way, even if the customers make some amendments, you'll end up with a more powerful and useful piece of communication that's more likely to influence the way in which customers and clients see your organization.

Contact information

It may sound like a small point, but it can be deeply frustrating for customers if they want to talk to someone at your organization but there's no telephone number given. It's all too easy to provide a contact e-mail address or a web enquiry form but sometimes a phone call is all that's required in order to close a sale.

It's also useful to have a link to frequently asked questions (FAQs) near to where the telephone number is communicated on the site, as this may alleviate the need for the call to be made in the first place.

Layout strategies

Research shows that visitors to a website tend to eyeball what's written at the top left of the screen if they read from left to right; they tend to skip banners or what looks like advertising and don't pay too much attention to what's written further down the screen. A key reason for this is that visitors to a website are usually looking for something in particular and don't want to waste time searching for it.

It's worth bearing in mind that not every word you'll write will be read so it's best to help navigate the visitor with clear directional copy positioned in high-visibility parts of the website. For example, using hypertext links in the body of the copy creates more multiple paths for visitors to access the information they're looking for in other places on the website.

It's best to use simple words, short headlines, short sentences and short paragraphs. If you want to convey more detailed or complex copy about your products or services, then think about providing a PDF download or a 'printer-friendly' button so that it makes it easy for visitors to print off a document.

Search engine optimization (SEO)

It's clear that search engines drive the internet and are the key information aggregators for just about any subject under the sun. They are also the primary conduit for customers and prospects who may be searching for a particular product or service and are more likely to find you as a result of a search rather than by typing your URL into the browser.

Search engines use mathematical algorithms to analyse a user's question or search query in order to provide web pages that attempt to most closely answer the question or relate to the search term.

Given that we can't control how search engines work, it's important that all commercial websites are constructed in such a way that web pages are returned first (or on the first results page) for any relevant search, since most users rarely look beyond the first page of search results and as a result you may never be found.

Search engine optimization (SEO) is critical when planning and designing a website. An optimized website will attract more traffic than its rivals because it achieves naturally high search responses and as a result doesn't need to rely on paid-for search results in order to drive traffic to the site.

Even if you're able to hard-wire SEO into your website, the effects of this time and investment may not necessarily come through immediately and may take between six and 12 months to be realized, as a website takes time to register with all relevant search engines.

- Take the longer-term view when engaging with SEO for your website. There are no short-term fixes that will propel your website to the number one spot, and in fact older websites tend to get higher rankings than newer ones.
- Track the number of unique visitors to your website as a result of natural search results. Any half-decent web analytics tool will be able to provide you with this data.
- Track the number of key phrases that are driving traffic to your website.
- Track the number of inbound links to your website.
- Track the number of indexed pages by search engine.
- Try to link traffic data with number of sales successfully transacted on your website (where this is relevant).

Online newsletters

Let's face it. Most online newsletters are nothing more than a glorified advertorial that's nakedly attempting simply to get you to buy something, go to an event or subscribe to something, which will open up another screen that will try to up-sell and cross-sell to you at the same time as asking for your permission to opt in. While all of this activity can be rationalized on the basis of trying to 'sell', it may in fact alienate a large percentage of those potential customers and clients who don't like to be sold to and in fact are seeking insight and knowledge from an online newsletter.

The starting point is what's in it for them. Why would they want to spend any time reading your newsletter as opposed to doing something else on a rainy Friday afternoon?

Value in the communication will sell it, not making it a sales piece

The online newsletter should be 'what it says on the tin' and deliver topical, well-observed, insightful knowledge and practice that demonstrate that your company or organization knows what it's talking about.

It's more about influencing the way that your prospective customers and clients will think in the future – and why they'd want to come and talk to you – that will be the real power of an online newsletter.

Too little thought goes into understanding what outcomes are required from something like an online newsletter, and instead salespeople think it's to be treated like another piece of direct mail.

Typographical considerations

When it comes to the design and typography of an online newsletter, everyone has an opinion but very few learn anything before offering their opinion. Some will say they prefer light blue to light yellow, Times New Roman looks terrible, and underlined words help to provide emphasis. Blah, blah, blah. This level of ignorance makes even less sense given how people like to obsess about style rather than substance.

Table 7.6 provides some general guidance on the use of typography and layout.

Table 7.6   Typographical considerations for the online newsletter

Fonts	Serif typefaces like Times New Roman are readable and are useful where you need to have continuous text.
	Sans serif typefaces like Arial and **Arial Black** are good for headings. Don't have more than two typefaces on the page – one serif and one sans serif.
	For continuous text, avoid upper case (although it's acceptable for short headings) and avoid italics, especially with small font sizes.
	For added emphasis, consider choosing a different font instead.
	Avoid underlining – it looks ugly in a newsletter.
Aligning text	For continuous text, avoid centre or right alignment. If you justify text, it's a trade-off between look and readability. Don't justify text that is too narrow.
Borders	Don't butt words up to lines, text boxes and cross-heads. Also, make their thickness appropriate to the text they are near – only use thick lines with large fonts.
Headings	Keep these clean and preferably short.
White space	Allow copy and pictures to breathe, and consider space as 'thinking time' for the reader.
Line length	Avoid long lines of text. The eye gets weary reading them on-screen or on a smartphone – a maximum of 12 words is about right.
Line spacing	Use 1.5× spacing for continuous text, smaller spacing for headings that stretch over more than one line, and smaller still for big headings.
Colour contrast	Consider colour contrast in order to create visual interest and also to help the reader navigate through the content of the newsletter.
Navigation	Consider using on-screen turning page technology where the online newsletter mimics the look and feel of a physical newsletter and is easy to flip from one page to the next.

In terms of the actual content of an online newsletter, the following points should be observed:

- Use simple, jargon-free and colloquial language.
- Offer an industry perspective and latest statistics on changes happening in that market segment.
- Signpost the reader to other relevant resources.
- Provide insight on issues and challenges faced by many customers and clients and currently what's being done to meet them.
- Provide one or two case studies and testimonials that deliver key sales messages through the lens of the customer or client.
- Give an update on news, events and views.
- Have a maximum of only 25 per cent of the space in the online newsletter devoted to sales promotional copy.
- Keep the tone of the newsletter open and friendly and invite feedback and sharing of thoughts and ideas with the audience.
- Think of changing the format for subsequent online newsletters to keep it fresh, and consider using mechanics such as prizes, promotions, competitions and awards that help to collect data on a permission basis, provide a reason for the reader to return, and maintain the dialogue with the reader via the online newsletter.
- Consider using info graphics, data visualization, interactive charts, drawings and photographs.
- Include a picture and full contact details of the person with whom readers can engage on any of the material presented in the online newsletter.
- Ensure that there's a statement on data protection that's written in a friendly and jargon-free way.

For more guidance on data protection compliance, refer to Guru in a Bottle®'s *Essential Law for Marketers* (2nd edition).

Google AdWords

Google AdWords are a paid-for advertising product and, as with any other form of copywriting, the intention is to grab attention and influence behaviour. The ads appear as four-line text items on the right-hand side of the Google search results. Google works on the principle of relevance and, depending on what users are searching for, Google only wants to return websites and AdWords that specifically deal with what they're looking for.

Given that you have to bid for the use of certain Google AdWords in competition with other brand owners, you should only bid for the most specific and relevant keywords you can think of, and these must also be included in your ad copy.

The major difference with other forms of online advertising is that the brand owner only pays if the user clicks on the Google AdWords – referred to as pay-per-click (PPC).

Importance of Google AdWords copy

The copy used for Google AdWords plays a vital role in the success of any PPC campaign. There's no guarantee that simply using the best keywords and most compelling sales copy will increase the response rate of any PPC campaign, as the Google AdWords may simply fail to deliver the customers you're looking for.

The following tips will dramatically improve your response rate and chances of reaching your desired customer and client segments.

Google AdWords tip 1: Be specific

Don't write generic ad copy for all your keywords. You should try to be as specific as possible so that your Google AdWords can deliver the right message to your desired customer and client segments.

For example, take men's shoes. If you're retailing shoes and you've different types of shoes in your inventory, you should make a few sets of keywords for each of the different types of inventory that you have and then write compelling Google AdWords for each of those sets. The best way to do this is to have multiple ad groups for your different sets of keywords so that you can easily write specific ad copies for the different ad groups.

Google has several utilities that can help you in this task, including a keyword ideas tool that will allow you to put in the parameters you want, and the tool will suggest keywords on the basis of what the competition are using and the level of global and local monthly searches against those most popular keywords (Table 7.7).

Many brand owners believe that copying Google AdWords of the top-performing advertisers can make their PPC campaign a success. Wrong. Certainly you can take ideas from your competitors while you're writing your Google AdWords copy. But blatantly copying a competitor's Google AdWords makes your Google AdWords insignificant. Many search queries today show near-duplicate Google AdWords with the same title and some minor changes in the Google AdWords body and a different display URL. This is definitely not helping the brand owner, because users get confused when they see the same kind of Google AdWords lined up in a column. Users tend to go for the one that stands out and is different from the rest of the group.

Table 7.7 Keyword ideas

Keyword	Competition	Global monthly searches	Local monthly searches
office shoes	Low	368,000	201,000
vans shoes	High	673,000	201,000
dr martens	High	1,500,000	301,000
hotter shoes	High	90,500	74,000
wedding shoes	High	823,000	201,000
new look shoes	Medium	60,500	60,500
wynsors	Low	49,500	49,500
doc martens	Low	1,220,000	246,000
skechers	High	1,220,000	135,000

Source: https://adwords.google.co.uk (accessed 18 August 2012)

Google AdWords tip 2: Highlight your unique selling proposition (USP)

Given the high degree of commoditization in certain markets, brand owners are often left fighting it out over price. In order to combat this downward spiral, having a USP is a key offensive sales strategy in order to compete on value rather than price.

Consider the following:

- How different are your products and services compared with those of your competitors?
- What makes your product or service unique?
- What benefit would the customer get after buying what you sell?

The Google AdWords chosen must encapsulate your value proposition and ideally shouldn't be capable of being easily replicated by your competitors. They must be unique and something that your customers can relate to and benefit from.

Some examples of popular USPs:

- Olay: 'You get younger-looking skin.'
- Domino's Pizza: 'You get fresh, hot pizza delivered to your door in 30 minutes or less – or it's free.'
- FedEx: 'When your package absolutely, positively has to get there overnight.'

In all of the above examples, all the USPs are pretty straightforward and uniquely describe the value proposition in simple terms.

Google AdWords tip 3: Don't get carried away being too creative in the copy

Advertisers often try to make their Google AdWords copy very creative, but this doesn't translate into a higher return in terms of PPC rates and sales conversions.

Because of the nature of PPC ads, it's very important for you to grab the visitor's attention right at the beginning. Think of a traditional Google search page, for instance – when users perform a search, they're presented with a page full of blue-coloured links on a white background. They're looking for a particular solution to a problem and, even though you offer the solution and you've put up your Google AdWords on the right-hand side of the screen, the user may not be able to spot you. One reason may be that your Google AdWords copy doesn't include the words that users are searching for and as a result this makes your Google AdWords irrelevant to their search.

When you search for a term and you're provided with 10 results, you naturally go with the results that have exactly the same words of your search query on them.

Google by default automatically bolds your searched keywords in the search engine results page (SERP), so when writing your next Google AdWords copy make sure you include your main keywords in the ad headline and ad description so that they're automatically bolded when users include those keywords in their search query.

Having your keyword in the Google AdWords copy also makes your ad more relevant and as a result delivers a better click-through-ratio (CTR).

Google AdWords tip 4: Call to action

Many brand owners forget to include a CTA in their Google AdWords. Having a good CTA can increase your CTR and also increase your campaign effectiveness.

Users need to know what's in it for them if they click on the Google AdWords. They're already in a page full of related links that they were searching for and you're just one of those results. So, if you're going to attract them, you'll have to make sure that they know what they'll get from your page.

For example, if users are thinking of buying car insurance, they need to go to a destination where they can straight away get what they need: an insurance quote. They don't want to end up on a site where they'll receive an endless supply of insurance tips or articles. That's not what they're looking for.

Google AdWords tip 5: Get to the point

You don't have the luxury of a lot of space to write your PPC Google AdWords. Google AdWords allows only 25 characters in your title and 35 characters each in the one or two description lines beneath it, so avoid all the unnecessary words and fluff and include only things that add value to your advertisement.

You'll get only about 5 to 10 seconds before users abandon the page, so you really need to grab their attention the first time they see your Google AdWords. If you're selling a product, you may want to give away the unit price in your Google AdWords copy so that the users who find your product affordable will click on your Google AdWords and the rest won't – saving you some money, as it won't drive traffic that has a very low conversion rate for you.

No matter how good and convincing your sales copy, the conversion rate depends partially on how much money users can afford to pay at that very moment. If they've a maxed-out credit card and your product costs US$1,000, then your offer isn't any good and their click would be of no value to you.

It's always good to tailor your offer according to the user's query. For example, if someone is looking for 'cheap hotels', you might want to highlight the price factor in your Google AdWords copy. On the other hand, if users are looking for 'luxury hotels', you might want to highlight some of your premium facilities such as an outdoor heated swimming pool and an award-winning spa.

So think of some offers and specific details that you can give away right within your Google AdWords copy that will save users their time and your money.

Google AdWords tip 6: Make sure your ad is formatted properly

Typical mistakes include:

- the title is not proper cased;
- everything is written in small letters; and
- spelling errors.

You only get a very small window of opportunity when it comes to grabbing the attention of your customer or client via PPC, so make sure that the user gets a good first impression when looking at your Google AdWords copy. For example, capitalizing the first letter of each word is a common practice that makes your ad copy look attractive. However, you can test with various other methods and use the method that works best for you.

Google AdWords tip 7: Display the URL as part of your ad copy

Another common mistake made by brand owners is to pay little attention to the display of the URL as part of the Google AdWords copy, and yet this is vital for the effectiveness of the ad as well as CTR. You can put absolutely anything in your display URL, provided that the domain matches with the domain of the destination URL. No matter what your domain name is, you can include your primary keyword with a trailing slash in your display URL to 'assure' users that they'll indeed go to the right page.

Try to use keywords in your display URL, if that's possible – the page doesn't even need to exist on your website, as the display URL is for display purposes only. You can choose your display URL to be whatever you want and send users to your choice of destination – provided that both are under the same domain.

Google AdWords tip 8: Make sure that your ad copy and landing page are aligned

In the vast majority of cases the landing page will be prepared first before you get on to write your ad copy. But sometimes brand owners forget what's offered on their landing page and write their ad copy from scratch. As a result, even good ad copy with a high CTR may fail miserably, because after customers or clients go to the landing page they can't find what the ad copy has promised. You need to have some sort of correlation between your sales copy on the landing page and your Google AdWords copy. One easy way of doing this is to highlight and include your USPs and benefits in your landing page that relate to the promise that you made in your ad copy.

Google AdWords tip 9: Take account of day and time for running the ad campaign

Each market segment that you compete in is unique and has its own unique web traffic pattern. For example, depending on the type of products and services you're selling, some days of the week may be better than others. Equally, some times of the day may be better than others. A combination of optimum days and times is likely to yield a higher CTR.

The default scheduling made by Google is to allow you to run your ads every day of the week, or just on weekdays or weekends. This may be sufficient for your purposes. Alternatively, it may be in your best interests to set your campaigns up to run at dates and times of your own choosing and spend more or less on specific days of the week or hours of the day. For example, you may find that your company or organization's web traffic and sales are strongest during the week and sharply drop off over the weekend. If this is the buying pattern you face, then you might want to set up your campaigns to reflect these traffic flows so that when customers and clients are online they can find your ads quickly and easily and you don't have to stretch the budget over gaps of time that bring you poor-quality traffic that has a low CTR and poor conversion rate.

Google AdWords tip 10: Keep the campaign constantly under review

The entire success of your Google AdWords copy is dependent on the CTR and conversion into sales and so it's sensible to carry out some form of testing of your ad copy:

- Test your Google AdWords copy headline. Create a few variations of the headline and see which brings you more CTR and more sales conversations. Don't get fooled by high CTR – high CTR doesn't necessarily mean that your ad is performing well. Rate of conversation is what it's all about.

- Test different offers. Each of your ads might include an offer, and you may create a few offers to see which one works the best. For example, does an offer of '20 per cent off' perform better than 'qualify for an immediate $50 discount'?

- Test your USP. Sometimes even after you've identified a unique strength of your product or service, it may not be the best one in terms of converting interest into sales, so always test with different value propositions and see which one works for you.

- Run multiple split tests of your Google AdWords copy. Have at least three ads set up in each ad group and run them for a considerable amount of time before coming to a conclusion about their performance.

- Make small changes at a time. For example, start with the Google AdWords headline first. When you're changing the headline, don't make any other changes. Run that test for a while and find out the best headline that gives you a good CTR. Once you achieve an acceptable result, move to the next item and test it thoroughly. Continue this until you've refined what is working well. CTR is an important indicator for your ad's effectiveness because CTR is directly related to your ad copy whereas conversion is only partially related. Conversion depends a lot on your sales copy and landing page as well, so concentrating more on CTR initially would be a better idea, and slowly you can work your way up to increase your sales conversion rate.

- Even the slightest of changes matter. You might not find all tests worth doing, but you should know that even a single punctuation mark can make a significant difference on your CTR.

- You should make sure that you test every single dot in your ad copy thoroughly. Some basic items to be tested include:
  - www versus non-www in your display URL;
  - different use of caps in your headline and description;
  - trailing dots (…) at the end of your ad copy; and
  - the use of other punctuation and special characters within the Google AdWords copy.

Sales letter

There's an old saying in sales and marketing: if you try to sell to everyone, you'll end up selling to no one. No matter how universal your product or service happens to be, customers and clients want to be able to feel you're connecting with them. Before you write a sales letter, stop. Think about the person at the other end who's going to receive it. Earlier we talked about a market segment of one. Even in B2B sales and marketing, it's a real person who shows up to the sales meeting, reviews the products and services on offer and ultimately writes the cheque.

'Each of these people is a real person with a unique background, hopes and dreams. Just like the path in life that led you to where you are now, they've walked their own path', observes British sales training guru Sean McPheat.

The same principles that apply to an online newsletter apply to the construction of the sales letter.

'The sales letter is probably the most powerful piece of copywriting ever to have been invented. By its very nature personal – if written properly – it takes your sales pitch directly to each and every one of your prospects', observes Andy Maslen.

The reality is that most sales letters are junk mail that ends up in the recycle bin.

As we've said earlier in this chapter, in order to improve the chances of the sales collateral being read, there needs to be a strong narrative. Creating a compelling story that delivers your key sales messages not only delivers greater impact but also is more memorable for the recipient.

Print or e-mail version of the sales letter?

There's no straightforward answer, and it really depends on whom you're trying to communicate with. Revenue per message is shrinking – whether delivered by physical direct mail through the letterbox or delivered by e-mail to an individual's PC, laptop or mobile device. As a result, many salespeople feel they must send more and more messages to compete. Wrong. Volume is a detriment, not an asset. In the battle to win the hearts and minds of recipients, relevance has become even more important in the 'war of words'.

In many respects the sales letter – whether in physical or soft-copy format – can be relatively quick and inexpensive to produce, but it's often hard to beat the odds of it actually being opened and read (Table 7.8).

From reviewing Table 7.8, it's clear that typical response rates for any type of sales letter are likely to be low, and they're getting lower. One reason why so many sales letters fail to drive sales is that they don't cut to the chase or get to the point fast. In this respect sales letters aren't that different from many other sales channels, such as e-mails, web pages or press ads.

Table 7.8 Typical response rates for the sales letter

Type of sales letter	Typical response rate	What you can expect
Sales letter individually addressed to a named recipient	6.7 per cent of the names mailed to	67 responses per 1,000 pieces posted
Sales letter B2C campaign	7.1 per cent of those mailed to	71 responses per 1,000 pieces posted
Sales letter B2B campaign	6.2 per cent of those mailed to	62 responses per 1,000 pieces posted
Sales letter door drop to households but not named individuals (otherwise known as 'junk mail')	5.0 per cent of those who receive the mail	50 responses per 1,000 pieces posted
Door drop to households but not named individuals (otherwise known as 'junk mail')	40 per cent is put in the recycle bin unopened	Of the 60 per cent that does get opened by the householder, 20 per cent doesn't get read
E-mail sales letter campaign	Open rates for segmented and named individuals versus non-segmented campaigns can vary as much as 20 per cent	A carefully segmented and named e-mail campaign will perform 20 per cent more effectively in the first 30 days

The ultimate sales letter will address the following questions that will be in the mind of intended recipients:

- What keeps them awake at night giving them indigestion, boiling up their oesophagus, eyes wide open, staring at the ceiling from the 'can't sleep at night' experience?
- What are they afraid of?
- What are they angry about?
- With whom are they angry?
- What are their top three daily frustrations?
- What trends are occurring and will occur in their businesses or lives?
- What do they secretly and ardently admire most?
- Is there an inbuilt bias to the way they make decisions ('System One' or 'System Two' thinkers?)

- Do they have their own language or code?
- Who else is selling to them, what are they selling to them and how are they selling to them?

Product sales brochure

This tends to be the glossy, high-production variety of sales collateral where the ratio of words to pictures, diagrams and graphics could be as high as 10:90, whereas an e-mail newsletter may have a ratio of 70:30 words to pictures.

The product sales brochure tends to be less personal, although this can be overcome if the tone of the sales collateral is open, friendly and engaging.

Car manufacturers spend what looks like a small fortune developing beautiful-looking product sales brochures that give the prospective purchaser strong emotional reasons for wanting to buy what is a high-ticket item.

One major flaw in the whole process is deciding whether the product sales brochure is actually required and how it will be used to drive sales by those who receive it.

Not having clear, behaviour-orientated objectives can be a fatal flaw in the thinking that sits behind the investment required to print a large number of these glossy 'vanity sheets' that aren't measured in terms of the value they deliver to the company or organization. But that doesn't mean they can't be.

A product sales brochure can be an appropriate piece of sales collateral in a variety of contexts:

- generating sales leads, for example for holidays abroad;
- winning orders, for example, B2B markets such as expensive yachts;
- driving free trials, for example test drives of the latest car model;
- improving perception of the company or organization, for example showing how it manufactures its products and the quality of raw materials used;
- gaining new members or supporters, for example a professional body, university or private members' club; and
- providing something to salespeople that they can hand out with pride at conferences, exhibitions, events and hospitality functions and to senior-level individuals within 'traditional' market segments such as law, accounting, medicine, insurance and other professions or in the luxury goods market such as clothing, watches, hi-fi, jewellery, apparel and high-end accessories where the expectation is to receive a well-designed and high-end product sales brochure.

International Chamber of Commerce Code (2011)

Background to the Consolidated ICC Code (2011)

The International Chamber of Commerce (ICC) Code sets the ethical standards and guidelines for sales and marketing, including the production of sales collateral, around the world. Developed by experts from a wide range of market and customer segments, the ICC Code (2011) is a globally applicable framework that harmonizes best practice in sales and marketing from the Americas, Africa, Europe, the Middle East and Asia Pacific. The ICC Code applies to all sales and marketing communications in their entirety, including all words and numbers as well as material originating from other sources.

The Code is voluntary but has been incorporated by industry regulators across the world. For example, in the UK, it's been adapted by the Committee on Advertising Practice to produce its own CAP Code, overseen by the Advertising Standards Authority (ASA).

For a detailed explanation of the codes of practice that affect this area of sales and marketing practice, refer to Guru in a Bottle®'s *Essential Law for Marketers* (2nd edition).

The ICC Code is relevant for B2B as well as B2C sales and marketing collateral and takes account of social, cultural and linguistic factors in the production of such materials. For example, when judging communications addressed to children, the ICC Code provides that their natural credulity and inexperience should always be taken into account in any determination as to the appropriateness of those communications.

Assumptions made by the ICC Code

The ICC Code makes a number of assumptions that are relevant when producing sales collateral: from a B2C perspective, individual customers and prospects are assumed to have a reasonable degree of experience, knowledge and sound judgement and to be reasonably observant and prudent when making purchasing decisions; and, from a B2B perspective, companies and professional organizations are presumed to have an appropriate level of specialized knowledge and expertise in their field of operations.

These same assumptions are applied in the CAP, BCAP and Direct Marketing Association codes of practice in the UK.

The ICC Code is structured in two main parts: general provisions on sales and marketing communication practice that contain fundamental principles; and then a series of detailed sections that cover particular activities such as direct marketing, sponsorship and sales promotion.

For a detailed explanation of data protection controls and laws, refer to Guru in a Bottle®'s *Essential Law for Marketers* (2nd edition).

General provisions of the ICC Code

Basic principles

All marketing communications should be legal, decent, honest and truthful, should be prepared with a due sense of social and professional responsibility, and should conform to the principles of fair competition as generally accepted in business (Article 1).

Decency

Sales collateral shouldn't contain statements that offend standards of decency currently prevailing in the country and culture concerned (Article 2).

Honesty

Sales collateral should be framed so as not to abuse the trust of consumers or exploit their lack of experience or knowledge. Relevant factors likely to affect consumers' purchasing decisions should be communicated in such a way and at such a time that consumers can take them into account (Article 3).

Social responsibility

Sales collateral should respect human dignity and shouldn't incite or condone any form of discrimination, including that based upon race, national origin, religion, gender, age, disability or sexual orientation. In addition, such activities shouldn't without justifiable reason play on fear or exploit misfortune or suffering, or appear to condone or incite violent, unlawful or anti-social behaviour or play on superstitious beliefs (Article 4).

Truthfulness

Perhaps the most important principle in the ICC Code and one that goes to the root of the production of sales collateral is that all such activities must be truthful and not misleading (Article 5). Any form of sales material shouldn't contain any statement or claim that directly or by implication, omission, ambiguity or exaggeration is likely to mislead the consumer.

The ICC Code spells this out in some detail, and although not exhaustive the following is a useful checklist as to what 'truthfulness' means in practice when writing sales materials:

- Characteristics of the product that are material in influencing the consumer to make a purchase, for example the nature, composition, method and date of manufacture, range of use, efficiency and performance, quantity, commercial or geographical origin or environmental impact must be clear.
- The value of the product and the total price to be paid by the consumer must be clear.
- The terms for delivery, exchange, return, repair and maintenance of the product must be clear.

- Other information, including terms of guarantee, intellectual property (IP) rights and trade names, compliance with international and national standards, awards, and the extent of benefits for charitable causes as a result of making a purchase, must be truthful.

Use of technical or scientific data and terminology

In much the same way that Article 5 provides for 'truthfulness', this principle (Article 6) captures situations where sales materials may 'sail close to the wind' without actually being dishonest and may be 'economical with the truth'.

In practice, copywriters shouldn't engage in the following activities:

- Misuse technical data such as research results or quotations from technical and scientific publications.
- Present statistics in such a way as to exaggerate the validity of a product claim.
- Use scientific terminology or vocabulary in such a way as to falsely suggest that a product claim has scientific validity.

Use of 'free' and 'guarantee'

This is perhaps unusual, as it's a specific rather than a basic point of principle, but it addresses the temptation to use words like 'free' and 'guarantee' within sales literature. In order to stem underhanded and oblique sales and marketing activities, the ICC Code provides that the term 'free', as in 'free gift' or 'free offer', should only be used in very limited circumstances (Article 7):

- where the 'free offer' involves no contractual obligation whatsoever; or
- where the 'free offer' involves only the obligation to pay shipping and handling charges, which shouldn't exceed the cost estimated to be incurred by the marketer itself; or
- where the 'free offer' is in conjunction with the purchase of another product, but provided that the price of that product hasn't been inflated to cover all or part of the cost of the 'free offer'.

Such a provision closes the door to many 'sharp practices' where the consumer is led to believe that there's a value-added benefit (for example, a significant financial saving) when in fact it's nothing of the kind and instead the copywriter is treating the consumer as gullible to such a tactic.

The provision also states that use of the term 'guarantee', 'warranty' or any such expression in such copy shouldn't give the impression that consumers will enjoy additional rights over and above their statutory rights.

The terms of any guarantee or warranty, including the name and address of the guarantor, should be easily available to the consumer, and any exclusion clauses or limitations on consumer rights or remedies must be clear, conspicuous and in accordance with national and international laws.

Substantiation

Sales materials often include claims, descriptions or illustrations that are communicated to consumers in order to influence them in making an informed choice. The ICC Code provides that such claims, descriptions and illustrations should be capable of both verification and substantiation (Article 8).

Identification

About a decade ago or even longer it was the fashion to place 'advertorials' that were paid-for advertising but made to look like editorial with the veneer of 'independence' about the content in the advertisement. Thankfully, this type of sales copy is losing its appeal, as there should be clear water between sales copy and genuine editorial content.

The ICC Code specifically states that such sales copy should be clearly distinguishable as such. When paid-for sales copy appears in a medium containing news or editorial matter, it should be readily recognizable as a paid-for inclusion, and the identity of the brand owner should be immediately apparent (Article 9).

Such sales copy shouldn't misrepresent the true commercial purpose and, as a result, copy that's promoting the sale of a product, for example, shouldn't be disguised as 'market research', 'consumer surveys', 'user-generated content', 'independent blogs' or 'independent reviews' where in fact these are far from being unsolicited or independent points of view.

Identity

This is linked to Article 9, and the ICC Code provides that the identity of the brand owner should be apparent in such sales materials and where appropriate should include contact information to enable the consumer to get in touch without difficulty (Article 10).

Comparisons

The ICC Code provides that any comparison of a competitor's products or services in sales materials mustn't mislead and must comply with the principles of fair competition (Article 11). Points of comparison should be based on facts that can be substantiated and shouldn't be unfairly selected.

Denigration

The sales material shouldn't denigrate any person or group of persons, firm, organization, industrial or commercial activity, profession or product or seek to bring it or them into public contempt or ridicule (Article 12).

Testimonials

As discussed earlier in this chapter, testimonials and case studies are some of the most powerful ways of getting a message across to a desired market and customer segment, as they have a quality of independence about them. The

ICC Code recognizes the potency of such content and provides that such sales materials shouldn't use or refer to any testimonial, endorsement or supportive documentation unless it's genuine, verifiable and relevant, as to do otherwise would be dishonest (Article 13).

The ICC Code adds that testimonials or endorsements that have become obsolete or out of date and therefore misleading through passage of time should be removed from all sales and marketing collateral.

Environmental claims

Given the increased importance of environmental issues within a sales context, the ICC Code was updated in line with international standards.

Copywriters need to ensure that any environmental claims or messages made in the sales literature hold up to the basic principles of truthful, honest and socially responsible communications and avoid misleading consumers.

Whilst the principles in the ICC Code appear simple, applying them to make new environmental claims, often based on terms that aren't universally understood, is much more complicated. ICC guidance maps that process for companies and provides a standard for brand owners to evaluate such claims should they be challenged under national and international laws and regulations.

An environmental claim refers to any claim in which explicit or implicit reference is made to environmental or ecological aspects relating to the production, packaging, distribution, use or disposal of products.

The ICC Code guidance on use of environmental claims includes:

- ensuring that all statements and visual treatments don't mislead, overstate or exploit consumers' concern for the environment;
- avoidance of general claims like 'environmentally friendly', 'green', 'sustainable' and 'carbon friendly' unless there's validation of such claims against a very high standard of proof;
- presenting qualifications in a way that is clear, prominent, understandable and accessible to consumers;
- presenting improvement claims separately so it's clear whether each claim relates to the product, an ingredient of the product, the packaging or an ingredient of the packaging; and
- the inappropriateness of emphasizing a marginal improvement as a major environmental gain, highlighting the absence of a component that's never been associated with the product category, or making a comparison with a competitor's product (unless a significant environmental advantage can be verified).

Portrayal or imitation of persons and references to personal property

The roots of this principle lie directly in the need to protect the personal privacy of citizens, and the ICC Code provides that sales materials shouldn't portray or refer to any persons, whether in a private or a public capacity, unless prior permission has been obtained; nor should such material convey the impression of a personal endorsement of the product without prior permission having being sought in the first instance (Article 14).

Exploitation of goodwill

In the same way that Article 14 is a principle about respect for privacy, the ICC Code on exploitation of goodwill prevents any unjustifiable use of a name, initials, logo and trademarks of another company, brand owner or institution (Article 15).

Imitation

Sales materials shouldn't in any way take unfair advantage of another's IP rights or goodwill in the absence of consent (Article 16). This principle effectively forbids copycat sales materials, as there may be an action in law for passing off.

For a detailed explanation on the tort of passing off, refer to Guru in a Bottle®'s *Essential Law for Marketers* (2nd edition).

Sales materials shouldn't imitate those of another brand owner in any way likely to mislead or confuse the consumer, for example through the general layout, text, slogans and visual treatment.

Safety and health

Sales literature shouldn't without justification on educational or social grounds contain any visual portrayal or any description of potentially dangerous practices or situations that show a disregard for safety or health as defined by national laws and standards (Article 17). For example, a sales brochure for a range of children's trampolines with children playing on the products should be shown to be under adult supervision, as the activity involves a safety risk that could potentially pose a hazard for children if they are not supervised by an adult.

Responsibility

Observance of the rules of conduct laid down in the ICC Code is the primary responsibility of the brand owner. Other parties also required to observe the ICC Code include copywriters and subcontractors (Article 23), who should also exercise due care and diligence in the preparation of sales material.

Employees of any of the above who take part in the planning, creation and publication of such materials are also responsible – commensurate with their pay grade – for ensuring that the rules of the ICC Code are observed and should act in the spirit and letter of the ICC Code.

Effect of subsequent redress for contravention

Subsequent correction and appropriate redress for a contravention of the ICC Code by the party responsible are desirable but don't excuse the contravention of the ICC Code (Article 24).

Implementation

The ICC Code and the principles enshrined in it are typically adopted and implemented nationally and internationally by the relevant local, national or regional self-regulatory bodies (Article 25).

References

Books

Kennedy, D (1990) *The Ultimate Sales Letter*, Adams Media
Kolah, A (2013) *Essential Law for Marketers*, 2nd edn, Guru in a Bottle®, Kogan Page
Maslen, A (2011) *The Copywriting Sourcebook*, Marshall Cavendish Business
Maslen, A (2011) *Write to Sell*, Marshall Cavendish Business
Mitchell, A (2001) *Right Side Up*, HarperCollins Business
Moon, J (2008) *How to Make an Impact*, FT Prentice Hall
Zyman, S (2000) *The End of Marketing as We Know It*, Harper Business

Websites

A best-practice guide to e-mail sales and marketing: http://www.mailermailer.com (accessed 15 August 2012)
A good example of handling data protection issues on a website: http://ebay.com (accessed 16 August 2012)
For a discussion on e-mail sales copy: http://www.marketingsherpa.com (accessed 15 August 2012)
Information on Google AdWords: https://accounts.google.com (accessed 18 August 2012)
US Direct Marketing Corporation: http://usdirectmarketingcorp.com (accessed 18 August 2012)

Power of word of mouth:
"I'll have what he's drinking!"

The power of business networking

Introduction

As the economies in the Eurozone go into reverse gear with virtually no growth expected throughout 2012 and no end of the recession in sight until at least 2014, European brand owners are facing the prospect of a depressed market for their products and services coupled with the need to diversify in the hope of attracting new customer and client segments in order to survive.

China, by contrast, is forecast by the IMF to grow by 8.2 per cent in 2012 and beyond, despite widespread fears of a slowdown, and economies such as Brazil, Russia, India, Indonesia and Nigeria are racing ahead with growth rates of 6 per cent and higher. The mighty United States may only just manage a meagre 2 per cent of growth in comparison, if it's lucky, over this same period.

Against this backdrop it's becoming clear that the ailing economies of old Europe and the Western hemisphere are rapidly losing their dominance. For example, for the first time in decades, exports to the 27 European Union member states are smaller, in cash terms, than those to the rest of the world.

Multinational companies haven't been slow to react to such changes and have been diversifying their sales and marketing efforts in order to reach more valuable customer and client segments in the emerging economies.

In the UK, some of the biggest companies operate almost exclusively in these fast-growing emerging markets. For example, global banks HSBC and Standard Chartered make most of their money in Asia; insurance giant Prudential has a near-monopoly position in some of the fastest-growing economies of south-east Asia; and the likes of GSK, BAE Systems and Rolls-Royce seek growth in almost every booming corner of the world as well as their own backyard.

Yet none of this new business activity could have been achieved simply through more efficient operations, IT, people, strategy and processes. At the end of the day, much of the growth in incremental sales has been generated as a direct result of the power of business networking.

But it's not only large corporates that need to use the power of business networks – it's every company and organization. In this increasingly competitive global marketplace where relationships matter, doing business has increasingly become dependent on who you know rather than just what you know or the quality of the product or service you deliver. As a result, business networking has become the fastest and most cost-effective way to build an enterprise in these challenging times. Yet networking isn't always considered that important by many executives, who tend to spend far too much time stuck inside their own organizations dealing with internal politics.

Networking with customers, clients and prospects, on the other hand, increases the available pool of contacts, builds awareness of what you deliver for customers, clients and stakeholders and motivates valuable referrals that can open the door to new sales opportunities.

Historically, networking was viewed as an activity that could only be conducted face to face, from informal breakfasts through to formal black-tie dinners. Indeed such practices continue today and remain important for the vast majority of small and medium-sized businesses, which rely on such forums as a way of interacting with their peer group as well as prospecting for business leads.

But the opportunities for business networking have expanded beyond these horizons, and as you'll read in this chapter 'virtual' networking has come into its own as a result of the rapid growth of social network sites and online community forums.

British business coach Heather Townsend, who's worked with entrepreneurs as well as multinational company executives to help them improve networking skills for business advantage, warns:

> *Most professionals know that effective networking is vital if they want to be successful in what they do. Some may have years of experience of networking in person but be daunted by the world of online networking. Others are a whiz at social networking on the web but enter a room full of strangers with extreme trepidation. It's a fact that many professionals don't network well at all. And this is dangerous: get it wrong and at best you'll lose out on opportunities; at worst you can severely damage your professional credibility.*

This chapter provides insights and expert guidance on how to develop the natural communication skills we all possess in order to be an accomplished business networker, helping you to feel equally at home building business relationships face to face or via online networks.

Face to face

As a salesperson, you can choose how much time you want to devote to business networking as part of the working week, by what means you'll network and how much success you'll generate for yourself when networking.

One of the most influential face-to-face business networks in the world today is the exclusive Young Presidents' Organization.

Young Presidents' Organization (YPO)

This is a global network of high-achieving young chief executives that connects them with their peer group in more than 110 countries to learn, exchange ideas and address the challenges that leaders face today. There are several around the world and an annual conference that brings members together in a different host city every year.

Guided by the mission of 'building better leaders through education and idea exchange', the organization provides members with access to unique experiences, world-class resources, alliances with leading business schools, and specialized networks to enhance their business, community and personal leadership skills.

There are currently over 25 such face-to-face business networks covering everything from apparel, beverage and construction through to IT and real estate business networks.

YPO was founded in 1950 by men's accessories manufacturer Ray Hickok who at 27 years old inherited his family's 300-employee company in New

York. He and other young business leaders began meeting regularly as a way to become better managers by learning from each other, and this founding principle continues to guide the organization in the wake of Ray Hickok's death in 1992.

To join this exclusive business network, you need to be a president, chairman of the board, CEO, managing director, managing partner, publisher or equivalent under the age of 45 and satisfy the following requirements:

- If you work within the sales, services or manufacturing sector, then the company must have at least US$8 million in gross annual sales.

- If you work within the financial services sector, then the company or institution must have average annual assets of at least US$160 million.

- If you work for an agency-type business, then annual fees or commissions billed must exceed US$6 million.

In total, there are 6,000 YPO individual members, and on reaching 50 years of age they moved to the World Presidents' Organization (WPO), a group founded in 1970 by 200 former YPO members that facilitates the continuing lifelong learning experience with access to the YPO–WPO global network and other benefits.

In aggregate, the companies run by YPO and WPO members employ more than 16 million people and generate more than US$6 trillion in annual revenues, making it a highly valuable and important business network.

As discussed in this chapter, whether you work for a small or medium-sized enterprise, a charitable organization or a multinational company, business networking shouldn't be a 'nice-to-have' but rather an essential component of daily business life.

As the YPO example illustrates, there's more to successful networking than meets the eye, and it can't be measured simply by counting the amount of business cards you end up with when you head for the exit door at the end of a networking event.

On the surface, most face-to-face business networking is about people standing around talking to each other. The real skill is how you pull this off and whether you join the 'super-league' of networkers who know how to 'work a room'.

As we discuss later, face-to-face networking must be in sync with online networking and vice versa. Whereas you may be tempted to exclusively use LinkedIn and Twitter in order to widen your reach to prospective customers and clients, you should consider face-to-face business networking at the same time. There's no 'one-size-fits-all' answer to the question of how much face-to-face versus online business networking is the right balance to strike. The answer is 'It depends', and this comes back to your objectives for business networking in the first place. For example, in the UK, mothers with pre-school-age children tend to be online much more than other sections of the British population, so it's vital for a salesperson to be part of this community by having some form of online presence.

MamaBabyBliss (2012)

This new British company has tapped into the highly lucrative market of 'yummy mummies' by offering baby massage and yoga classes. Instead of advertising in trade or mainstream parenting publications, the company has focused its efforts on using Google AdWords, social media including Twitter, Facebook and blogs, and PR directed towards local and national magazines, newspapers and parenting websites in order to reach desired customer segments. All these activities are underpinned by face-to-face networking activities around the UK that include mother-and-baby shows at the Birmingham National Exhibition Centre, as well as London's Earls Court and ExCel in the Docklands. Taken together, these activities help to establish credibility with consumer groups.

'It's about finding innovative and imaginative ways to keep spend down and return on investment high. That's why a lot of brands in this market have moved away from mainstream advertising', explains Kerry Haynes, marketing manager at MamaBabyBliss.

Word of mouth in the form of endorsements from happy parents has a significant impact for the bottom line, as mothers with pre-school-age children tend to listen to other mothers in the same position more than any other group.

'It's the biggest word-of-mouth market there is – if you get one mum signing up, the chances are that more mums will sign up for classes too', Kerry Haynes says.

In regional areas, local events and summer fêtes provide a cost-effective opportunity for display stands with goody bags and promotional offers such as trial classes. But networking has to be about more than a free promotional offer. It's the quality of the networking experience that counts.

Pioneering research in the area of behavioural economics by Nobel laureate Daniel Kahneman, professor of psychology at Princeton University in the United States, shows that this isn't as straightforward as it sounds.

Behavioural economics

Daniel Kahneman and his colleague Amos Tversky undertook a study over two decades that explored the largely uncharted territory of behavioural economics: an understanding of the exercise of human judgement and typically how decisions are reached.

The core of their hypotheses is that the majority of judgements made every day by ordinary people are based on data of limited validity. For example, the apparent distance of an object is determined in part by its clarity. The more sharply the object is seen, the closer it appears to be, which is why the passenger wing mirror of cars manufactured in the United States, Canada, India and Australia carry the warning 'Objects in mirror are closer than they appear.'

Although there's some validity in such a 'rule', because more distant objects can appear blurred to the eye, over-reliance on this 'rule' can lead to systematic errors in the estimation of distance, so the 'rule' has limited validity. For example, distances can be overestimated when visibility is poor and conversely can be underestimated when visibility is good. So the reliance on clarity as an indication of distance leads to common biases.

Taking that one step further, the research discovered that such biases are also found in the intuitive judgement of probability ('Shall I purchase or shan't I purchase?') and that in each of us there are two 'selves': the experiencing self (known as 'System One') and the remembering self (known as 'System Two'). These two 'selves' are relevant when considering the outcome from a face-to-face meeting with a customer, client or prospect.

Daniel Kahneman, in his book *Thinking, Fast and Slow* (2011), explains:

> *For example, we can expose two people to two painful experiences. One of these experiences is strictly worse than the other, because it's longer. But the automatic formation of memories – a feature of System 1 – has its 'rules' which we can exploit so that the worse episode leaves a better memory. When people later choose which episode to repeat, they're naturally guided by their remembering self and expose their experiencing self to unnecessary pain.*

When this theory is applied to the measurement of well-being, it creates a surprising result.

'What makes the experiencing self happy isn't quite the same as what satisfies the remembering self', claim the psychologists, acknowledging the dichotomy that such a theory creates – how two selves within one body can pursue happiness in completely different ways.

What's certain from the fascinating, ground-breaking study is that when we are in System One mode we do the fast thinking, whereas in System Two thinking is much slower and more deliberate and it monitors System One, trying to maintain control as best it can within its limited resources.

So, in essence, the salesperson needs to engage with the experiencing self (System One), which does the living, and the remembering self (System Two), which keeps score and ultimately makes the choices as to whether to buy or not.

The following key points will help you to improve your face-to-face networking skills:

- Keep your contacts book up to date – it's hard work, but keep notes on everyone you like or find interesting. Usually the back of a business card is a good place to write where you met, the date and other pertinent details. Then enter this into your Outlook contacts as part of a living database when you get the opportunity to be in front of your PC, laptop, tablet or smartphone.

- Take time to nurture people – remember important events, such as a job promotion or job move to another company or organization, where sending a short 'congrats' e-mail can be an appropriate way to keep the channel of communication open.

- Arrange an informal gathering – known as a 'salon' – for a small group of people to enjoy topical conversation either over lunch at a nice restaurant where there's a guest speaker or over evening drinks at a nice venue. Don't feel you must pick up the bill – make it clear that everyone must pay for themselves, but you do the hard bit by organizing the gig. In the UK, networking guru Carole Stone runs a salon every four weeks on the same date, at the same time and place. It only ever needs to be an hour and a half – and it works.

- Use your business cards sparingly. Never thrust your business card at someone – it's not effective. Always ask for other people's business cards and enquire whether they'd like to have yours. If they say 'yes' then give it. Alternatively, simply ask for theirs and wait to see if they ask you for yours. If they don't, then that should tell you something and it's unlikely that they'll be on your Christmas card list.

- Follow through with a contact within 24 hours by sending them a message via LinkedIn, Twitter, Facebook or e-mail – we all lead such busy lives and are constantly meeting new people, so it's important you're not forgotten and avoid having your business card end up in the bin.

- Have a reason for wanting to get in touch. Reflect on the conversation and how this was interesting or useful; find common ground and always have in the back of your mind why they'd want to spend time with you again – make it worth their while, so to speak.

- Realistically, you won't get round to meeting everyone you may have hoped to see at a conference, symposium, seminar or event, so an e-mail to someone referencing the fact that there wasn't time to meet but that you'd be interested to have a coffee with him or her can sometimes be far more complimentary and flattering than the outcome had you met them at that event in the first place.

- Don't be short-sighted – share your contacts with others on LinkedIn or Facebook and be prepared to assist your contacts by making introductions to others. You'd be surprised how often this is reciprocated without you having to ask for a return favour.

- Take a genuine interest in people – don't have a conversation with someone whilst at the same time looking over his or her shoulder to see if there's someone more important you feel you should be talking to. It's the surest way of being identified as feckless or a 'social butterfly', and people will start to avoid you, so don't do it.

- Show the world what a gracious and charming person you really are. If you see people standing on their own, go and introduce yourself to them. Find out about them, what they're interested in and their reasons for coming to the event – you'd be surprised that your friendliness can translate into a genuine bond that could deliver much more than you bargained for. Feel free to network such people with others whom you feel they could get on with. It'll do wonders for your own 'personal PR' and is very empowering.

Word of mouth

The temptation for many sales and marketing professionals is to splash the cash on a new shiny sales promotion in the hope of driving sales fast. This is particularly evident at Christmas and other religious holidays and festivities celebrated around the world. In fact, the entire global advertising industry was built on the ability of a one-way communication channel to help shift products and services to the widest number of consumers. Today, such channels have become so much more sophisticated that it's hard to recognize what we used to do in the past as a result of technological advances made, particularly in mobile communication.

For a review of how advertising has become a two-way channel of communication, refer to Guru in a Bottle®'s *High Impact Marketing That Gets Results*.

Savvy sales and marketing professionals have started to see things differently, and there's a general realization that traditional sales and marketing isn't enough. The need for two-way dialogue is now the order of the day. For example, recent research shows that the primary influence behind 20–50 per cent of all purchase decisions made by customers and clients is word of mouth.

In many respects, word of mouth is the 'purest' form of business networking, leading some commentators to claim that it's the world's most powerful sales tool. And they have a point.

The influence of word of mouth is at its greatest when customers and clients are buying a product or service for the first time or where it's a relatively expensive purchase decision requiring more research, so the purchaser actively seeks more opinions and there's a longer period of deliberation than would be the case for a much less expensive purchase decision.

Product reviews are constantly being posted online and opinions disseminated through online networks, often shared with thousands of people from all over the world. Some customers even create websites and blogs to praise or criticize brand owners that fail to live up to their promises. Sites such as Trip Advisor are testament to the spread of consumer activism on the web.

As all of these online communities increase in size, scale and character, sales and marketing professionals now place a higher degree of importance on relevant and appropriate interaction with these forums.

For a detailed discussion on e-marketing, m-marketing and direct marketing, refer to Guru in a Bottle®'s *High Impact Marketing That Gets Results*.

McKinsey Research (2010)

Research by global strategy consultants McKinsey has examined what makes effective word of mouth and how this can help to drive sales of products and services.

There's a world of difference between idle gossip and word of mouth. In the case of the former, it's questionable whether there's any residual value for the consumer in relying on it. However, more credence is given to word of mouth.

From a sales perspective, word of mouth is the desirable 'by-product' of delivering excellent service and product to an existing customer or client, who in turn is a willing brand ambassador or brand advocate to other potential customers and clients. This generates exponentially a greater number of recommendations, which can then convert into sales, as well as driving deeper brand loyalty amongst those who fall under the influence of word of mouth.

As discussed in Chapter 2, the sheer volume of information available today has dramatically altered the balance of power between brand owners and consumers. As consumers have become overloaded, they've also become increasingly sceptical about traditional advertising and marketing and increasingly prefer to make purchasing decisions largely independently of what a particular brand owner may say about its products and services.

According to the researchers at McKinsey, this tectonic power shift toward consumers and away from brand owners reflects the way people now make purchasing decisions as a matter of course.

Once consumers make a decision to buy a product, they start with an initial consideration set of brands formed through product experience, recommendations or awareness-building marketing. Those brands and others are actively evaluated as consumers gather product information from a wide variety of sources and decide which brand to purchase. Their post-sales experience then informs their next purchasing decision, and so forth.

While word of mouth has different degrees of influence on consumers at each stage of this sales journey (Figure 8.1), uniquely it's the only factor that ranks among the three biggest consumer influencers at every step of that journey.

Word of mouth can prompt a customer, client or prospect to consider a brand, product or service in a way that other channels such as advertising can't deliver. The right messages resonate and expand within interested networks, influencing brand perception and consideration as well as propensity to purchase and ultimately the brand owner's market share.

The growing importance of online communities and communication has dramatically increased the 'momentum effect' of word of mouth.

'In the mobile market, for example, we've observed that the pass-on rates for key positive and negative messages can increase a company's market share by as much as 10 per cent or reduce it by 20 per cent over a two-year period. This effect alone makes a case for more systematically investigating and managing word of mouth', claim the McKinsey researchers.

Not all word of mouth has the same impact on consumer behaviour and, unsurprisingly, messages delivered by word of mouth from a trusted source, such as a friend or close acquaintance, are up to 50 times more likely to trigger a purchase response than the low-impact recommendation of a complete stranger.

Figure 8.1   Influence of word of mouth in sales of consumer products

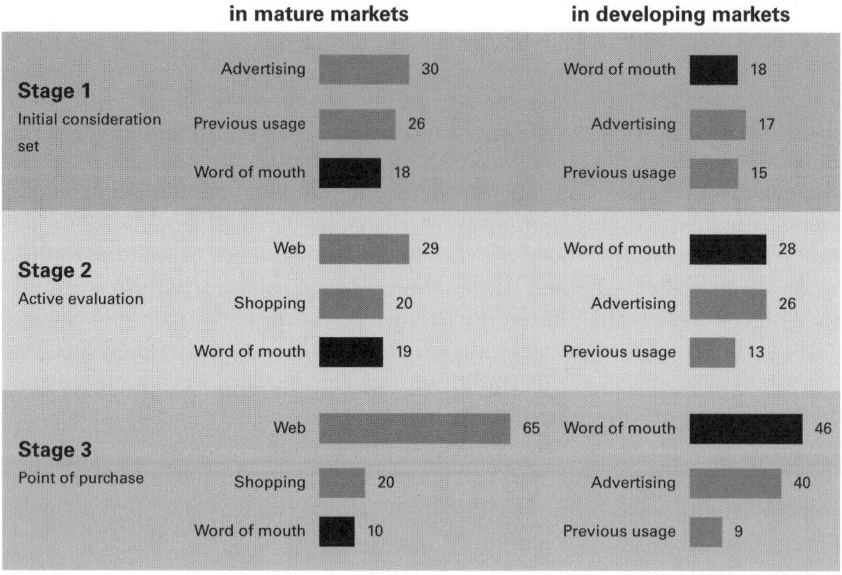

	in mature markets		**in developing markets**	
Stage 1 Initial consideration set	Advertising	30	Word of mouth	18
	Previous usage	26	Advertising	17
	Word of mouth	18	Previous usage	15
Stage 2 Active evaluation	Web	29	Word of mouth	28
	Shopping	20	Advertising	26
	Word of mouth	19	Previous usage	13
Stage 3 Point of purchase	Web	65	Word of mouth	46
	Shopping	20	Advertising	40
	Word of mouth	10	Previous usage	9

Source: Bughin, Doogan and Vetvik (2010)

In an attempt to prove this hypothesis, McKinsey carried out research that showed that 'word-of-mouth equity' is the sum of the volume of messages multiplied by the impact of those messages. Although this may appear straightforward, there are a large number of variables that can affect the outcome of word of mouth.

The impact of those messages can be evaluated in terms of:

- where the person is talking, such as in a social media network, and whether this is a close and trusted source or whether it was word of mouth provided by a large and unconnected number of people;
- whether the close and trusted source of the word of mouth is influential in his or her own right;
- in terms of what's being said, whether the word of mouth is a relevant key buying factor for the consumer; and
- the value of word of mouth in light of the consumer's own experience with that product or service.

The latter is a potential purchase 'trigger', and of course from the consumer's point of view it will either confirm or deny his or her experience of the product or service or simply be a matter of hearsay and not be that compelling. The impact of the word of mouth therefore reflects what's said, who says it and where it's said. It also varies by product and service category.

What's interesting is that the content of the word of mouth is generally the most persuasive feature, and in the McKinsey research study this appeared to be confined to rational rather than emotional benefits of products and services. Next came the identity of the person delivering the message, and a higher value was attached to those who were more influential, such as bloggers, who tended to generate three times more word-of-mouth messages than those who were less influential. Finally, where the word of mouth circulates is crucial to the power of those messages.

From a business networking perspective this is very important. Messages that circulate within tightly knit and trusted networks, such as trade or professional bodies, tend to have less reach but greater impact than those messages circulated through dispersed communities. One reason is that there's usually a high correlation between people whose opinions we tend to trust and the members of a network we most value. That's why old-fashioned 'kitchen table' recommendations and their online equivalents are so persuasive. After all, a person with 800 'friends' on Facebook may happily ignore the advice of 795 of them. It's the small, close-knit network of a handful of trusted friends that has the real influence.

Word of mouth and Apple (2010)

At the time of the iPhone launch in Germany, Apple's share of word-of-mouth volume in the mobile phone market segment was about 10 per cent, or a third less than the market leader Samsung. On the surface, it looks as though Apple was being squarely beaten by its rival.

However, a closer look tells a very different story. The McKinsey research showed that the buzz accompanying the iPhone's messages was about five times more powerful than average. This translated into a word-of-mouth equity score for Apple that was 30 per cent greater than that of Samsung, with three times more influential customers such as bloggers recommending the iPhone over other handsets such as Samsung's Galaxy smartphone. As a result, sales directly attributable to the positive word of mouth surrounding the iPhone outstripped those attributable to Apple's paid marketing sixfold and, within 24 months of launch, the iPhone was selling almost 1 million units a year in Germany.

The flexibility of word-of-mouth equity allows salespeople to gauge the word-of-mouth impact on products and services regardless of the category or industry. And, because it measures performance rather than the sheer volume of messages, it can be used to identify what's driving – and hurting – word-of-mouth impact.

What Apple did rather brilliantly was to manage consequential word of mouth by using the insights gained by word-of-mouth equity to maximize the return on sales and marketing efforts. Understanding the dynamics of word of mouth allowed Apple to evaluate the most appropriate channels and messages employed and allocate its marketing accordingly to help drive sales.

In summary, the McKinsey study shows that marketing-induced peer-to-peer (P2P) word of mouth, particularly within social media, generates more than twice the sales of paid advertising in many market segments, including mobile phones.

Power of social media

The new challenge for the vast majority of salespeople is how to turn conversations within social media into hard cash.

With the convergence of technologies rapidly becoming a reality for millions of consumers around the world, mastering how to connect word of mouth in social media to the sales and marketing engine could make the difference between success and failure.

Brands and their fans

For example, global brand owners such as Disney, Adidas and Nike have built 'fan' pages on Facebook and get people to 'like' them in much the same way that rock band the Grateful Dead pioneered the way to use the web to get their millions of fans around the world to 'follow' them.

The experience of new consumer brand owners such as Zynga and ASOS, which grabbed a US$500 million share of the fashion industry in less than three years, demonstrates that brand owners across all market segments have the opportunity to turn social media engagement into meaningful revenue streams.

'Marketing's no longer about pushing messages and hoping for sales leads, nor does just using the tools guarantee people will listen. It's all about engaging customers in meaningful and advantageous conversations', observes social marketing guru Michael Saylor, CEO of MicroStrategy.

There are several key ways in which salespeople can rewire their approach in order to harness the power of social media:

- creating a space in the 'online ecosystem' that reflects your business and organization and cultivates your customers' and clients' trust and earns their loyalty;
- actively participating in the unique culture of each available social media platform to engage with your desired customer and client segments;
- establishing an organizational structure that constantly targets the next new media trend;
- attracting online champions and change agents who'll uncover the social networks you need to reach;
- motivating the key influencers who'll help build your reputation in the networked world; and
- adapting your company or organization to consistently identify market needs and trends, based on the invaluable connections you forge and the empathy and insight you obtain in the process.

Social CRM

The above strategies are part of 'social CRM', which seeks to address the shortcomings of traditional customer relationship management (CRM) that tends to be focused on promoting what the company wants to sell rather than what the consumer wants to buy.

Michael Saylor explains:

> *The best way to serve customers is to understand their preferences, but traditional CRM doesn't do this, so they feel ignored. Response rates drop while costs rise. On the other hand, social CRM is a world where your database is continually updated by the people on it. People on social networks openly share information about themselves, from the banal to the intimate: their location, their age, what they like to eat, where they like to eat, where they go on holiday and how they like to relax. Their lives are played out on their Facebook pages, videoed on YouTube and continually tweeted – a goldmine of information that a social CRM system can help you open up.*

The benefits of social CRM in the context of business networking include:

- segmenting and building content campaigns that drive better customer engagement because they're based on facts rather than assumptions;
- measuring the success of word of mouth in real time;
- reducing the cost of customer and client acquisition;
- creating offers that are highly targeted; and
- improving the way you can collaborate with your customers and clients profitably by empowering them in the process.

'Unless you've a clear understanding of your customers or clients' interests, biases, habits, followings, preferences and trust circles, as well as the best time and place to make them, any offers you make are likely to be inappropriate', concludes Michael Saylor.

Brand advocacy

As discussed in this chapter, word of mouth has risen to the top of the sales and marketing agenda, and in the United States alone over 500 billion word-of-mouth impressions are generated across social media networks every year.

Turning highly satisfied customers and clients into brand advocates can create a point of differentiation for a brand owner that's not easy to dislodge or remove. And, whereas all marketing and advertising can be copied up to a point, selling a product or service to a brand-loyal customer of another supplier is a completely different matter.

Brand advocacy research (2007)

A few years ago, US researchers at the University of Connecticut set out to prove something of a paradox – that the most valuable customers for any business aren't necessarily those who buy the most products or services. The results of the research study, conducted in the telecommunications and financial services sectors, showed that the most valuable segments were those whose word of mouth brought in the most profitable new customers, regardless of how much the brand advocates may have spent themselves.

The study found that many high-spending customers who said they'd recommend a product or service and then subsequently didn't weren't as valuable to the business as those customers who may have spent less but nonetheless were active brand advocates and good sources for referrals.

The research study concluded that salespeople should focus their efforts on those customers who bring in the most sales referrals rather than investing time and resources on those who don't, although intuitively this may not feel the right thing to do.

Word-of-mouth research (2010)

US brand advocacy specialists Zuberance set out to test this hypothesis by identifying the monetary value that could be attached to word of mouth in helping to drive incremental sales.

'Our analysis is similar to the study conducted by the University of Connecticut and published in the *Harvard Business Review*. We found that if companies systematically identify and energize brand advocates they receive at least 10 times the return on investment (ROI) in media and sales value', explains Rob Fuggetta, CEO of Zuberance.

He points to several reasons for this:

- Consumers trust word of mouth at least five times more than advertising, paid search, e-mail and other sales and marketing tools. As a result, sales and marketing programmes that energize brand advocates achieve substantially higher conversion rates than other comparable campaigns, and in some cases this can be as much as 6 per cent higher.

- Unlike the case for paid media, brand owners don't financially reward brand advocates for spreading the word about their products and services.

- Energizing brand advocates creates long-term value, as the experience of Apple, TiVo, Harley-Davidson and Four Seasons Hotels testifies.

For a further discussion on customer loyalty and advocacy, including the net advocacy score, refer to Guru in a Bottle®'s *High Impact Marketing That Gets Results*.

Customer and client feedback

As can be seen in Figure 8.2, there are four parts to customer and client feedback, starting with the scope of the review.

Figure 8.2 Four-step customer and client review process

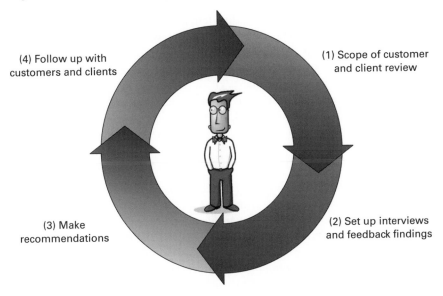

(4) Follow up with customers and clients

(1) Scope of customer and client review

(3) Make recommendations

(2) Set up interviews and feedback findings

In one sense, getting quality customer and client feedback is a more formal method of business networking.

There are several reasons why actively seeking customer and client feedback is a great idea:

- It shows you want to listen actively.
- It shows you actually care what customers or clients have to say.
- It allows you to demonstrate that you value the relationship.
- It allows you to demonstrate that you want to follow up if there are teething issues and show your desire to fix them straight away.
- It is a pre-emptive step where a complaint from a customer or client could be coming your way, and seeking feedback can defuse a potentially inflammatory situation that may have resulted in the spread of negative word of mouth.
- It allows you to demonstrate 'customer service in action' by actively seeking ways in which you can improve what you deliver.
- It allows you to understand how well you've done and what you could do to improve the delivery of the product or service to the customer or client.

- It is a way of continuing the dialogue where you can qualify other interests and requirements without actually 'selling' but could come away with a new sales opportunity as a result.

- It helps to increase awareness of your other products and services that the customer or client may not be aware of or may not have considered in the past but may now.

As discussed at the beginning of this chapter, the sheer volume of information available today has dramatically altered the balance of power between brand owners and consumers. However, companies and organizations still try to operate on their own terms – pushing products and services at customers and clients in the vain expectation that these segments will buy from them. As we've said in other parts of this book, the perspective 'inside out' should be 'outside in' instead. It's more about 'pull' and less about 'push'. Getting the balance right is critical, particularly as customer and client expectations are rising and trust in major institutions and organizations is rapidly falling.

British customer and marketing guru Peter Fisk observes:

Emotions drive customer attitudes and behaviours like never before. At the same time that more choice and broader experiences have driven higher expectations, falling trust in business has led to significant decline in customer loyalty. Business transparency and the media's obsession about the negative aspects of business have fuelled this decline in trust in brands, whilst the abundance of choice and speed of innovation accelerates the promiscuity of customers.

Types of customer and client feedback

There are about half a dozen different types of feedback, as described in Table 8.1.

From the list of possible forms of customer and client feedback, a regular review of the relationship is possibly the most effective, as it can act as an 'early warning light' should there be problems with the relationship that may have been missed or gone unchecked.

It's important to consider what the objectives are before commencing on any customer or client feedback exercise, as well as what you'll do with the information once you've got it. This will determine the nature and type of questions that you'll want to seek answers to.

If you wish to use customer or client reviews as a benchmarking exercise then you should consider a mix of quantitative and qualitative questions so you can measure the health of that relationship over time. It's also important to limit the number of reviews that you may want to conduct with customers and clients, as follow-ups can be time-consuming and could be perceived as a burden if not handled appropriately. By asking customers and clients to respond to a list of questions, you're indicating that you value

Table 8.1 Six typical forms of customer and client feedback

Type of feedback	Description of formal networking opportunity
Customer and client relationship reviews	An annual health check of your existing relationships.
Other external stakeholder reviews	Uncover external perceptions about your brand and uncover untapped sources of referrals.
Internal reviews	Uncover internal perceptions of your brand; identify any disconnects between what your customers and clients experience and what your employees are able to deliver; and make employees feel listened to and valued.
Project/matter reviews	End-of-project debriefs to ensure that learning is applied to future work.
Win/loss reviews	Reviews carried out routinely as part of your pitch process.
Testimonial/case study interviews	Obtaining compelling information and insight that you can use in your request for tender (RFT) responses, credential statements and other marketing materials.

your relationship with them. You need to act on any feedback promptly, so overstretching your resources by conducting numerous reviews all at once can end up being counter-productive and not achieve the desired outcome.

The account manager or account director may not de facto be the best person to conduct a customer or client review even though that person may have the best working knowledge of the customer or the client. The reason is that customers and clients may not be willing to be forthright or say what they may be thinking – they may feel obliged to say what they think the account manager or account director wants to hear. This is dangerous, as it may have the effect of storing up problems for the relationship in the future if they decide to duck out of dealing with these issues now.

Alternatively, the account manager or account director may feel obliged to defend past work should the feedback be less than positive, and again this will alter the complexion of the exercise, which should as far as possible be quantitative rather than qualitative. This isn't the purpose of the review, and it may result in the customer or client shutting down and being less open in the review process for fear of causing offence.

It's far better to have an independent reviewer, as customers and clients are generally much more comfortable in talking to someone who's an independent, external person, and customers and clients wouldn't necessarily always feel comfortable being openly critical with the account manager or account director.

The selection of which customers and clients you speak to should be done based on the criteria that are important for your company or organization, for example the size of the client, its financial value and its growth potential. Alternatively, it could be customers or clients whose fees are declining, and it's important to understand why.

Getting internal buy-in

Commencing on any type of customer and client feedback does require the buy-in of the CEO, as the process could uncover some nasty surprises and indirectly amount to criticism or lack of leadership of a senior person in the company or organization that may have been obscured from view for a period of time.

As far as it's possible, it's a good idea to avoid the office politics that could accompany such an exercise.

The following points are useful when seeking internal buy-in:

- If necessary, you may wish to identify a project sponsor or get the CEO's buy-in, as the customer and client feedback process needs to have credibility within the company or organization in order to be taken seriously.

- Give detailed consideration to likely objections that could be raised internally and how you'll need to deal with them.

- Acknowledge that some people will naturally feel uncomfortable with the process.

- Conduct a couple of test reviews with customers or clients that are broadly supportive of the process. Showcase the positive feedback to others within your company or organization. There'll always be issues to work on, and this should be seen as a positive way of further developing the relationship.

- Ensure the person conducting the review with the customers or clients is perceived as being independent in terms of having no vested interest in the feedback – good or bad.

Follow up with the customers and clients post-feedback

This final step in the process can so easily be forgotten and yet in many respects it's the most important – what is the company or organization going to do now as a result of having got this information? This provides the context for networking with the customers and clients who have freely given their time in order to take part in the exercise.

- Thank customers and clients for participating and let them know the next steps and time frames.

- Ensure follow-up takes place and that customers and clients are kept in the loop – this is vital in ensuring that they feel the process has been a valuable investment of their time.

- Use the positive messages and inputs that came out of the process within sales and marketing activities – but always seek permission from the customer or client first before doing so.
- Review the process – understand what worked well and what could be improved if the exercise was rerun with a different set of customers or clients in order to get a deeper granularity of detail from the findings.

LinkedIn

There are two types of sales professional – those who are on LinkedIn and those who are still thinking about being on LinkedIn! Unbelievably, there are sales managers out there still undecided about whether they should engage on LinkedIn with customers, clients and prospects as part of their everyday business networking activities. The root cause of standing at this crossroad is something much deeper than LinkedIn. It's fear – and yet there's nothing to be frightened of. It's hardly up there with being in the dentist's chair!

Despite countless books, articles and blogs on the subject, most people still don't fully understand what LinkedIn or online networking is all about. One belief commonly shared by sales professionals is that LinkedIn is an excellent substitute for face-to-face networking. Well, it isn't. As we said earlier in this chapter, offline networking needs to be supported by online networking and vice versa.

Part of the problem why online networks are so misunderstood is that the user interface on some of these sites may appear simple (Twitter and Sina Weibo), appears far too complex (Facebook and Google Plus) or doesn't offer enough guidance in order to maximize the value of the experience (LinkedIn and Quora).

On the other hand, there are some generations of sales managers who are still intimidated by any form of online networking and steadfastly hide behind their 'scepticism' of the value of such networking as part of their daily sales activities. Had they lifted the scales from their eyes, they would've seen that LinkedIn is a global business-to-business (B2B) marketplace populated with budget holders, line managers and decision makers ready to be influenced to make intelligent and effective buying decisions.

Currently, there are 161 million LinkedIn members in over 200 countries and territories who are set to exceed 5.3 billion professionally oriented searches on the platform by the close of 2012. These billions of connections are based on finding the 'trigger points' for engagement with a colleague, friend, associate, customer, client, sales prospect and even potential employer – and at the end of the day this always comes down to having shared and common interests.

LinkedIn makes this easy to discern by providing a valuable pool of information and sales intelligence through personal profiles of key decision makers as well as through LinkedIn groups and channels.

LinkedIn speaker Adam Gordon, based in the UK, remarks:

LinkedIn isn't just for the most senior executives. Any organization would do very well to engender an 'entire firm' approach to business development and sales. If your most senior people connect on LinkedIn with your clients' and targets' most senior executives, your mid-ranking client teams connect with their peers and your early career professionals link to their upwardly mobile counterparts, you'll have created a true 'man-marking' approach. That way, you'll get a true and full picture of your markets and be in a position to enhance customer and client relations not just now but also for the future.

Needle in a haystack

It used to be the case that it was difficult to track down people when you didn't have their precise name or other demographic details – in fact, it was equivalent to searching for a needle in a haystack. LinkedIn changed all that for ever. It's now highly conceivable that you'll be able to track down a key decision maker using LinkedIn's extremely powerful search facility. The reason is that LinkedIn users tend to maintain full profiles on the site, and this enables others to find them.

Try this exercise. If you're already on LinkedIn, then put your name into Google. You'll find that your LinkedIn profile is likely to come up in the first three results on Google. What this means is that your LinkedIn profile is likely to be the first place where someone checks out your online identity in order to get an impression of you, assuming that you're a total stranger and unknown to that person. LinkedIn enables you to make a good first impression. And you only ever get one chance to make a good first impression, so don't blow it!

Managing connections

If you've been using LinkedIn for years, you've now become accustomed to receiving invitations to connect to people who feel they've something in common with you. They may have done business with you in the past or could be former colleagues. In such cases, it's acceptable to connect. However, if you're looking to build a relationship or dialogue with a prospective customer or client whom you've never done business with but think you may in the future, then sending an invitation to connect on LinkedIn isn't going to work. In fact, your invitation to connect may be seen as being presumptuous, and it's preferable to get introduced by one of your contacts who's connected with the individual, as that's likely to be more successful.

Avoid trying to connect with people on LinkedIn whom you don't know or haven't bothered to get to know. Around 25 per cent of LinkedIn users will never connect with you if they don't know you, and 50 per cent will only accept your LinkedIn invitation if they feel they may benefit from getting to know you. It's these segments that you need to reach, as they're discerning about their contacts and are potentially more valuable to your business or organization provided that you can cultivate the relationship. Try to find them on groups or channels on LinkedIn and start a dialogue with them about topics and issues where there's a community interest in learning and understanding more. Get to listen to what they have to say. Ask questions.

Whether you decide to connect to someone or offer the opportunity for someone to connect to you boils down to one thing – your objectives. In order to make LinkedIn networking work for you, it's important to have a clear set of objectives or criteria for giving and accepting invitations to connect. These can include any of the following:

- Build a network only of people and contacts whom you already personally know.
- Build and maintain a specific in-depth network of influencers, specifiers and authorizers around one market segment.
- Build a broad network that shares or reflects your own attitudes, values, beliefs, perceptions and behaviours.
- Only add people to your network who may offer an immediate benefit or solution to some aspect of your professional work.

Research suggests that a LinkedIn connection with another person simply means that the person has given you permission to speak to him or her – and nothing more. It doesn't mean the person wants to meet you and it certainly doesn't mean he or she wants to buy from you (well, not yet anyway). It's up to you to use your skill in influencing and selling in order to try to convert this relationship into a commercial one.

Quantity versus quality

The folks at LinkedIn would prefer that we only connect with those where there's a genuine connection rather than selecting 'colleague' or 'friend' as the basis for the connection when patently we've never met them before. You need to decide what your own criteria will be in evaluating such requests:

- What level of interaction needs to have taken place for you to feel comfortable agreeing to an invitation to connect to you on LinkedIn? To have a face-to-face meeting, a phone conversation or simply an e-mail exchange?
- How important is it that you get to know someone before you agree to link to that person?
- How important is membership of a specific group or association in order for you to add someone to your professional network?

One of the most effective ways of using LinkedIn is in creating acknowledgement between you and others and taking these new relationships offline, such as face-to-face networking.

LinkedIn groups

Admittedly there's a limit to the number of groups you can be a member of on LinkedIn (currently it's 50 maximum), so applying to the 'owner' or 'moderator' to join a group and being accepted is a mark of your standing and the value that you're expected to bring to the group.

It's important that you contribute to the thinking of the group, and it's always preferable that you share links to interesting content or articles (preferably not just your own but those of other commentators too) that add to the 'knowledge capital' of the group. If you take such an approach it won't be long before you're engaged with other members and able to demonstrate your expertise and insight across a range of issues that are pertinent to all members of the group.

Over time, you'll discover that some of the members of the group could potentially become your customers, clients or supporters and, because you've taken the time and trouble to engage, they'll be more receptive to wanting to discuss their own issues and challenges with you.

If a LinkedIn group doesn't provide you with an opportunity for regular dialogue or appears dormant, then you're best leaving it and joining one that does. If you can't find one that meets your needs and requirements, then you can create one from scratch.

Building your own LinkedIn group

There are a number of considerations you need to make before taking the plunge and creating your own LinkedIn group:

- Ensure the title of the group is compelling, authoritative, relevant and timely. It needs to contain a phrase that will make invitees believe the content and experience of membership will be of major interest and benefit to them. Avoid overtly branding your LinkedIn group as your company's group, as this isn't inclusive and will have the effect of turning off potential members who'll see through it as a sales exercise and as a result will give it a wide berth.

- Ensure that you or someone high-profile within your company or organization takes on the 'owner' or 'moderator' role for the group. This is a figurehead position but doesn't necessitate that the owner or moderator does all (or any) of the work.

- Ensure the group description acts also as a 'welcome' message, is informative and clearly describes the benefits to LinkedIn members of their participation.

- Pre-load between two and four 'discussions' on the appropriate section so there's already content for the members to comment on when they first enter the group. Make sure these discussion topics are relevant to the members, give them information, demonstrate your knowledge, know-how, insight and expertise, and encourage them to get involved.

- Once you've established the framework for the group, it's important to recruit members. Using the powerful search functionality on the platform, create a list of prospective group members. Make sure that you've thought about the guest list carefully. Ideally, members should have something in common with each other; they could work in the same sector or be at the same functional responsibility within companies and organizations within the same market segment.

- Invitations to join the group should come from the 'owner' and, if that's not you, perhaps you should volunteer to do this for him or her.

- Unless you're already connected to those whom you wish to invite to join your group, you will require an e-mail address in order to invite them to join, provided they are on LinkedIn.

Recommendations

This is the LinkedIn equivalent of 'word of mouth', and having genuine recommendations that add value in terms of what you actually delivered and what your key attributes are will be more valuable than bland recommendations that fail to tell a story as to why the person is recommending you.

Some commentators suggest that you should write your own recommendation, but that should be avoided in all but extreme cases, as this isn't a genuine recommendation and actually it will be transparent to those who know you that in fact you were the author of the words chosen – which could be damaging for your relationship and credibility with them. So don't do it!

General housekeeping

Keeping your 'status' up to date allows your contacts and connections to know what you're up to – LinkedIn has a very efficient way of transmitting your updates to all those you are linked to.

It's also useful to ask your current connections to make introductions to other members, which creates a multiplier effect. For example, if you've 30 connections and 20 of them introduce you to three new connections each, that has the power of tripling your total LinkedIn connections in one go!

Finally, always respond to all questions you receive from members as well as provide unsolicited 'answers' to questions posted by members seeking solutions to issues or problems. If you give the benefit of your expertise and experience, you'll be amazed how this can be repaid many times over – all because as a member of the community you helped another member and that in turn helps to build trust and reputation over the long term.

Twitter

In 2006, three Americans, one of them a vegan called Biz, had a 'daylong brainstorming session' and came up with the idea for Twitter. They called it Twitter because it means 'a short burst of inconsequential information' and 'chirps from birds'. Fast-forward to 2012 and 140 million people worldwide send 340 million tweets a day, and most of these tweets were sent via a mobile device or smartphone.

Twitter is direct, 'over-the-garden-fence' chit-chat with 140 million neighbours – from rock stars, film stars, politicians, hacks, fundamentalists and preachers to companies, organizations, business leaders, thought leaders, commentators and journalists plus the occasional sales and marketing guru.

'If Facebook and LinkedIn are the adults of the social media revolution, Twitter is still very much the teenager of the family', observes Heather Townsend.

It's true that, if you go looking for it, you'll stumble across a lot of content that's easily forgettable. However, at a face-to-face networking event, a lot of what's said is drivel and perhaps 10 per cent of what's said is relevant within a business context. Twitter isn't that different. That's because social interaction online mimics the way we behave as social animals when we're offline.

People don't like demanding, confrontational, face-to-face interactions. On the whole they prefer side-by-side, random interactions around gradually discovering things that they share in common. Routine, random, low-level interactions are the foundations for building trust and for creating a sense of community, free from political interference, propaganda, censorship and control.

Twitter also creates an environment of random interactions that's really conducive to meeting new people with shared attitudes, values, beliefs, perceptions and behaviours. From that perspective, it's a lively, engaging channel for online networking.

In many respects, Twitter is tribal, as it appeals to our tribal instincts in our desire to 'follow' a leader.

It's all too easy simply to dismiss Twitter as a 'fad' or as an 'irrelevancy' if all you do is associate it in your mind with what you had for breakfast yesterday. Yet it's spawned its own language, such as those who use the service being known as 'peeps' or 'tweeters', and of course all of this can appear mildly banal and even irritating depending on your point of view. But salespeople ignore Twitter at their peril. All these negative perceptions of Twitter belie its real strength as one of the most influential short-hand channels of communication on the planet.

Getting your message across in no more than 140 characters should be taught in every classroom, in every school in every country in the world – that takes skill and focus of thought and imagination, not just abbreviation. It's these abilities that are going to be increasingly in demand of a successful salesperson, as the attention span of customers and clients will get even shorter in the future.

Twitter subculture

Networking on Twitter is a subculture in its own right – you have 'followers', but not in the biblical or religious sense! Unless you choose to protect your tweets so that only people you have approved can read them, then everyone can see what you have to say. To succeed on Twitter, you need to show your whole personality and engage with the Twitter community as an individual, whereas LinkedIn expects professional rather than personal updates on its site.

Heather Townsend warns:

It's very easy to use Twitter ineffectively as a networking tool. Before you start tweeting, it's essential that you know what you are trying to achieve by being on Twitter. For example, if you want to build relationships with people with a desired market segment, you need to be actively looking to follow and engage with your desired customer segments on Twitter. It's very easy to get seduced into trying to build up a follower base fast. It's not the number of followers you have that counts; it's the number of engaged followers you have.

Many brand owners have found value in Twitter as a way to build awareness of their brands, products and services, as well as helping to drive traffic to their websites in order to boost sales.

To find out how engaged someone's follower base is, take a look at the number of lists that they've been included on. The higher the number of lists someone is included on, the greater the level of engagement within their follower base.

Twitter for profit

Some companies, such as Starbucks and footwear and apparel online retailer Zappos, have embraced Twitter so that it's become integrated into their culture.

Zappos (2012)

Not only does the company monitor and use Twitter for customer service and feedback, but its CEO Tony Hsieh encourages all employees to participate on Twitter to keep its followers posted on what's going on in the company. Of nearly 1,600 employees, more than 500 are on Twitter, and this is used both as an external communication channel and the unofficial company noticeboard. Tony Hsieh often responds personally to Twitter users if they tweet him about a particular issue or problem they need help with.

A dedicated microsite, http://tweetwall.apps.zappos.com, features Twitter searches for every brand Zappos sells, and collects tweets about Zappos and an amalgamation of every employee's tweets and profiles.

This openness with customers and employees has helped to give Zappos a unique competitive edge in its own market segment, as well as creating exceptionally high levels of loyalty amongst employees and customers alike. It's a lesson that many other brand owners should take heed of and follow, and has similarities to the way that the Grateful Dead rock group grew its worldwide fan base.

Twitterquette

The following rules of social etiquette on Twitter are worth bearing in mind the next time you're tempted to write a tweet or tweet your blog post:

1 *Don't over-tweet.* The number one reason to stop following someone is because the person tweets too often. It's just annoying when your timeline starts filling up with aimless tweets because someone is stuck on a train or at the airport, bored.

2 *Don't humble-brag.* Re-tweeting praise is the preserve of pond life – don't do it! The rest of the world frankly doesn't care, nor do peeps want their timelines cluttered with re-tweeting 'Loved the blog this week, you're a genius xxx'.

3 *Don't plug.* While e-mail dies a spam-induced death, so far Twitter remains a commercially light zone.

4 *Do have a picture, not an egg.* It's just bad manners not to have a picture of yourself on Twitter rather than the default blue egg icon. It sends the wrong message – that you wish to remain anonymous. Some peeps also think it's bad form to lurk, that is, to follow lots of people but never tweet yourself. It does sound creepy.

5 *Do remember that everyone can see what you're saying.* Therefore avoid saying anything that could raise even the slightest question mark over your integrity, your reputation, or what you get up to in the privacy of your bedroom. If it's salacious, you could find yourself trending on Twitter for all the wrong reasons!

6 *Don't make social or networking arrangements.* It's very annoying for your followers to find their timelines clogged with you arranging to meet a friend or business acquaintance (Shall we go for drink? – Which bar? – What time can you...? Zzz). Use direct messaging, text or even the mobile for such purposes.

7 *Don't tweet about stuff that makes you look as though you need to get a life.* If you're tweeting about washing the car on Sunday morning, then think again.

Facebook

The world's largest social network is set to top over 1 billion users by the end of 2012, but it hasn't been an easy ride. Partly bruised by the criticism of its management style, Facebook recently declared it was seeking to become 'easier to work with' for brand owners, a goal partly resting on striking a balance between consumer privacy – a major hot topic – and the insatiable appetite of brand owners in search of ever more detailed demographic and psychographic data about customers, clients and prospects.

Leaving aside the obvious social networking function that Facebook delivers to millions of people around the world, brand owners often question the business value of Facebook and actively stop employees from accessing the site for fear that no work would ever get done. As a result, the perception of many brand owners in the past was that Facebook wasn't for them. That's all about to change.

One of the powerful advantages of Facebook is its ability to engage on a one-to-one basis with your desired customers, clients, prospects and supporters. Admittedly, those brand owners that are B2C are more likely to want to use Facebook, whereas interactions that are B2B tend to be conducted more often than not on LinkedIn and Twitter. However, Facebook is fast evolving to address the opportunity for B2B brand owners to engage with their desired customer and client segments. For example, about 40 per cent of B2B brand owners acquire a customer or client by using Facebook.

Very often, B2B prospects will want to dig a bit deeper and find out what others are saying about you – good or bad! Facebook's open network allows people to see whom their peers are interacting with and what they're talking about at any given time, providing a highly useful pool of market and customer intelligence.

By asking questions, encouraging conversations, and creating personal engagement with your customers, clients and prospects, Facebook is an excellent networking tool allowing you to build relationships in a way that wasn't possible even a couple of years ago as a result of the vast amount of data it holds about its users.

As a permission-based sales and marketing platform, Facebook is one of the most powerful networking tools in the world. Facebook shouldn't be treated as a marketplace where you're looking to make a fast buck. It should be remembered that most people log on to Facebook to have fun and connect with friends. Interacting with brands and organizations isn't the primary reason for visiting Facebook each day. However, that doesn't mean that users aren't a captive audience or capable of wanting to make a purchase of a product or service whilst at the same time hanging out with friends on the Facebook site.

Red Bull (2012)

This brand owner understands how to connect with its customers and fans without boring them into submission or bombarding them with sales and marketing messages and blatant advertising. Red Bull is the expert in creating experiences around its audience's desires and interests, and its Facebook page offers custom apps for download as well as unique content that in turn has become a hallmark of the brand. For example, its 'Procrastination Station' is a series of online games for fans, who now have a reason to return to the site again and again, which helps to turn them into brand advocates with a high degree of customer loyalty compared with other Facebook users, which will translate into recommendations and incremental sales.

A key feature about Facebook is its flexibility, and its business pages now look much more professional for the audience it is trying to appeal to.

As in face-to-face networking, Facebook places a high importance on getting up close and personal. A method to achieve this is to ask fans questions as well as reward them for their time. In short, Facebook networking is all about taking part and getting your fans to take action by posting a comment on your wall and clicking the 'like' button next to your post or content so that others may pay a visit too. This may sound straightforward, but it's not child's play. It takes dedicated hard work and effort to update content constantly and show up daily in order to engage with your fans.

Some of the most successful brand owners on Facebook, such as Zappos and Amazon, provide an opportunity for fans to share photos and talk about their likes and dislikes, as well as send messages to each other, rather than create a site as a showcase for flogging their products. But if people do buy a product, then they encourage them to talk about it, making word-of-mouth advocacy part of the Facebook experience and integral to the way the brand owners network with their customers.

In order to maximize the value of the social networking power of Facebook, the following tips will help steer you in the right direction:

1 *Manage your presence on Facebook carefully.* Avoid corporate-speak or overt selling. Think of it as a community of like-minded people whom you want to hang out with. Use colloquial rather than formal language and ensure that your tone of voice is friendly – this is really important. Be open to listening to others, so asking for opinions, thoughts and ideas is the right direction to go in.

2 *Refresh content and don't let your site go stale.* Facebook may look relatively straightforward, but it will consume a vast amount of time and energy to keep it updated and fresh. Be prepared to maintain it; otherwise you'll find you won't have many friends left at the end of the week.

3 *Make your site less about what you want to say and more about what your fans want to talk about.* Facebook can be one of the most valuable instantaneous market research tools available – and it's free! Don't feel afraid to solicit opinions. You won't agree with everyone but

you'll earn respect and enhance your reputation by being prepared to listen to comments – good or bad.

4 *As with all good sales activities, create consistent 'calls to action'.* Get your fans to take action by offering prizes, promotions, discounts or competitions or ask them to sign up for a newsletter – all of this is valuable networking time and allows you to communicate with them in the future on an ongoing and consistent basis.

5 *Encourage word-of-mouth advocacy.* It's very important to make it easy for your fans to talk about you by asking them to share your content, getting them to engage in competitions, promotions and other special events and, as we've said earlier, making the experience on your Facebook page more about them and less about you.

6 *Be generous.* Take the position of facilitator or 'host', where you actively encourage your visitors to exchange thoughts, ideas and information that are of benefit and value to the community you are appealing to rather than having some ulterior commercial motive.

7 *Be street-wise.* Treat your Facebook page as a mini-site of your own website. The key is to create a presence on Facebook that sparks familiarity with your brand when your existing customers or clients visit your page.

8 *Keep a clear set of objectives at the front of your mind.* You must decide why you are on Facebook in the first place. When you understand the 'why' it's much easier to understand the 'how'; otherwise you could stumble around and in fact lose sight of the purpose for all of this activity in the first place.

9 *Measure and evaluate.* There needs to be a sense of effort versus reward, so don't treat Facebook any differently from how you would treat any other aspect of a sales and marketing campaign. There are plenty of free tools that you can use that'll deliver the metrics you need in order to manage your presence on Facebook. Use them!

10 *Think of Facebook as part of your networking mix.* Remember to integrate offline networking with online networking. Both need the same love and attention, so don't neglect one in favour of the other.

And remember – this should be a natural and enjoyable experience, so don't be tempted to over-analyse everything you do on Facebook. Just do it.

References

Books

Fisk, P (2009) *Customer Genius*, Capstone
Kahneman, D (2011) *Thinking, Fast and Slow*, Allen Lane

Schaffer, N (2009) *Understanding, Leveraging and Maximizing LinkedIn*, Windmill Marketing
Townsend, H (2011) *Business Networking*, FT Prentice Hall

Articles

Bolger, M (2012) Early adopters, *Marketer Magazine*, July/August
Bughin, J, Doogan, J and Vetvik, OJ (2010) A new way to measure word-of-mouth marketing, *McKinsey Quarterly Review*, April
Kumar, V, Petersen, JA and Leone, R (2007) How valuable is word of mouth?, *Harvard Business Review*, October

Reports

Guide to Getting Quality Client Feedback for Your Firm (2012) Kaleidoscope Marketing
The ROI of Energizing Brand Advocates (2010) Zuberance Report

Websites

A US social networking site for working and sharing content that works on a question-and-answer format: http://www.quora.com (accessed 28 July 2012)
Baby massage, yoga and pre-school retailer: http://www.mamababybliss.com (accessed 10 July 2012)
Become a friend of Ardi Kolah on Facebook: https://www.facebook.com/ardi.kolah (accessed 28 July 2012)
Follow Ardi Kolah on Twitter: https://twitter.com/ardikolah (accessed 28 July 2012)
Google+ is another social networking site: https://plus.google.com (accessed 28 July 2012)
LinkedIn is one of the world's leading B2B networking platforms: http://www.linkedin.com (accessed 28 July 2012)
Online retailer Zappos has embraced Twitter: http://twitter.zappos.com/employees (accessed 27 July 2012)
The UK's biggest parenting website: http://www.netmums.com (accessed 10 July 2012)
The US-based Word of Mouth Marketing Association (WOMMA) provides its members with best-practice guidance and advice: http://womma.org (accessed 10 July 2012)
The world's largest micro-blogging site is a hybrid of Twitter and Facebook and has more than 300 million registered users: http://www.weibo.com (accessed 10 July 2012)
The Young Presidents' Organization (YPO) is one of the most influential face-to-face business networks: http://www.ypo.org (accessed 10 July 2012)
US-based brand advocacy experts in the field of word-of-mouth marketing and research: http://www.zuberance.com (accessed 10 July 2012)

"No more calls please – I can't believe the lengths some sales people will go to grab my attention!"

How to get senior-level appointments in your diary

Introduction

No salesperson is ever short of prospects. You can buy lists or even trawl through the phone book (definitely not recommended!), but turning these names into actual sales is a completely different matter. You might as well walk around New York's Times Square and accost the first person you meet on the off-chance that he or she would be interested in buying what you have in your suitcase. Well, don't be surprised if that doesn't work.

Making appointments with key decision makers isn't a random exercise like picking the lucky numbers for a national lottery. Success is dependent on doing your homework.

Doing your homework

As discussed in Chapter 2, preparation and planning can make the difference between success and failure.

The art of prospecting and getting appointments with key decision makers is about having a funnel of qualified leads, excluding no-hopers, and only approaching those actually in a position to buy your service or product. It's about being ruthless in qualifying in and qualifying out and only focusing resources where there's a good chance of achieving a sales outcome, as discussed in Chapter 10.

However, it's not all plain sailing, and securing an initial senior-level appointment in your diary can be subject to a number of other factors, including:

- how easy or complicated it is to sell the product or service in the first place;
- the time it takes for implementing the solution;
- the time it takes for delivering the physical product; and
- the timescale that's important to the customer, client or prospect and whether this can be met.

All of these have an influence on the outcome of the initial sales appointment, as the inability to meet the expectations of the customer, client or prospect won't result in a sale, no matter how well the initial meeting went. This is why doing your homework is so important. And, if all of that wasn't enough and you're confident you can meet every detailed requirement, there's still no guarantee that a carefully crafted pitch will convert a prospect into a customer or client.

Although it's often said that 'A pitch is the hinge on which the door opens' – and if you've ever watched television's *Dragons' Den* then you'll know exactly how important a 'perfect pitch' can be – it's not the whole story. In many sales situations it's unlikely that you will have met the person you're doing business with unless he or she is an existing customer or client.

It's worth remembering that, although you may be ready to sell, you do not know whether the customer, client or prospect is ready to buy. This is worth considering before you push ahead on your sales mission.

If timing is an issue – and it could be as simple as the budget planning cycle of the company or organization – don't give up before you've even begun. Just because a purchase order isn't signed off as a result of all the hard work you've put into the early stages of the sales process it doesn't follow it won't ever happen. It could happen in six days, six weeks or six months. It depends on whether this is a significant-value contract or one that can be signed off relatively simply. Bear in mind that many companies and organizations employ procurement and purchasing professionals, which can add a layer of complexity to the sales process.

When you weigh all this up, getting that first appointment with a key decision maker is a very important first step in the journey to closing a sale.

As discussed in Chapter 3, a lot depends on your ability to be in 'receive mode' rather than 'transmit mode'.

Ask any experienced salespeople what the key is to a successful sale and they'll say it's creating a good first impression. Making an impact within a minute can open the door to the rest of the sales process. If you come over badly, the door can be slammed in your face and you may not be invited back.

A golden rule is to approach customers, clients or prospects with the intention of finding out as much as you can about them, such as their needs and requirements, as well as their attitudes, values, beliefs, perceptions and, ultimately, purchasing behaviour. Yet landing a senior-level appointment presents something of a stumbling block for so many salespeople, who could be much more successful if they were better at doing this.

Let's be clear. Success in getting a senior-level appointment has nothing to do with luck and everything to do with the approach you choose to adopt, as well as meticulous planning and attention to detail. This chapter explains tried and tested appointment strategies that will achieve a first appointment as well as subsequent meetings that may be required in order to get the customer, client or prospect 'over the line'.

The good news is that it's completely in your power to achieve a significantly improved 'strike rate' for securing first appointments with key decision makers that'll have a major impact on your ability to close a sale. Irrespective of whether you're a small, medium or large company or organization, the same principles apply.

The basic etiquette of making an appointment

Out of all the challenges that sales professionals and business owners face, one of the toughest is getting a face-to-face appointment with customers, clients or prospects. We all know that, once we're in front of customers, clients or prospects, we'll have something valuable to share with them, so it's about getting to first base.

The reality is that you'll never get a chance to work your magic as frequently as you would wish unless you can figure out a way to increase the chances of securing a first appointment with a decision maker. And 9 out of 10 times that means getting past a gatekeeper in order to reach a key decision maker (see below). Cold callers are used to dealing with gatekeepers – around 45 per cent of all cold calls are answered by a switchboard receptionist. Where there's a direct-dial telephone number, it's likely that you'll get the voicemail of the person you're trying to contact – this applies to a further 45 per cent of all calls. So that leaves just 10 per cent of all calls made being answered by the person you intend to speak to – and this doesn't leave any room for a margin of error.

How to have a successful blind date

In the words of US singer-songwriter Billy Joel:

> *Get it right the first time. That's the main thing. I can't afford to let it pass. Get it right the next time. That's not the same thing. Gonna make the first time last. I'm not much good at conversation. I never was much good at comin' on real strong. If all it takes is inspiration, then I might have just what it takes. If I don't make no bad mistakes.*

Thanks, Billy.

Of course, Billy Joel was singing about being on a first date – but then so are you when you're trying to get that first important appointment with a key decision maker whom you've never met! Comparing your pitch for a first meeting to a blind date may seem far-fetched, but it reinforces the point that the day of the 'hard sell' is firmly in the past and, as we've said throughout this book, selling is now much more a people business.

Hang-up risk

A common pitfall is to launch straight into a prepared script with the intention of getting an appointment in the diary, particularly if this is done on the phone. The reason is that a key decision maker will always be able to tell whether the person on the other end of the phone is reading from a script – and if you're reading, then you're not listening. That's a disaster and it won't work. The other person will hang up.

Customers, clients and prospects are much more sophisticated in their purchasing now. They don't like the 'hard sell'. You have to involve them in the process: ask questions, establish their real needs and then 'pitch' in terms of the benefit you can offer and how you can meet those needs.

Politeness always pays

It's always polite to ask 'Are you in the middle of something?' as well as asking 'And is this a good time?' The fact that you've demonstrated politeness and consideration for the other person creates a positive atmosphere, and it's much more likely that you'll be invited to make another call if it's not convenient right now.

There are other advantages, too. If the decision maker picks up the call and he or she is in the middle of an internal meeting – which can often be the case – then taking such an approach also avoids the potential embarrassment and irritation that can so easily be caused when someone's least expecting a call from a sales rep.

Sadly, thoughtfulness is often lacking when it comes to cold callers, who for the most part read from a prepared sales script in the vain hope that the other person will submit to their will and agree to a meeting. Yeah, right. Whoever told them making appointments with key decision makers was a 'numbers game' needs to think again. It isn't.

Such an approach – if still practised – is reminiscent of how timeshares were marketed in the late 1990s. The cold caller would offer the prospect some 'high-value gift' as a thank-you for making an appointment to attend the timeshare presentation. In some cases, this could be a free flight for two people to the timeshare location, where the couple are expected to sit through a cheesy film presentation as part of the terms of accepting the high-value gift or risk having to pay back the cost of the free flights. Such high-pressure tactics have long been abandoned and are a million miles from taking the trouble to listen actively to prospects as opposed to holding a metaphorical gun to their head. It's the former that's likely to yield superior results. The latter simply doesn't work and in any case may now fall foul of anti-bribery and corruption legislation in many jurisdictions.

For a discussion on the provision of hospitality and its legal implications, refer to Guru in a Bottle®'s *Essential Law for Marketers* (2nd edition).

The 'perfect pitch' requires prior preparation in order to avoid poor performance. Getting an appointment in the diary after an initial telephone conversation allows for the conversation to continue. For the conversation to take place in the first instance, you must be prepared to listen.

What's keeping them awake at night?

If the hot prospect has landed in your lap through a recommendation from another customer or client, then you may be able to share the issues, challenges and problems faced by others and how they overcame these if it's relevant to the conversation and in order to land the face-to-face appointment with this prospect.

One technique to ensure you 'get it right the first time' is to attribute a score for every attribute that makes a promising customer, client or prospect, sometimes referred to as 'lead scoring'. One of the top indicators is the source of the lead, as in the above example. If the prospect name is taken from a purchased list, it scores zero, but if the prospect has been recommended to you then it scores maximum points.

Don't denigrate or criticize their decision to go with another provider

A fair assumption to make is that prospects are very comfortable with the product or service they are using right now, so rather than trying to run down the competition why not enquire gently why customers or clients feel it works. What's good about the product or service they currently use, and what would it take for them to consider changing their mind? In this way, it's about qualifying a future sales opportunity and getting a rough timescale for doing so.

Try to avoid relying on price as the main point of differentiation between your product and service and that of the incumbent provider. Price may be relevant for any future sale, but it may not be the only significant factor in the decision-making process. Taking such an approach can assist in building a dialogue and also shows that you're solutions driven.

Stick with the facts, create a narrative and avoid the temptation to 'sell'. If hot prospects relate to the story, they'll definitely want to talk to you further.

The above is a good example of not selling the product or service, but 'selling' yourself, and increasingly this is much more important than the standard features of a product or service.

For a further discussion on this point, see Chapter 1.

A common thread running through all of the above approaches is that none of them are dependent on a prepared 'sales script', and the hard work starts before you get to 'pitch' for an appointment.

You have to really know your customers, clients or prospects: what their business is like and where they stand in relation to their own competitor set or peer group. Information on their personal background helps too.

As we discuss later in this chapter, you should have a look at LinkedIn, Facebook and other networking sites that are popular in your country. Here you'll find a lot of information about the individuals you may be pitching to – even things about their hobbies and interests. It's all interesting stuff. You need to start to build a dialogue with them if you're to sell to them, and so this information is extremely useful in that regard.

Find the common ground

Wherever possible, it's always a good idea to find some common ground. Perhaps the approach to the hot prospect had been suggested by another customer or client as a result of the benefits and service that person had received. Alternatively, career background, professional associations and interests can be vital clues in how to approach people.

It's far better to have done your homework on each individual prospect before you pick up the phone if you want to land a senior-level appointment. And that's the point. It's a senior-level appointment you're after. The more you know and understand the better.

It's also very important that the initial telephone call is short and you get to the point very quickly.

Provided you've done your homework, the conversation should allow customers, clients or prospects to initiate the idea of meeting if what they hear strikes a chord with them. It's worth recalling the old adage that 'time is money', so there needs to be a compelling reason why customers, clients or prospects would want to agree to a meeting. You need to listen, interpret, evaluate and then respond rather than jumping in before they've had a chance to impart vital clues that you can pick up on in order to land the appointment.

Your place or mine?

When making a face-to-face appointment with senior decision makers, it's important to accommodate them and their diary – after all, at this stage of the process, their time is more valuable to you than your own – so make it easy for them to say 'yes'. That may mean meeting them at their office or premises or, if more convenient, at an airport terminal, where they may have time to squeeze in a meeting before taking a flight.

It's also vital to find out beforehand who else is likely to be at that initial meeting. For example, if the finance director is likely to be present, then you'll need to focus on the cost of your product or service a bit more and conversely, if the operations director is there, you'll need to focus on other technical issues such as usability and logistics, where relevant.

It's important to set out an agenda, but also let the customer, client or prospect feel involved. It's always a good idea to give case studies that demonstrate the value of the product or service being offered, and also allow a reasonable time for questions and for dealing with objections.

For further guidance on how to make an effective sales presentation, see Chapter 6.

Expect at least 30 per cent of all appointments you make to get moved, postponed indefinitely or even cancelled. This is a typical attrition rate for salespeople and shouldn't be taken personally!

If you've made the appointment for the face-to-face meeting by calling the hot prospect, then don't forget to thank the person for his or her time and say that you'll follow up with a short confirmation e-mail of the points discussed and the agreed date and time of the face-to-face appointment and will also double-check nearer the time to ensure that it's still convenient to keep that appointment. Also invite the prospect to send any additional information or clarification that came up during the call, which can help the chances of the initial face-to-face appointment being successful.

Being courteous and well-mannered throughout the interaction with a customer, client or prospect goes a very long way to establishing you as a professional salesperson, and as a consequence you'll see an improvement in your personal strike rate for closing sales.

If you want to get more appointments with key decision makers, then you need to start setting appointment goals based on identifying the appropriate decision maker in each company or organization that may be interested in buying your product or service.

Identifying the appropriate decision maker

When it comes to making a pitch, it's important to establish that a lead is qualified and that you're talking to the appropriate decision maker – usually the one who pays the bills or can authorize the expenditure you seek from the company or organization.

Job titles

The job title of the appropriate decision maker can vary depending on the type of product or service that you're selling. You may have an inclination to go to the top floor to look for the decision maker, but that may not always be the best strategy. You could be looking in the wrong place! While the president, chief executive, managing director or owner typically oversees the entire company or organization, it doesn't mean that this person is the most appropriate person for you to pitch to. For example, if you're selling office supplies, then the senior decision maker that you're looking for is unlikely to be the CEO but rather the office or operations manager.

If you pitch to the wrong people, don't rely on them passing on the word to one of their colleagues. This isn't likely to happen and in any event, even if your business card was passed on, it's unlikely that the other colleague will call you for a follow-up meeting. It's always preferable that you get the details of the appropriate decision maker and make use of the fact that you've met this person's colleague and would now like to follow up with the decision maker based on a deeper understanding of his or her needs and requirements.

Pitching to the wrong person is guaranteed to decrease dramatically your likelihood of making the sale, so don't do it. The key is to find out who the appropriate decision maker is for your product and service and pitch to that person.

Check the website

When going after hot prospects it's important to do your homework to identify the key decision maker. It's surprising how much information can be gleaned through a Google search, the company or organization's website and also appointment tools like LinkedIn.

Start with the customer, client or prospect's website. There's generally a page that lists the key leaders and decision makers in the company or organization. You can often get the name and title of the person who would be responsible for the department that you need to speak with. In some instances, you can also get an e-mail address and/or telephone number to make an introduction prior to your pitch. If you can't locate the name and details of the appropriate person you need to pitch to, then you may need to take another route.

News releases

A good secondary source of information is a company or organization's news releases. For example, if you're approaching a company or organization because it's just started a project for which your product or service would be a perfect fit, then there's usually a quote from the person responsible for heading up that project in a news release that can be found on its website. Even if this person ends up not being the key senior decision maker you need to track down, it's a good starting point.

Don't check – double-check

When you think you have the appropriate decision maker in your sights, take a minute to determine that you truly have the right person. During your first contact with the appropriate decision maker, try to establish answers to the following questions:

- Does the person control the purse strings of the relevant budget?
- Does the person make the purchasing decisions for these types of products and services?
- Who else might need to be involved in the decision-making process?
- What's the internal process for sign-off on such agreements?

Based on these inputs, you should be able to establish if you've reached the right decision maker or whether you need to find another person within the company or organization.

For decision makers in large companies and organizations, a personal referral or recommendation can be very powerful, which is why LinkedIn can be so effective in achieving an appointment with a key decision maker. You'll be surprised when you use LinkedIn at how often you do have a common contact who'd be willing to introduce you.

When in doubt, a good rule of thumb is that it's easier to get buy-in going down the food chain rather than getting sign-off from the top. However, through the entire vetting process, one thing to be cognizant of is that decisions are rarely made in a vacuum. Lower-tier managers may play a vital role as key influencers to the ultimate decision maker. For this reason, treat everyone whom you approach in the appointment journey as being important in helping you achieve your goal.

Once you establish the decision maker for your deal, you'll be well on your way to closing that sale!

Don't be short-term in outlook

US venture capitalist Carol Roth, who's worked with entrepreneurs and multinational companies to raise more than US$1 billion in capital, advises salespeople to switch from short-term goals of pitching a product or service to establishing a relationship with the prospect. She says:

> *Purely transactional business is a bit passé. To initiate that relationship with the decision maker, get introduced through a shared connection. It will lend credibility to help bridge that initial trust gap, plus move you to the 'top of the pile' so the decision maker gets back to you more promptly. You can check LinkedIn to see if you have a relevant connection or ask around in your professional alumni, personal and social networks to find someone who can provide that critical introduction.*

Voicemails and e-mails

Other sales gurus advocate sending a series of e-mails and voicemails to a key decision maker inviting a meeting focused on the business outcomes that will flow from using your product or service. These messages should pique the interest and curiosity of the key decision maker, particularly if you offer to share the results that similar customers and clients have achieved by working with you. It also demonstrates that you've done your homework and are not wasting time trying to offer a product or service that won't be vaguely relevant.

'Decision makers are busy people with their own goals and problems. Getting to know their situation before you approach them is critical to having a context in which to listen', adds Liz Strauss, a US blogger on business strategy and selling. She advises that, rather than chasing 500 decision makers, it's preferable to identify five key decision makers and get to know their business before you approach them. She says:

> *Meet someone who knows the decision maker to find out the venue in which the person most likes to consider new sales offers. Turn your pitch into an invitation. Suggest a way that you might meet or talk for a limited time (15 minutes) to see how your offer can move the decision maker to achieving their end goal. Then listen.*

Following such an approach will navigate around the potential barrier that a key decision maker can put up about having an initial sales meeting. Some commentators label this 'consultative selling', but in reality it's all about listening, building rapport and establishing trust and credibility. The selling of a service or product comes next, when this has been established.

Building rapport with a key decision maker can take place by e-mail, phone, video-chat or face to face – the key is to use a multifaceted strategy that works for that person's preference of communication.

'You should first develop relationships via the internet and social media and then you really have a valid reason for your call', advises British telesales guru Sean McPheat. The time of day could be important too. If the key decision maker is an entrepreneur, then a phone call before 7.30 am, at noon, or after 5.30 pm may be appropriate, as many business owners work longer hours than normal.

Getting past the gatekeeper

Key decision makers are unlikely to be acting on their own and will rely on colleagues in the management of their responsibilities. These can range from the receptionist on the switchboard through to an assistant or a deputy of the function. This is to be expected. You need to be consistent in being courteous to the gatekeeper – after all, gatekeepers have been given their instructions, and they're doing their job by being the person between you and the key decision maker.

Often, you won't be able to get a direct line or even an e-mail address, but don't let that put you off. Try to be helpful by understanding these are the protocols, but provide cogent reasons why you feel it would be advantageous to get to speak to the boss and seek guidance as to how best to get some information across to that person.

Alternatively, suggest that you can call back at a different time of the day if that's more suitable. Very often, key decision makers like to start work early in the morning and will often answer the phone if they are in the office at say 7.30 am. If you're getting nowhere in being put through, try calling early in the morning – it's also impressive that you are at your desk and ready to do business.

Another strategy is to think of inviting the key decision maker to some type of invitation-only event where a small group of key decision makers will also be present. This could be a breakfast briefing with an eminent speaker, for example. If the subject and invitees are of interest, this will increase the chances of the message getting through the gatekeeper and to the decision maker, as well as improving the chances that the decision maker will attend.

Leaving a message for key decision makers is always a possibility, but probably the last resort, because if they feel it's a sales call they won't bother returning it and will assume that you'll behave like a dog with a bone and chase them for another telephone conversation.

Tools to get appointments – LinkedIn

The fact remains that, unless you're able to connect with the decision maker, then despite however many assistants and receptionists you may end up speaking to, your sales efforts may not come to anything.

In Chapter 8, we discussed how to use LinkedIn to ask for and drive referrals, but it's also an excellent tool in getting sales appointments with key decision makers.

Don't forget to manage your own profile

There's no point in prospecting for customers or clients unless your own public profile is up to date and gives a positive account of your career history, experience and expertise. Given that LinkedIn is probably one of the best business-to-business (B2B) networks in the world, whilst you can check out key decision makers' profiles they can check you out too.

Something as small as an up-to-date photograph can make all the difference – and not having a photograph on your LinkedIn profile can send an un-intentional cue such as making you appear as if you have something to hide. Putting a face to a name is particularly important within the online social network environment, as it can often provide reassurance to someone who, frankly, doesn't know you from Adam but can see from your photo that you may be someone he or she feels comfortable doing business with. A lot of people are reluctant to post a photo of themselves but on balance you'll be at a disadvantage if the box where your picture should be is simply a grey head-and-shoulders stock image.

Whatever happened to your 'personal brand'? LinkedIn gives you the golden opportunity to project your personal brand in more interesting and engaging ways than an advertisement in the local newspaper or *Yellow Pages* ever can. And the best bit is it's free. If you blog, LinkedIn can provide you with the opportunity to import your articles to your profile, and it can allow you to get followers from Twitter to connect with you on LinkedIn, to speak publicly through discussion groups, to project yourself, your expertise and your business, and to build a network.

Check out what information there is on the company or organization the key decision maker works for

Companies and organizations tend to want to manage their profiles on LinkedIn very carefully. With large organizations, vast numbers of employees will use LinkedIn as a way of keeping in touch, so the profile of the company or organization tends to be kept up to date.

If you're trying to reach a key decision maker, first check the company profile page. This is an excellent starting point, as not only do you see who works for the company or organization you're interested in doing business with but you can also check out individual profiles. The immediate benefit is that you'll instantly see if someone in your own network has a connection with the company or indeed an individual – it may be with the key decision maker or someone else in the company or organization.

If you have the good fortune to know someone who's also connected with the key decision maker, then you can send an InMail to your own contact and seek advice as to the best way to reach the key decision maker as well as get introduced to that person. It immediately implies that you are a trustworthy individual and worth speaking to if someone who knows the key decision maker is prepared to make the introduction.

Using Advanced Search

This is a very useful utility of LinkedIn, and the specific name of the key decision maker can reveal a lot of detailed information, as well as whether someone in your network has a link to this individual. Rather than trying to connect with the key decision maker first off, it's preferable to use your own personal contact to help make the introduction by sending an InMail asking the person to do this for you.

Where your own network is connected to someone other than the key decision maker you're wanting to reach, then it's all right to request your network contact to get in touch with his or her contact to help make an introduction to the key decision maker on your behalf.

Reading and following recommendations made by the key decision maker

This is a minor treasure trove of information – it may list people you know but didn't realize had a commercial relationship with the decision maker you're trying to reach, or indeed it may reveal that some of your competitors have got there first. Either way, there could be vital clues as to what the key decision maker rates as excellent in terms of individual qualities he or she might be seeking in a supplier.

Having harvested this insight, you should consider contacting someone who's in a similar position to the key decision maker you're trying to reach and get that person to write a recommendation for you that when read could influence the opportunity to meet the senior decision maker.

Questions and answers

This is fascinating, as senior people like to feel they are able to help people by exercising their knowledge and experience to point people in the right direction. The senior-level decision maker could well be one of those people, so it's worth checking out his or her profile page and Q&A section, where you can see what questions the person has asked and also answered on LinkedIn.

There's nothing to stop you posting a question on a group page that you're a member of if you're seeking some insight into a particular organization and want some guidance as to whom to contact and how best to approach the person to secure an appointment. The LinkedIn community has professional groups that you should join, where you can exchange information, ask questions and even collaborate or find a business or organization that could use your services and would be prepared to meet to discuss their needs and requirements.

Creating a discussion on LinkedIn

This is a great way to open a dialogue about a problem, issue or challenge that many key decision makers may be grappling with right now, such as how to manage employees' motivation in an economic downturn. You may be able to help, as you could run a motivation and training company that uses leadership and motivation games in order to encourage team work and loyalty – something that could be under threat within the company or organization you feel able to help.

By posting a simple question under the heading 'Managing morale in an economic downturn' you could ask group members what they do to manage the motivation of their employees in order to hear other perspectives and offer your own, and hopefully this will reach the key decision maker if he or she is part of the group, as the decision maker can follow the thread of the discussion on LinkedIn. This helps to position you as an expert in the field without screaming this from the roof tops.

If there's enough interest, you could create an evening event with a client with whom you're currently working, invite prospects to hear first-hand how such a situation was successfully managed and invite key decision makers to discuss their own challenges with you at separate one-to-one meetings.

A positive sign of success will be the number of connection requests you receive as a result of the above activities. If you're seeing a steady stream of connection requests, then you're well on your way to landing a senior-level appointment in your diary.

In summary, some key points to remember are:

- Regularly update your status on your LinkedIn profile and ensure that you have '100 per cent profile completeness' before you seek appointments with key decision makers.

- Ask your current connections to introduce you to their key decision maker contacts or those who know the key decision maker you want to reach. If you have 50 connections and 40 of them introduce you to two connections each, you'll have almost tripled your total connections in just one stroke.

- Join groups on LinkedIn in order to expand your network and increase the possibilities of being connected with a key decision maker.

- Do your homework and actively seek out company and organizational information, as well as individual profiles of key decision makers.
- Take part in discussions.
- Ask questions within discussion groups in order to engage, listen, evaluate and respond.

References

Books

Jarvis, J (2007) *85 Inspiring Ways to Market Your Small Business*, How To Books
Kolah, A (2013) *Essential Law for Marketers*, 2nd edn, Guru in a Bottle®, Kogan Page
Parkinson-Hardman, L (2010) *LinkedIn Made Easy*, Crystal Clear Books
Schiffman, S (1990) *The 25 Sales Habits of Highly Successful People*, Adams Media

Articles

Allen, M (2012) Sales 101: appointments: http://www.ezinearticles.com (accessed 24 June 2012)
Cannon, D (2011) Identifying the decision maker: who's in charge here?: http://www.ezinearticles.com (accessed 24 June 2012)
Gordon, A (2012) LinkedIn for business success: http://wwww.winningwork.com (accessed 24 June 2012)
James, C (2007) Scheduling the meeting: http://www.eyesonsales.com (accessed 24 June 2012)
Shanto, T (2012) Five proven ways to get more appointments: http://www.ezinearticles.com (accessed 24 June 2012)

"We've been closing down for two years -
it's the only way we can keep going"

Closing a sale and follow-up

Introduction

At the time of writing this book, a quick search for books about 'sales' on Amazon elicits 211,655 results, compared with 'marketing', which gets 190,344 results, perhaps reflecting the relative importance placed on selling stuff.

As you've read throughout this book, qualifying a prospective customer or client is a key selling skill for any business or enterprise, but the acid test is the ability to graduate the suspect into a prospect, from prospect into a strong lead, and then from a lead into a real opportunity leaving you to close the sale.

In any group of businesspeople – and this could be just about anywhere in the world – half will identify customer segmentation as the hardest thing they need to be able to do, and the other half of the room will identify closing a sale as the toughest part of their job.

Those who find segmentation difficult often complain that in many cases they are starting from a position of ignorance; they need to compile a list of prospects, then find out details of these companies such as size, market focus, specialism, needs, challenges or issues, as well as what makes them successful, and then track down the names of the right people within those businesses, all of which is a time-consuming and frustrating process.

Others in the same room won't agree that this is the stressful bit. Their view is that closing a sale only becomes hell when the prospect hasn't been properly qualified. Contrary to the first group, they take a methodical approach and are persistent and even creative in how they qualify leads. The challenge for them is in understanding the psychology of the buyers, of putting pressure on them, and themselves in the process, and asking for money – ironically, something that not all salespeople are good at doing.

In an ideal world, quantifying and closing a sale should be a seamless process. It's often observed that good salespeople begin by making small closes as soon as they engage with customers, not to get them to pay money at the earliest opportunity but to build trust and dialogue with them, when the chances of closing a sale are dramatically improved.

So why do businesspeople struggle to close a sale? One answer lies in the way we are wired. The fear of rejection is deep rooted in all of us, from birth in fact. A newborn baby is programmed to do everything it can in order to be accepted by its parents. It's a matter of survival for the baby that it's not rejected by its mother, and this primeval fear is in our subconscious for the rest of our lives. What happens as we grow older is that the fear of rejection transforms itself into fear of failure. It's something successful entrepreneurs often point to as the biggest motivating factor for them in business.

Yet fear of failure also creates a psychological barrier for many people in that it frightens them from even asking prospective customers or clients whether they'd like to buy the product or service. In the UK, we put this down to being a 'British thing', as talking about money and stuff like that makes us feel uncomfortable, even awkward, whereas Americans are brilliant at selling, aren't they? They don't have any inhibitions whatsoever when it comes to wanting us to open our wallets.

Well, that's complete nonsense. The ability to close a sale isn't dependent on where you happen to work in the world. You respond to those situations according to the map of the world you hold in your head. The map is based on what you believe about your identity and on your values, attitudes, beliefs and behaviours, as well as your memories and cultural background. It's complicated and contradictory. Sometimes our map of the world makes no sense to us.

Successful salespeople tend not to be afraid of failure or waylaid by undesirable results. Instead they tend to learn the lessons from setbacks, pick themselves up, dust themselves down and have another go. And everyone's capable of doing the same. Let's face it: can you imagine a world where you gave up learning to walk simply because you fell over the first time you tried it?

Take Thomas Edison as the grown-up example of this phenomenon. Although he's famous for inventing the light bulb, he had less successful ideas in the course of his lifetime too. His genius lay in trying out ideas, learning from unexpected results and recycling concepts from an experiment that didn't work in other inventions. Where others saw his thousands of attempts at inventing the light bulb as failure, Thomas Edison saw these attempts as new learning experiences that ultimately took him closer to a successful outcome. So take a leaf out of his book; you need to stop worrying about failure, as this keeps you focused on the past. If you examine the results you've already got, even if you've been unsuccessful in closing a sale, you can learn a lot from this, shift your focus to possibilities and move forward to achieving a successful outcome. This is what will help you close that sale – or even get that dream job you've always wanted.

You've one chance to make a good first impression

Trying to convince or cajole people to do something they may or may not want to do won't always be successful.

'The first thing you should do is stop selling. Selling is about the seller. It focuses on you and what you need. If you're thinking about what you need to do next to make the sale, you won't be focusing on your customer', says US entrepreneur and business guru Michael Gerber.

Closing a sale starts at the beginning of the transaction, when you first make contact with your prospect. If you're weak on making that initial contact, on qualifying or handling objections, on presentations or on any other aspect of the sales process, then you're unlikely to be effective.

First impressions last, and from the moment you approach or talk to a prospect the selling begins. If the relationship starts off badly, turning it around at the end in a 'closing' style will be hard if not impossible. It takes time, effort and practice in order to improve your success rate at closing a sale. And, as in the movies, a perfect ending needs a perfect beginning.

When looking to make a good first impression, remember to do four simple things:

- *Focus on the outcome*. It's important to understand precisely what it is you are trying to achieve. This chapter will help you do just that.

- *Be proactive.* Unless you take the first step and then the following ones, nothing will happen to help you towards that outcome, no matter how clearly defined it may be.

- *Borrow from neurolinguistic programming (NLP).* If you have the awareness to see, hear and feel what isn't working, you can modify your behaviour to steer you towards the desired outcome.

- *Maintain behavioural flexibility.* In interactions amongst people, whether in a business or a social context, the person with the most flexibility of behaviour can control the interaction.

When you make a sale you don't always create a customer or client. Selling has a short horizon and focuses on a single transaction. However, a customer isn't or at least shouldn't be a one-night stand – well, at least the customer you want. Depending on your business, your contact with your customer may be fleeting or prolonged, daily or irregular, but when customers have a need for your product or service you want them to come to you, not your competitor. You want and seek a relationship, and in the vast majority of cases that's what your customers and clients are looking for – the confidence to trust you.

'The help they need to make the right purchase decisions for themselves will come from you. At least, they hope it will. It's your job to make them believers – to convert their interest and hope into the conviction that you can give them what they need', observes Michael Gerber.

It's about selling the advantages of cooperation rather than demanding it that will help close a sale.

- You close prospective customers or clients by helping them to be open to you personally as well as your ideas.
- You close them on arranging a time to meet that's convenient for them.
- You close them on allowing them to answer your questions on their business.
- You close them on your product or service during your presentation.
- You close them on the answers you give in response to their questions and concerns.
- You close them by making it easy to do business with you.

Asking for what you want

It may sound stupid, but many sales simply don't get done because the customer or client wasn't asked to sign on the dotted line. All too often, salespeople will assume that all they have to do is turn up, demonstrate the benefits of a product or service and answer any questions or objections that may arise.

Making an assumption that the sale will automatically follow is a wrong assumption. There are a number of strategies that you can employ to assess the prospect's level of interest, which will help you gauge when the moment is ripe for closing the sale.

Reading the signs

Excellent salespeople have an inbuilt antenna for detecting just when the right moment has arrived in order to attempt to close the sale. That's because they are constantly reading the signs – verbal and non-verbal.

Verbal signs

By listening to prospective customers or clients rather than being in 'transmit mode' you can quickly tell whether they are open to being closed, so to speak. A good indication of this is when they start to ask more pertinent questions or questions around how the product or service can help them achieve certain challenges, issues or problems they may have failed to tackle previously.

- Clarify your customers' or clients' needs by playing this back to them.
- Address any concerns that they may have with respect to the product or service.
- Make sure you take their point of view (POV) in determining the value of the product or service as a solution to their needs and requirements.
- Although you're ready to sell, you need to determine whether customers are ready to buy and whether they have the financial means to do so.

As a general rule of thumb, few people ask technical questions unless they're seriously thinking of buying a service or product – and it's a strong clue that it may be time to close.

Visual buying signs

Visual buying signs are often much more subtle than verbal signs, and you have to read people's body language to uncover what they really feel subconsciously, which they will find it difficult to mask. For example, take facial expressions. They can convey many different intentions and, because we learn to mask our facial expressions at an early age, anything you observe on the face should be compared with the non-verbal signs of the rest of the body.

Researchers have discovered that as much as 80 per cent or more of communication is non-verbal. Former FBI agent Joe Navarro says:

The face can reveal a great deal of information, but it can mislead. You need to look for clusters of behaviours, constantly evaluate what you see in its context and note whether the facial expression agrees or is in contrast to signals from other parts of the body. Only by performing all of these observations can you confidently validate your assessment of a person's emotions and intentions.

Knowing how to distinguish between comfort and discomfort will help you to focus on the most important behaviours for decoding non-verbal communications and assist you in deciding whether a prospective purchaser's body language is suggesting it's time to close that sale (Table 10.1).

Table 10.1 Interpreting body language

Body language	Technical term	Interpretation
Nostrils flaring	Nasal wing dilation	Known as an intention cue, as it gives away that the person is oxygenating in advance of taking some action.
Leaning away from you	Distancing	This is an age-old flight response where the person leans away from you subconsciously because he or she disagrees or feels uncomfortable.
Clasping of the knees and shifting of the weight on the feet	Intention cue	The person wants to get up and leave.
Crossed legs	Territorial imperative	Usually signals that a person is comfortable.
Interlocking of legs	Intention cue	Suggests discomfort or insecurity.
Leaning towards you	Mirroring and matching (isopraxis)	Suggests high comfort and agreement.
Crossed arms	Torso shield	If it happens in the course of a conversation it's likely to indicate discomfort.
Self-preening such as dusting off a sleeve or the collar of a jacket	Preening behaviour	Usually a sign of dismissiveness if done during a conversation.

For more guidance on non-verbal communication, see Chapter 6.

Over time, you'll be able to read people by noting their body language. Remember that decisions are made on an emotional basis, so asking an open question about how people feel about everything they've heard so far or discussed is a useful indicator for whether to close the sale.

Overcoming objections and concerns

It's unlikely that in attempting to close a sale you'll get an unqualified 'yes', although anything is possible. The more likely scenario is that prospects will raise some objections or concerns that you'll need to understand and respond to in order to convince them that these issues are totally solvable.

Objection-handling process

How you handle objections or concerns can make all the difference as to whether you close the sale or not. It pays to make sure you are equipped and prepared for any contingency within the sales process, so this last hurdle is in many respects the most important to get over.

Remember, objections can be transformed into an opportunity. For example, you can increase understanding of the other person's circumstances and get closer to him or her, building a more trusting relationship (Figure 10.1).

Figure 10.1 Objection-handling process

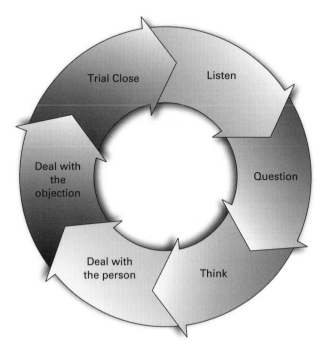

1 Listen

Stop. Don't try to jump in at the beginning – this may cause further objection. When you interrupt people, you are objecting to their concern. Before you can act on the objection, it helps a great deal if you can understand properly not only the objection but also the thought and emotion behind it.

Use active listening methods, nodding and physically showing interest. They're trying to tell you something that will help you sell to them, which is a gift from them to you. If you don't listen, then their next step may well be towards the door and you'll have lost the sale.

2 Question

Before you question, listen some more. Questions should elicit the background and detail of the objection or concern. Listen not only to the objection but to the emotion behind it. Seek to 'read between the lines'. The objection as stated may well be a cover for the real issue that's troubling them.

Where appropriate, it's all right to ask some questions. This not only shows you're listening and interested in what they have to say, but also gives you more information with which to make the sale. As you question them, watch carefully for body language that gives you more information about what they are thinking and feeling.

Remember that this isn't an interrogation, and that giving them the 'third degree' will turn them off, so keep your questions light and relevant. You might also tip the bucket at this time, asking them if there are any more concerns (ie objections) that they have. If you can resolve such concerns, you might gain a close. It's not always necessary to ask questions. Be deliberate about what you are doing if you do.

3 Think

Now, before you dive into objection handling, think before it's too late. What methods will work best with them? Should you take a direct and confrontational approach or should you use the soft-soap approach to finesse the situation? Or maybe you should put it off to another day – but only if you can be sure that you can return to the selling situation.

Thinking is a good thing, in that you are adding a little pause into the proceedings, which helps to demonstrate how you are taking their objections or concerns seriously.

Once you have discovered the objection, the next stage is to acknowledge not only the objection but the person too.

4 Deal with the person

It's important to accept the person. Accept that the person has a right to object. Accept that you've not fully understood the person. You don't do this by saying 'I accept you're right' or anything like this. The simplest way is through your attitude and behaviour (your body language).

Objecting can be a scary act, and people can fear your reaction. By not reacting negatively and by accepting the objection, you also accept the person.

When you accept people, you build both their trust and their sense of identity with you. You also set up an exchange dynamic where they feel a subconscious sense of obligation to repay your acceptance. Accepting the objection means understanding how it's reasonable, at least from their current POV, for them to object to what you may believe is an excellent offer.

It also means accepting the work that addressing the objection will require of you. Objections can be frustrating, and if you object to their concerns you'll end up in a stalemate.

5 Deal with the objection

There are two types of objections or concerns you're likely to face when attempting to close a sale: real ones and 'accidental' ones.

A real objection is based on the facts and reflects a deep concern about the proposed solution or product being offered. Real objections take work, but if they can be resolved you've got the sale.

On the other hand, 'accidental' objections are where the objection is due to a misunderstanding and this is usually very easy to address, with an apology for not being as clear as you could've been as well as a more helpful explanation of your 'pitch'.

Persuading your way through an objection means working to change the way they view the objection in the first place. You can wear them down such that they no longer view the objection as being worth pursuing. You can change the way they view the objection more positively such that they have a 'light bulb moment' that leads them to perceive the objection as being no longer important.

You can also concede your way through, giving in and effectively buying their commitment. This will almost always happen when it comes to price. If they object to the price, you can always lower it. If they don't want it now, you can come back next week, next month or next quarter. Concession can be both a useful approach, especially if you're in a hurry, and a threat. If you give them an inch, then they may want to take a mile, but this isn't always the case, and a prepared concession strategy can pay dividends. It's what experienced negotiators have worked out before they enter into any negotiation. The price they want to achieve and ask for and the 'hidden' price point they are willing to accept have been calculated in advance. In this way, prospects think they've 'won' by extracting a key concession on price. This may be the only barrier left to closing the sale and so it's worth considering carefully.

Go for the 'trial close'

Get a commitment from them such that, if you can satisfactorily address their objections, they will agree with you and make the purchase. This is also a good method of identifying further objections. If they say no, then loop back and elicit these. Eventually, they will run out of objections. If you can address these, it's in the bag.

This is also the point where you may well be making a commitment to them, to resolve their objections. This may be difficult and cost you in various ways, from calling in favours from other people to putting in additional effort.

The decision you have here is to decide whether it's profitable to make the concessions asked. Persuasion is often an exchange, and you are always at liberty to back out.

Typical objections faced in a sales situation

If you can classify how they object then you are on the first step to handling the objection. There are many types of objection, and Table 10.2 lists some of the main ones.

Table 10.2 Typical objections

Type of objection likely to be encountered	Examples
Need They say that they don't need your product or service for some reason or another, or perhaps have a need that you can't satisfy.	'I have one of those already.' 'My car works just fine, thank you.' 'I have no space for any more.' 'Sorry, I just don't want it.'
Price The objections here are about the price of the product or service.	*'How* much?' 'I've already spent my budget for the month.' 'Your competitors sell a better product for less.' 'I could get it cheaper on the web.' 'I didn't realize that service wasn't included.'
Features They object to some element of what you are selling, whether it's aspects of a service or details of a product.	'I don't like that style. It looks rather modern for me.' 'It doesn't have the latest gadgets.' 'The guarantee is only six months.' 'It's far too big.' 'It's not good enough quality.'
Time In this, the objection is around time, such as the person not being ready to buy.	'I don't know. I need to think about it.' 'I won't have the money until next month.' 'I'm moving next year – maybe then.' 'I need to talk to my manager first.'
Source They question the source of the product, often its credibility. This may include questions about you, too.	'I don't know you from Adam. I prefer to buy from people I know.' 'I saw a report about how badly your company treated its workers.' 'How will I know if you are around to service this in five years?'

Objection-handling methods and techniques

There are literally hundreds of objection-handling methods and techniques, which have spawned thousands of sales techniques training programmes – each claiming to be better than the other.

It's highly likely that if you work in a sales-orientated role within your organization or enterprise then you will be attending both internal and external sales training courses on a frequent basis throughout your career.

Table 10.3 highlights some of the more popular methods and techniques for handling objections, although these are not exhaustive; you mustn't feel you need to use all of them at once, and your own company or organization will have procedures that you should follow in the first instance. These procedures can generally be found on your company or organization's intranet.

Remote closing

Not every closing sales situation takes place face to face, and in fact in many sales situations the buyers and sellers never get to meet in person. Closing a sale where there isn't face-to-face physical interaction has its own particular requirements.

Closing a sale via the phone

There may be situations where there's been a sale meeting and customer or client prospects say that they'll get back to you. The following will help to make you proactive rather than waiting for the phone to ring:

- Call prospects to check to see if they had any remaining questions about the product or service to satisfy their needs.
- Arrange a specific time for the follow-up call.
- Reread all the information on this account so that the details are fresh in your mind.
- Refer to a brief summary review that should list everything they agreed that they like about your product or service. Check you have captured the emotional triggers that make them feel some ownership over the product or service to be delivered.
- Prepare a titbit of information that's new and/or interesting and picks up with something that was said to you by them in the last conversation.
- Prepare a closing question for the phone call that you have prepared and rehearsed that asks for a firm commitment today.

Table 10.3 Objection-handling methods and techniques

Technique	Description	Examples	How it works
Boomerang	When people object, turn the objections around by using what they say to prove that they are wrong. Use their own arguments like a boomerang, so they go around in a circle and come back to persuade them.	'Yes, it is expensive, but I don't think you would want to buy your wife a cheap present.' 'Indeed, the house does need work but, as you said, you are very good at do-it-yourself work.' 'Certainly, if you don't have the money today then we can arrange it all for tomorrow.'	By using what they say, you're saying that they are right. And when you attach what you want to what they say, then by association what you want is right.
Objection chunking – both up and down	You can take a higher, more general viewpoint or a more detailed focus. Chunking up (also called 'helicoptering') lets you see more and understand the big picture. When you chunk up, specific issues seem small and insignificant. My worries about a scratch on a car are nothing in comparison with world peace. You can expand the pie, showing them how they are getting not only the basic product, but other things as well. You can add widgets and warranties. You can add emotions like the added peace of mind they will have from your product. Chunking down drills into the detail, highlighting and addressing significant concerns. It also distracts attention from more difficult concerns in other areas. You can reduce the apparent size of the objection, for example by changing dislike of a town into dislike of a neighbourhood or just a street.	'Let's look at the big picture. What do you really want to achieve by using this?' 'That's interesting. Tell me more about that.' 'How does your CEO think about this?' 'Tell you what: let's get one of your engineers to consider the situation.'	Taking a different perspective has a dual effect: first, of reframing to create a different focus and a new understanding; second, of distracting from what might be a difficult issue to resolve.

Table 10.3 *continued*

Technique	Description	Examples	How it works
Conditional close	When others offer an objection, make it a condition of resolving their objection that they make the purchase. You can also use this approach to make any trade; for example, if you want them to watch a promotional video, offer a cup of coffee. Always, by the way, phrase it in the form 'If I... will you...?' rather than 'Will you... if I...?' This is because our brains work very quickly, and starting with 'Will you' causes them to begin thinking immediately about objections, and they may miss the exchange. On the other hand, starting with 'If I' will cause psychological closure on what you are offering, thus drawing them in to the close.	'You say you want a red one. If I can phone up and get you one, will you take it today?' 'If we can figure out the finance for you, will you choose this one?' 'If I get you a cup of coffee, would you like to sit down and look through the brochure?'	The conditional close uses the exchange principle to build the social agreement that, if I solve your problem, you will buy the product in return.
Curiosity	When they declare that they don't want to buy from you, act curious. Don't just ask 'Why?', but express a curious interest that says 'How interesting – I wonder why.' Getting the objection out before they leave then gives you one last shot to keep them there. Even if they still leave, it also lets you know why you failed to sell to them today and so improves your sales skills.	'I know you don't want to buy this, but before you go could you just let me know what your reason was?' 'I was just wondering what led to your decision not to buy this today.' 'Most people really go for this one. I'm a little curious as to how you decided otherwise.'	Being curious appeals in part to their child-self, whereby you say 'Wow, isn't that interesting!' and invite them to a game of exploration and discovery. Curiosity also evokes their need for novelty in their life. When you are non-threatening and not in 'closing mode' they may well relent and give you the information you need.

Table 10.3 *continued*

Technique	Description	Examples	How it works
Deflection	Avoid handling an objection by deflecting it such that it doesn't hold up the proceedings. Listen to it. Show understanding of the concerns. Then carry on as if nothing had happened. Say that you'll come back to it later. Maybe you won't have to. Give an excuse, such as not having information or having to talk to somebody else later.	'Yes, I see what you mean... mmm... Now let me show you the range of finishes you can have.' 'Good point. Can I come back to that later? Thanks. Now what I was saying was...' 'Yes, I've got some information about that back at the office somewhere. Can we carry on now?'	By accepting someone's objection you are accepting him or her as a person, and the additional harmony and rapport created may be enough to overcome the objection. Refusing to answer people's objections now may also be a power play, where you are demonstrating authority and control over the situation. If you can get away with it, they may cede more power to you.
Feel, felt, found	First empathize with them, telling them that you understand how they *feel*. Then tell them about somebody who *felt* the same way. Then tell them how that other person *found* that things were not so bad and that when they did what you want the buyer to do they found that it was actually a very good thing to do.	'I understand how you feel about that. Many others have felt the same way. And what they have found is that...' 'I know how you feel that it looks rough. I had someone in here yesterday who felt the same when she first looked at it, but when she tried it on she found that it was so comfortable.'	By empathizing with how people *feel*, you are building harmony with them to create rapport. When you talk about how somebody else *felt*, you move the focus to a more objective place, which they are likely to trust more. This also makes them a part of a group such that they don't feel alone. When they are attached to that group, then you move the whole group by telling how the person in the group changed his or her mind. The buyer, being attached to the group, should change his or her mind at the same time.

Table 10.3 *continued*

Technique	Description	Examples	How it works
Humour	When they object, don't respond with negative emotions such as anger or frustration. Defuse the tension with gentle humour, maybe feigning shock or otherwise poking fun at yourself. Be careful about making them the object of humour. It can be done, but you need to be sure first that they won't be offended, so it should be avoided.	'Oh no! What will we do?' (Smiling) 'Well, I think this car would be very sad to see you go home without it.' 'I think I've lost my touch.' (Looking at your hands with a puzzled expression)	When you receive objections it can be very frustrating, and it's very easy for these emotions to leak out. By reframing the situation with gentle humour, you can show that you're not offended by their refusal. Remember that they, too, may find objecting embarrassing and uncomfortable, with the result that they may well want to get away from you (and the embarrassment) as soon as possible.
Justification	Rather than fight the objection, justify why it's reasonable. Tell them how you have deliberately made what you are selling this way for a particular reason. If they complain about price, tell them the product is built for a superior market. If they complain about quality, tell them that this is to allow you to charge a very low price.	'Yes, the car is expensive, but it's a rare import and cost a lot to bring over here.' 'I know it's not new, but it will give your image depth, making you look more established.' 'It's large, which is why most people who buy it find that visitors notice it at once.'	When people object, they often are saying that what you are offering is somehow unfair or wrong. If you can subsequently show that it is fair and reasonable, then they no longer have reason to object. Using the argument that it's 'fair and reasonable' makes it difficult to argue against.

Table 10.3 *continued*

Technique	Description	Examples	How it works
Objection writing	When they object, tip the bucket to get all the remaining objections, writing these down as you go on a clean page of paper. Then show it to the other person and verify that, if you address these, then there are no reasons for them not to buy. Then, as you handle each one, cross it out. You can ask the person before this is done. A variant of this is to summarize the objections into one word or a short phrase. Thus you write down 'price', 'size' and so on. This allows you to reframe slightly what they are saying.	'So, we've addressed this. Can I cross this out now?'	Writing things down is useful for a visual thinker. It also moves the problem on to the external, objective sheet of paper (from a person's subjective thinking). And then it allows you to cross it out. The act of crossing it out causes closure, on eliminating the objection.
Pre-empting	Tell them about a possible objection before they object. Then handle the objection so it can't be brought up again. Make the objection rather weak and the handling rather strong. Tell them stories of other people who objected and then looked foolish.	'I had one person who didn't like the shade, but then he hadn't realized that this was the latest fashion.' 'You might find this expensive, but we can find the right deal.'	If you answer the objection before they bring it out, then they are unable to voice the objection without appearing not to have heard you.
Push-back	Don't accept the objection. Push back assertively rather than aggressively. Object to their objection. If they are wrong, tell them. You can push back either directly, by telling them they are wrong, or indirectly, by showing them that they are mistaken. Indirect push-back is usually likely to reduce further objections, unless you have concluded that a 'short, sharp shock' is likely to be more effective.	'That's not right. This product is the most competitively priced on the market today.' 'I can see that you might think that, but the latest survey has shown that we are the lowest-cost supplier.' 'Would you like to check those figures again? I think you'll find you'll reach a different conclusion.'	A direct response to an objection can be a shock that the other person will accept.

Table 10.3 *continued*

Technique	Description	Examples	How it works
Reframing	When they object, reframe their objection as something other than a 'no' so you can continue with your selling. Reframe the objection as a misunderstanding (and take the blame for this yourself). Reframe the objection by taking the subject and turning it around. Reframe a small difference as being the critical difference. Reframe 'required specific experience' to 'relevant experience'.	'I can see that this isn't making sense. Sorry – let me put it another way.' 'The cost may be high, but the cost of inaction may be higher.' 'Yes, blue is an unusual colour. It will make you look really original.'	Reframing uses what the other person has given you, which makes it more difficult for him or her to deny it.
Renaming	A simple approach to handling objections is to change something in what you are presenting. Some examples are given below, but you can think of more, of course. Objections have names. It may be price, worry or something even more specific. Turn price into cost of ownership. Turn worry into reasonable concern. Words have very individual meanings, which means that changing 'heavy' into 'weighty' or 'strong' into 'powerful' can change the meaning of a whole sentence. Renaming the objection changes it, or should I say 'putting the problem into new words creates a whole new world'?	'You say you are worried and I can see you are concerned and that tells me you are interested in good-quality products.' 'When you consider about how long it takes, you may also think about the free time it will give you.' 'You said you would talk to your partners. Could you think instead of discussing it with them?'	Words are 'little packets of meaning' and can have a complex schema associated with them, as the deeper aspects of linguistics show. Changing just a word changes the meaning of what's being discussed, showing it in a different light.

Table 10.3 *continued*

Technique	Description	Examples	How it works
Reprioritize	When they have a priority that is stopping them from buying from you, find ways of changing the priority. Explore the criteria they are using to decide. Probe to find how important each criterion is to them. Appeal to their values, which include a system of prioritization. Reframe their arguments so they naturally change their priorities. At the same time, increase other priorities so as to lead them to buy from you.	'You're very loyal to your current supplier, but should you be more loyal to your family?' 'You are right, price is important. But how much more important is quality to you?' 'A big picture would look nice, but with smaller pictures you can show more of them.'	When evaluating between different choices, we use different criteria and different weighting of those criteria. We also get fixated on particular solutions and forget about other criteria. If you can change criteria, change weights or remind the other people of forgotten criteria then you can get them to reprioritize.

Holding the customer's or client's attention

Ideally you'd want to communicate using all five senses in order to get your points across and close the sale, but because of time and money pressures, as well as convenience, a lot of business is conducted via the phone. However, that doesn't mean that using other forms of communication is out of the question:

- Visually engage prospects by e-mailing material to them ahead of the call and ensure they receive this in plenty of time prior to any attempt to close the sale.

- In any material sent, ensure that the business or consumer benefits are upfront and expressed in a way that the prospect prefers rather than wrapped up in technical gobbledegook.

- An alternative way of seeing prospects is via a Skype videoconference call, which is free and becoming much more common in business use. If this isn't available, then many hotels offer a videoconference facility at an affordable price, which may be better than a conversation over the phone (if appropriate).

- If it's a conference call, it may be appropriate to have a technical person available to answer any technical questions about your product or service that are beyond your own competence.

Closing via e-mail

Like the phone, an e-mail may be the way in which a potential sale is closed, so it's important to be meticulous in the way the e-mail is constructed, despite the fact that you appear to have spent your working life writing e-mails:

- Prepare the e-mail as you would a formal proposal or document. Use bullet points, summaries and plenty of white space, which makes it easier to read on the screen (you will need to switch into HTML format in order to carry this out).
- Use capitals for section headings and extra spacing between sections or important points for emphasis.
- Always double-check the document before sending it. It's probably sensible to print this out, as it's likely to be printed out at the other end, and double-check for typos and grammatical errors. If figures are used, double-check the maths.
- Double-check that vital information, such as the date and contact information including phone numbers and e-mail addresses for responses, is included.
- Pay particular attention to tone and the use of language depending on the intended audience for the communication.

Closing via the website

Today's websites are sophisticated shopfronts, where a multiple number of processes take place, including closing sales (Figure 10.2).

However, the days of people randomly surfing the net have long gone, and today your website will be found through search on an internet browser such as Google Chrome or Microsoft's Bing. It's therefore essential that, if using the website for closing sales, it first of all needs to be found. This may sound obvious, but so many businesses fall at the first hurdle because they forget a basic tenet of marketing – promotion – and try to leapfrog straight into sales because they have a website. If the website can't be found, no one will come. Ironically, the web address needs to appear on all offline or more traditional media, such as brochures, advertisements, leaflets and flyers, and increasingly at point of sale in order to drive traffic.

Other strategies include online channels such as Facebook, YouTube, LinkedIn, Twitter and other online networks provided that these are appropriate for the desired audience and customer segment you are trying to attract and close a sale with. The website should have social media buttons so that customers can easily share information about your products and services by one click on the relevant page.

In addition, contact details, frequently asked questions (FAQs), online forms and confirmations must be easily laid out.

Figure 10.2 Functionality of a typical website

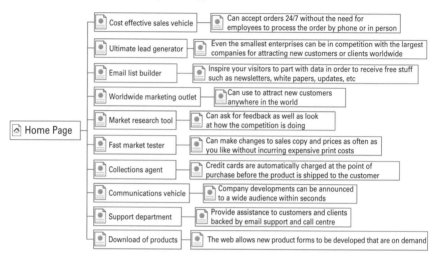

The site also needs to protect users' personal and financial information from falling into the wrong hands, so the website needs to be a secure and trusted site in order to encourage this type of transactional behaviour.

Back-end selling

When people become associated with your business or enterprise, whether as customers or clients or even simply as newsletter subscribers, you've got the opportunity to offer products and solutions to them. Back-end selling is promoting your products and services on the 'back end' of an action they took with you.

There are so many giveaways of information and tangible items on the web that could otherwise be sold for money. However, organizations have come to realize that there's more value to be had in the back-end sale.

This is an important consideration for closing a sale on a website and could take many forms:

- an e-mail newsletter promoting a new product release offered only to current customers;
- a follow-up phone call or face-to-face meeting with a customer two weeks after the product has been received;
- a personalized letter specifically addressing the interests of the person who purchased the product; and
- other strategies for generating sales including up-sells and cross-sells (see Chapter 3).

Maintaining the customer or client through to the next sale

Sales and service go hand in hand. When your business relies on personal selling you can bet that you also need great customer service, because personal service keeps customers, plain and simple.

The old adage is that if you don't know how to keep your customers you shouldn't waste your time seeking new customers. You'll just lose them.

Maintaining customers or clients is one of the most important strategies in sales and marketing, and traditionally it's not an area of strength or expertise for most businesses or enterprises. Given that it's hard enough to close a sale, you really don't want customers to go elsewhere should a problem or issue occur when supplying the product or service to them. Remember, it costs seven times as much to acquire a new customer as it does to retain an existing one, so the maths for investing in good customer service post-sale is a 'no-brainer' from a financial perspective.

See also Guru in a Bottle®'s *High Impact Marketing That Gets Results*.

Many businesses struggle with understanding the customer churn rate: those customers or clients who leave each year. As a general rule of thumb, if the customer churn rate exceeds 5 per cent in the majority of customer segments, you probably have a customer service problem. In order to determine whether this is an issue for the business, you need to do a very simple calculation:

- Compare last year's and this year's customer or client lists to find out how many customers you lost during the year. Ignore new customers for this part of the calculation.
- Count the total number of customers on the first of the two lists (that is, the list from the previous year). This then provides a baseline for the calculation of churn rate.
- Divide the number of lost customers by the total number of customers to arrive at the churn rate.

For example, if you started 2012 with 1,500 clients and in 2013 this reduced to 1,250, you lost 250 clients. The churn rate is therefore 250 divided by 1,500 or nearly 17 per cent, which is indicative of a serious customer service issue that needs to be addressed.

There are a number of proven strategies that you can employ in order to reduce churn significantly within the business as well as improve the likelihood of making further sales to existing customers.

Persistent follow-up

Practising consistent and persistent follow-up is proven to be one of the most effective strategies in retaining customers and clients. It's important for any business or enterprise to develop an organized, systematic approach. Follow-up shouldn't be practised only for existing customers or clients but applies to all contacts you've interacted with, as maintaining contact will develop the relationship and make repeat purchasing from you much more conducive.

Given the competitive markets all businesses now operate in, it's become commonplace for sales professionals to practise aggressive, thorough follow-up methods that even a few years ago would have been considered unnecessary. The reason for this development is that without being persistent and visible you'll be forgotten about and lost.

To adopt effective methods of follow-up, you need to know the concerns that customers or clients have about service and follow-up, and you need a good handle on the challenges that they regularly face. You can only serve your customers or clients well when you know what they want. Some of the most common customer or client concerns about the selling and servicing of their accounts are:

- not receiving a call that a salesperson promised to make;
- knowing contact telephone numbers and best available times in order to reach customer services should something go wrong;
- having the ability to speak to someone in authority;
- feeling appreciated for their business;
- spending the minimal time 'on hold' in order to speak to a real person;
- having a call centre service in the country of their domicile rather than offshore where there could be linguistic and cultural challenges in being understood;
- being kept informed of ways to keep costs down and increase productivity;
- being informed promptly of potential challenges and getting any problems resolved quickly;
- being addressed appropriately and politely and receiving personal attention; and
- being given honest and realistic information about service and problem-solving issues.

By making follow-up and service a regular part of sales activities, you can efficiently address all of these customer concerns and maintain a competitive edge with your peers, who may not be as obsessive with their after-sales service.

As a general rule of thumb, you need to contact existing or prospective customers at least six times in the year in order to maintain or win them as customers. Phone calls, e-mails and direct mail are the most commonly used channels, but increasingly these are overused, so think more creatively about how you continue to keep in touch; for example, an invitation to your stand at a trade show where you can also conduct meetings with existing and prospective customers works extremely well, as it combines a number of activities in one go and adds value to the follow-up experience.

Other touches that show that you care include sending a thank-you note to customers for making the purchase and for opting in to receiving a regular newsletter and updates via e-mail as well as including them in the feedback loop when looking at launching new products and services.

In some cases, special user groups of customers or clients can be created on social media networks such as LinkedIn and YouTube, which allows for dialogue and interactivity between users, who can share experiences and tips in the use of your products or services.

Key account management (KAM)

As we've already discussed, the costs involved in acquiring new customers or clients is always higher than you think, so retaining them has an immediate bottom-line impact for the business. Plugging holes in a 'leaky bucket' of customer defections is a high-value activity and one made all the more so in the face of the many supplier reduction programmes that many companies have recently embarked upon in the ever-greater search for getting 'more for less'.

But there are also more positive advantages that can flow from KAM. For example, the longer a customer or client is retained, the more experienced you become in servicing that customer's needs and requirements and so the lower the costs involved as a result of moving up the 'experience curve'.

Despite all businesses being focused on the performance of profit and loss (P&L) over a 12-month period, the true value of customers and clients who stick with the business can be calculated in a different way – known as 'lifetime value'. The longer you retain a customer or reduce customer churn in the business, the better the lifetime value (Table 10.4). This isn't complicated or surprising mathematics: halving the defection of customers or clients doubles the rate of lifetime value of those who are retained. Yet, for all its simplicity, it's not a measure that's foremost in the minds of most senior managers. According to Peter Cheverton, one of the world's leading experts in KAM, 'one of the strongest arguments is that it has a beneficial effect on reducing customer defections and reducing the incidence of local defections in individual markets'.

Table 10.4 Calculating the lifetime value of a customer

Customer defection rate	Average customer lifetime	Annual profit	Profit over a customer lifetime
40%	2.5 years	1,000	2,500
20%	5 years	1,000	5,000
10%	10 years	1,000	10,000
5%	20 years	1,000	20,000

Source: Cheverton (2006)

As the marketplace approaches super-saturation of products and services – as the power in the sales and marketing equation shifts from product to consumer – brand loyalty starts to get eroded. In order to compete successfully, you have to create loyalty relationships with your customers or clients, one at a time. Good relationships win customer loyalty, and long-term loyalty is a very valuable commodity. Some businesses even calculate the premium won from the customer as a result of such loyalty, so measuring the reward for their investment.

The buyer's interest and involvement

In most of the sales situations you are likely to be involved with it's likely that there's going to be more than one person involved on the buyer's side of the table.

Academic research shows that there are typically four buyer 'modes', each resulting from the mix of the buyer's level of interest and involvement with the seller. In terms of involvement, this equates to how much time the buyer has spent understanding your sales proposition, for example whether the buyer was at every sales presentation or meeting or delegated this to others. Level of interest tends to reflect the importance of the proposition, and whether it's genuinely novel or creates a step change in business performance (Figure 10.3).

Figure 10.3 The buyer's interest and involvement

Level of Involvement		
	low	high
high (Level of Interest)	'Specifier' Buyer	'Lead Role' Buyer
low (Level of Interest)	'Gatekeeper' Buyer	'Service' Buyer

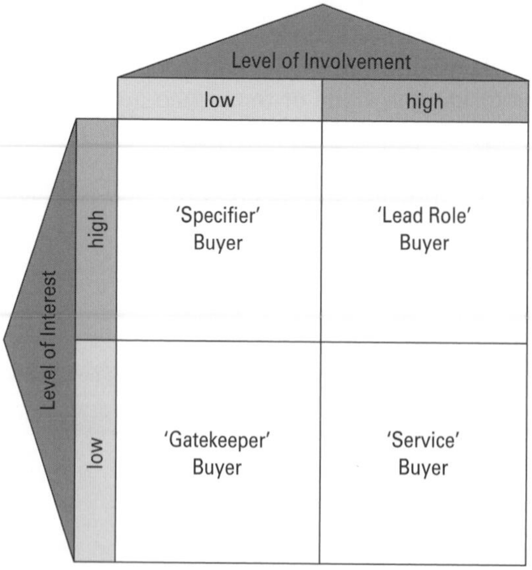

The lead role buyer

Lead role buyers have a high level of interest and involvement and so take a lead role, which is good for you in as much as they'll tend to keep you well informed as to developments within their business or the changing needs and requirements they may have, as well as be prepared to recommend you to others inside and outside the organization.

The gatekeeper buyer

At the other end of the scale are gatekeeper buyers, who tend to have neither interest nor involvement and are a classic challenge for you. Typically, they could be from a procurement or human resources department that may be involved in the decision-making process.

The only redeeming feature about this sort of relationship is that because their interest is so low you may have fewer problems talking to others within the customer or client organization as a result, although don't assume this will always follow.

The best option in such a situation is to be patient and persistent and to encourage all your team members to keep their ears and eyes open for opportunities to make other contacts elsewhere.

The service buyer

These people are performing a task for someone else's benefit, for example buying media advertising space. From your perspective as a seller, you should be thinking of ways to make it easy for them to do business with you.

A familiar challenge for you is the tendency for such people to revert to talking about price, while their internal client may well be interested in something else, such as quality of the product or service delivered. Getting to those interests and having them discussed is important to your goal as a seller, but you can become an additional burden on already-pressed buyers if you are then seen to be complicating their life. If there are lots of nitty-gritty details with your product or service proposition that require end-user evaluations, then you could try suggesting that you relieve them of this kind of detail by talking direct to the end user.

The secret is to keep things simple and straightforward for service buyers.

The specifier buyer

These individuals have high interest but low involvement and will tend to give you clarity on the requirement, but you need to ensure that you engage with them at the appropriate point, as they want others to handle the purchase of the product or service. Provided they encourage you to have contact with other decision makers in the buying process, you may be on your way to keeping them as customers or clients.

Ultimately you need to develop a strong relationship with the lead buyer, and the specifier buyer could be important in that regard.

The following checklist will ensure that you're successful in closing the sale:

- Ask for the business.
- Don't give away too much, too soon.
- Build rapport with the purchaser and read body language.
- Don't forget to get emotional buy-in, but emphasize the logical aspects of the offer.
- Ask questions of the buyer.
- Be confident in presenting your product or service.
- Invite questions and use this as a way of gaining buy-in.
- Test-close the sale.
- Address any final concerns.
- Close the sale.
- Follow up with excellent customer service.
- Keep the lines of communication open, frequent and relevant.
- Apply key account management principles in helping you keep the customer or client's business well into the future.
- Stay in control, learn from your mistakes when you don't close a sale so you do next time, and don't take yourself too seriously.

References

Books

Cheverton, P (2006) *Global Account Management*, Kogan Page

Gerber, Michael (2006) *E-Myth Mastery*, Collins

Girard, J and Shook, RL (2002) *How to Close Every Sale*, Warner Books

Karass, G (1987) *Negotiate to Close: How to make more successful deals*, Fireside

Navarro, J (2008) *What Everybody Is Saying*, Collins Living

Schiffman, S (1999) *Closing Techniques That Really Work*, Adams Media

Schiffman, S (2002) *Getting to 'Closed': A proven program to accelerate the sales cycle and increase commissions*, Dearborn Trade Publishing

Ziglar, Z (1985) *Secrets of Closing the Sale*, Berkley Publishing

Index

NB: page numbers in *italic* indicate figures or tables

Endorsements

This excellent book dispels commonly held myths about how to sell and provides a blueprint for driving incremental sales. Written in a highly engaging way, it is one of the best books on sales available and is a valuable addition to the highly successful Guru in a Bottle series. **Sir Paul Judge, President, Chartered Institute of Marketing (UK)**

This book makes a major contribution to the Chartered Institute of Marketing's Sales Leadership Alliance (SLA) initiative. It's totally unlike traditional books on selling, being an excellent manifestation of the fusion of the best of marketing with the best of selling. Every point the book makes is exemplified by real life examples from both marketing and sales best practice. I enjoyed reading this book and found it extremely useful. I wish it had been around when I was Marketing & Sales Director of a major company, controlling a sales force of over 200 people. **Malcolm McDonald, Emeritus Professor, Cranfield School of Management (UK)**

Much of the sales activity undertaken by companies and organizations is done in a disorganized, inefficient way. We often try to do too much at once. Emotions, information, logic, hope, risk and creativity are mixed together. This brilliantly written book provides a no-nonsense approach for the sales professional that shows how to effectively drive sales that will make a direct impact on the bottom line. An invaluable book for every budding entrepreneur. **Allyson Stewart-Allen, Programme Director, London Business School and Oxford University Said Business School**

Finally, a pragmatic and comprehensive framework to achieve the core and critical skills of sales effectiveness widely based on difficult intangible psychological work. **Roberto Abad, communication consultant & CEO, Ulled Asociados (Spain)**

In a book about the art of selling it's refreshing to see so much emphasis on listening to the customer, and collaborating to co-create products and services that they really want. Highly accessible and insightful, this book also encourages sales professionals to challenge assumptions about what motivates their customers and offers practical guidance on the approaches they are more likely to respond to. **Alex Evans, Editorial Director, National Sales Awards (UK)**

A comprehensive guide to selling, with lots of practical insight and tools to help you sell more and better. **Professor Merlin Stone, Head of Research, The Customer Framework (UK)**

Ardi is one of the most gifted media and marketing professionals I have met. He has boundless enthusiasm, a broad knowledge of the digital media world and the infectious charm that endears him to a broad range of people. It is indeed a pleasure to endorse his work because it is credible. **Neil Henderson, Head of Media Relations, MasterCard (Global)**

The sheer amount of practical advice on influencing and selling packed into this 'Guru in a Bottle' book must make it a magnum at the very least. Ardi Kolah nails some of the central issues for all sales and marketing people: the power and central role of emotion in buying decisions, the importance of listening and the need to focus, relentlessly, on your customer. It's a relief to read that I've been doing a few things properly over the years – I still wish I'd had this book from the beginning. **Andy Maslen, author of** *Write to Sell* www.copywritingacademy.co.uk

The Art of Influencing and Selling is a book you can pick up and put down as you develop your business or sales career. No matter how good you think you are at sales this practical guide will make you better and pay for itself hundreds of times over. **Michael Murphy, Global CEO, Grayling (Global)**

The key question that companies need to answer in the development of their sales strategy is: 'what do customers want?' rather than 'what do we want?' This book delivers the insights and processes to address this question. **Raoul Pinnell, Chairman, Bromley Healthcare (UK)**

Right from the very beginning, this book grips the reader – whether as a businessman or student. The content opens our minds to the realities of selling and reveals the art of how to engage and influence customers in a physical and emotional way. An excellent and brilliantly written book that will help me in developing the Café Spice Namaste and Mr Todiwala's Kitchen brands. **Cyrus Todiwala OBE DL, acclaimed chef and TV personality (UK)**

An indispensable guide for anyone who is selling a product, service or themselves. This is a truly multi-dimensional approach to selling that provides the theory, tools and techniques to enable everyone to become much more adept at selling. Written in an intelligent and engaging style, this book, part of the Guru in a Bottle series, will transform the way you approach sales and marketing – no matter what size organization or sector you work in. Packed with insightful truisms and numerous myth-busters, Ardi Kolah has managed to distil a lifetime's sales experience into one very readable volume – a must for anyone involved in selling. **David Doughty, entrepreneur and business mentor (UK)**

Everyone thinks they know how to place, market and sell themselves, their company, and their product. The reality is they don't, and they need to read this book. Marketing and selling isn't easy and it isn't a no-brainer; it takes expertise and skill. Most of us gain that experience and those skills in real time on 'the shop floor', but we too should have read this book. Packed full of insights and wisdom, this is a no nonsense volume that I wish I had had in my pocket more than once in my life! Read, remember, understand and apply, and then read again from time to time. You won't have wasted a moment; enjoy the book, and the results! **Professor Peter Cochrane OBE, former CTO, BT (UK)**

Comprehensive and in tune with the online, connected workplace, this book is essential for companies wanting to 'sell more stuff'. A combination of clear advice, up-to-date practical insights and references that distils the steps necessary to repeatedly make valued sales. Required reading for all those who want to make a positive difference to the bottom line. **Steve Dobson, CEO, The Marketing Medic (UK)**

What I love about this book is that it gives structure to intuition! For many who, like me, have spent a lifetime running their own business, selling and influencing is what they do, one way or another, every day. But it is easy – and wrong – to rely just on gut instinct. The Art of Influencing and Selling is like a mentor – it questions, challenges and makes you think.The book starts by talking about trust and, importantly, what trust means from the customer's point of view. If there is no trust then there is no sale. Indeed, a theme of the book is that everything should be seen from the customer's point of view. Intuitive, really. Some may say it is common sense, but sadly, while many organizations profess to see their business through the eyes of the customer, few actually do. This book asks why so few organizations see customers as individuals with differing needs. Having lived in France for 10 years, I appreciate how the book explores cultural differences. Many global brands struggle here and the book explains why it is imperative, in sales terms, to empathise with the culture of the country you are trying to sell to. It's a great book and a must-read for everyone who has customer contact – not just those in a direct sales role. **David Hammond, partner, Bringing Burgundy to You (France)**

This stimulating new book gives a fresh, updated view of the age-old business of selling. We all live in a rapidly changing world and this is particularly true for sales and marketing. This book addresses the shift in the balance of power from the seller to the buyer head on, and presents a new blueprint for sales professionals to adjust to this changing environment with lots of practical tips and techniques. Unlike many business books, this one is easy to read and understand, and I believe it is a must-read for both people starting out in sales and hardened professionals; in fact for anybody in business. I loved the cartoons by Steve Marchant – which added to the engaging feel of the book – and also the frequent case studies and examples used to illustrate the various propositions made in each chapter. I would suggest that this is a book to read and keep handy for quick reference when considering how to improve your sales figures. **Peter Phillips, partner, Synched Solutions (UK)**

The book is an invaluable addition for any sales professional who wants to learn how to improve their sales activities profitably and quickly. Up-to-date, highly relevant and brilliantly written. **Don Hales, founder, The Customer Service Training Network (Global)**

To achieve high impact marketing that gets results, we must become almost fanatical about walking in the footsteps of our customers and clients. Follow the approach advocated in this excellent book and you'll be on your way to creating more sales through better marketing of your business. **Keki Kolah, MD, Sai Advertisers (India)**